JUDGING THE JUDGES,
JUDGING OURSELVES

JUDGING THE JUDGES, JUDGING OURSELVES

*Truth, Reconciliation and the
Apartheid Legal Order*

DAVID DYZENHAUS

*Professor of Law and Philosophy,
University of Toronto*

HART PUBLISHING – OXFORD
1998

Hart Publishing
Oxford
UK

Distributed in the United States by
Northwestern University Press
625 Colfax
Evanston
Illinois
60208-4210 USA

Distributed in Australia and New Zealand by
Federation Press Pty Ltd
PO Box 45
Annandale, NSW 2038
Australia

Distributed in Netherlands, Belgium and Luxembourg by
Intersentia, Churchillaan 108
B2900 Schoten
Antwerpen
Belgium

Published in South Africa
(as *Truth, Reconciliation and the Apartheid Legal Order*) by
Juta and Company, Ltd., Cape Town
P.O. Box 14373, Kenwyn, 7790, South Africa
Telephone: +27-21-79-5101   email: cserv@juta.co.za

Hart Publishing is a specialist legal publisher based in Oxford, England. To
order further copies of this book or to request a list of other publications please
write to:

Hart Publishing, 19 Whitehouse Road, Oxford, OX1 4PA
Telephone: +44 (0)1865 434459 Fax: +44 (0) 1865 794882
email: hartpub@janep.demon.co.uk

British Library Cataloguing in Publication Data
Data Available

ISBN 1-901362-94-9

Typeset in Monotype Ehrhardt
by John Saunders Design & Production, Reading
Printed in Great Britain on acid-free paper
by Biddles Ltd, Guildford and King's Lynn

For Cheryl

And to the nurses and doctors of the Intensive Care Unit of St. Michael's Hospital, Toronto, especially Maureen Baye, Without whom not . . .

FOREWORD

Most of us these days are reared to know the majesty of the law. It was law, at Nuremberg, that delivered Germany from Nazism. And it was the loss of law, so vividly portrayed by Franz Kafka and others, that has been at the heart of 20th century totalitarianisms of all sorts. Again, certain celebratory traditions of United States legal history see U.S. constitutional law as a kind of secular religion and as the ultimate source of that nation's enduring strength: for better or worse, the major internal political struggles in America have been fought in the idiom of the law—as the phrase "civil rights" indeed suggests. Among the countries of the South, decolonisation after World War Two has meant a proliferation of constitutional experiments reflecting the new rulers' undiminished faith in legal solutions to the large problems of creating humane societies. Somehow, law is that to which we turn, these days, for collective self-expression— even if, by collective self-expression, we mean the right to be off, by ourselves, in the dignity of private dissent or eccentricity.

And yet, everywhere, the law has had another face. It is a familiar story: liberty for some alongside slavery for others; gulags alongside high-sounding declamations about equality; property rights alongside impoverishment and despair. If it is in the nature of Gods to disappoint, then certainly the deities of law have been no exception.

In South Africa, this disappointment—the distance between law's humanistic promise and its workaday betrayals—has been particularly stark over the last four decades. The question is whether we can change this, today, and how.

In Nadine Gordimer's novel, "The House Gun" (1997), a judge presides, with Olympian pomp and ceremony, over a murder trial. The judge seems the very image of the law's formality and Olympian grandeur; he commands the courtroom effortlessly, with good natured and officious bombast—and then we glimpse him, in an unguarded moment, furtively picking his nose with his handkerchief. For too long, South Africa had a judiciary populated by persons—

happily not without exceptions—who craved elegance, refinement and erudition, yet who end up revealed as upholders of an appalling system, apartheid, that was a crime against humanity. Some of these judges still wield power on the bench at the time of writing. What is to be done?

As part of a comprehensive review of the apartheid period, South Africans have been absorbed, for more than two years, by the work of the Truth and Reconciliation Commission, chaired by Nobel Laureate Desmond Tutu. Unlike similar bodies in Latin America and elsewhere, the South African Truth and Reconciliation Commission was given an expansive mandate. It was charged to investigate not only the deaths and disappearances of individual victims; the misdeeds of individual perpetrators. Its statutory mandate also required it to investigate the collective support that institutions and organisations within civil society proffered in advancement of apartheid. The business community, medical profession, churches as well as the legal profession—all had their day before the Commission.

Yet, as Professor Dyzenhaus notes, Archbishop Desmond Tutu began the hearings into the legal profession by suggesting that these hearings were the most important within the Commission's mandate. Apartheid was distinct from other twentieth century atrocities in that it was an extended system of socio-economic pillage based on race and—crucially—underpinned by the entire legal system. The legalised nature of racial segregation is what set apartheid apart. Thus apartheid is a case study in how legal norms and ideals—which ought to embody our common humanity at its most cultured and articulate—came instead to express violence, divisiveness and, in the end, lawlessness.

In its careful cataloguing, synthesis and comment on the various presentations made during the three days of hearings into the legal profession under apartheid, Professor Dyzenhaus's book represents a valuable resource of primary material, intelligently organised for future study.

As was often noted, the Truth and Reconciliation Commission managed to capture the imagination of the country in many ways. In the case of the hearings on the legal profession, potentially arcane jurisprudential debates found their way into the pages of the national media with unaccustomed clarity and thoroughness. And yet, as I read Professor Dyzenhaus's compilation and analysis of those three days, I realize with a jolt how much valuable material, how much nuance and close analysis, is lost even by the relatively thorough treatment that these issues have received in the South African media.

In short, this book represents an academic project of the most pleasing kind: it possesses an urgent relevance to pressing debates in the real world; it brings to these current concerns the scholar's virtues of distance, thoroughness and reflection; and it is marked by uncompromising intellectual integrity, which evaded certain participants in the hearings themselves.

A prime example of evasion was furnished by the judges themselves. As prime movers in the conversion of law to the ends of violence and lawlessness, the apartheid judiciary has much responsibility to shoulder for the ills of the past—and could have done much to enlighten the country about the inner workings of apartheid's administrative labyrinth. Yet, as emerges in the pages of this book, the judges declined to attend the hearings. They based this stance on spurious and misplaced arguments about judicial independence. And some of them dismissed the Commission and its work in openly contemptuous terms.

Judicial independence is a principle meant to insulate judges from the blandishments of the wealthy and of the state. It commits the judiciary to legal methodology and independent thinking in deciding cases. A major part of the indictment of the apartheid judiciary was exactly that it failed to exercise available areas of independence in ways that would have curtailed apartheid. It is therefore ironic that arguments based on judicial independence today should be used to defeat inquiry into the exercise of judicial independence in a historical perspective. According to this logic, judges may never be legal historians nor may they participate in countrywide debates over their own transformation.

This is not merely an academic or philosophical argument. In fact is goes to the heart of current debates over the future shape of the judiciary and the inclusiveness of judicial norms: their openness to the ethos of democracy, as opposed to what went before.

The apartheid judiciary was almost totally racially monopolistic and excluded women. The new South African judiciary must move away from this, but cannot effectively do so while the incumbent judges deny even the need for any reckoning with their racially compromised pasts. There is a direct link between the lack of repentance for past judicial misdeeds and the current tendency for certain judges to make the most extraordinary attacks on the constitution, most notably on its prohibition of the death penalty. Certain judges who happily sentenced black freedom fighters to hang in the past, now want to bring back the rope as a supposed solution to the country's crime problems. In making such public calls for the reintroduction of measures that the Constitutional Court has ruled against, these judges are committing nothing less than an act of judicial insubordination and an attack on the new constitutional order. The question, for present purposes, is: from whence come the resources of judicial self-assurance, the unchastened advocacy of inhumane policies, in simple terms, the *chutzpah?* I would suggest that the *chutzpah* of apartheid-era judges in current debates is intimately linked to their calculated refusal to take on board the full extent of their culpability in the policies of the past.

Given the inherent conservatism of judicial institutions, the painfully slow organic nature of their evolution, the refusal of the old guard to face up to its old self has created dilemmas for the well meaning new entrants into the judiciary, such as the Chief Justice and the President of the Constitutional Court. These new judges must combine the long-standing integrity of their anti-apartheid roles with the new administrative challenges of running a cohesive judiciary that retains and expands public confidence.

And this is in the end the key challenge: public confidence. This is not merely a public relations function, a creation of ad-men, something that image consultants can be hired to fix. Public confidence in a judiciary reflects far-reaching sentiments of belonging, identity and—ultimately—of justice among us all. These fragile sentiments were utterly destroyed in the South African past. It remains to be seen how far we can gather them together again.

Kader Asmal
Johannesburg
July 1998

CONTENTS

PREFACE
AND
ACKNOWLEDGEMENTS

The idea for this book was born in late October of 1997 in Cape Town in a conversation about the Legal Hearing which South Africa's Truth and Reconciliation Commission (TRC) was to hold in Johannesburg at the end of that month.

I am a former South African, now a Canadian citizen teaching at the University of Toronto. As a young law lecturer in South Africa in the early 1980s, I participated in the debates about the legitimacy of participation in the apartheid legal order, arguing that it was important for the overthrow of apartheid that lawyers and judges work against apartheid's legal order from within.

I had thought that such debates would end with the formal closure of the apartheid era, and my project for a six-month sabbatical in South Africa did not touch on such issues. As the Legal Hearing approached, I realised that these debates were still very much alive. I decided to attend the Hearing as an observer since, as neither altogether outsider or insider, I felt I had no place as a participant. However, a brief conversation with the TRC's legal officer, Mr Hanif Vally, convinced me to submit a written submission. It consisted of an argument in legal philosophy as to why most of the judges of the apartheid era had been in dereliction of the duty they assumed in taking their oath of office.

Few people, especially lawyers, think that philosophy of law matters. Thus I was, to say the least, surprised to find that I would make the first oral submission of the Hearing. This surprise was compounded after I had taken my seat at the table in front of the Commissioners, for their first question to me was whether I wanted to take the oath before God to swear the whole truth or the affirmation (the secular version of the oath). Convinced though I was of the soundness of my submission, I had not thought to submit it as evidence to whose truth I would have to swear. Nor had I thought that I would be questioned by the Commissioners, in effect cross-examined, once my sworn oral submission had closed. And as the Hearing progressed, I found myself riveted by the way in which participants either directly or indirectly engaged with some of the central questions of legal and political philosophy.

My initial thought had been to write a short article about the Hearing. But after its ambiguous course and conclusion, I realised that the article could not be short if only for the reason that the moral, political and legal issues were just too complex to be captured quickly. In addition, there is widespread international interest in the TRC since the topic of "transitional justice" has become urgent as new regimes struggle in the name of justice to come to terms with injustices of the past. And so I thought it worth attempting to respond to the need to provide a partial record of the Hearing.

When my first respectable draft ran to well over 100 pages, I began to think of the project as a short book, one that combines a narrative of the Hearing with moral, political and legal analysis. In particular, my ambition is to grapple as best I can with the issue which perplexed me during the Hearing, one which was raised time after time by many of the readers of various drafts of this work who felt a sense of personal moral disquiet as a result of their reading.

This issue was most perspicuously put by Mike Taggart, who said that the critique unleashed by the Hearing (at least in my hands) is like a wrecking ball demolishing on all sides. It is relentless, leaving no shelter behind which to hide, except finally fidelity to law.

Put differently, not only those who were involved directly in the Hearing, whether through participation or through being brought under its scrutiny, but all who can imagine themselves in their position, find that the process poses difficult and quite personal moral questions. South Africa's judges were in the limelight, but we cannot judge them without at the same time subjecting ourselves to judgment.

As someone who decided to leave South Africa in the 1980s, I failed to make the contribution to the new South Africa for which my education had prepared me, and now I choose—through publishing this book—to sit in judgment from the comfort of Toronto on those who stayed in South Africa. Others may judge me harshly for this. But my sense is that anyone who ventures along the path of critique will find him- or herself personally implicated, even self-incriminated, by the logic which the TRC relentlessly triggers. Since I have from the start thought that the Hearing was on the whole a productive process, I will in the end seek to defend the logic of the TRC's work in this very particular setting.

Many people have contributed to this book. Richard Hart's enthusiasm and his exceptional editing skills made swift production of the book possible. At a time when it seems increasingly rare for editors to care about the academic content of what they publish, it is a privilege to work with Richard.

I should also mention that this book has been written with two audiences in mind, international and South African. And here I must express my gratitude to Simon Sephton of Juta & Co. for making it possible to publish my book simultaneously in South Africa. While I was convinced early on that it was important to publish in South Africa as well as abroad, I have tried to provide information which will make the text accessible to an audience which is not very familiar with South Africa.

My debts in writing and revising this book are tremendous. Many of those who were kind enough to comment responded in great detail and with much thought, often passionately, sometimes vehemently. I have tried my best to deal with their criticisms. But in the nature of this enterprise, more than the usual disclaimer of the responsibility of any of those listed for any of the content of this book is in order.

I thank the following for comments on various drafts: Richard Abel, Carl Baar, Edwin Cameron, Sujit Choudhry, Stephen Clingman, Alfred Cockrell, Hugh Corder, Anton Fagan, Eduard Fagan, Robert Howse, Hudson Janisch, Jonathan Klaaren, Gilbert Marcus, Denise Meyerson, Jennifer Nedelsky, Toni Pickard, Sandra Prosalendis, Arthur Ripstein, Kent Roach, Craig Scott, Tony Sebok, Christine Sypnowich, Hamish Stewart, Scott Veitch, Danie Visser and Stephen Waddams. I have also had particularly helpful discussions about the TRC's work with Lee Bozalek, Mike Cherry, Zunaid Husain, Ian Marot, Christina Murray, John Parkington, Paul Taylor, David Schalkwyk, Nico Steytler, Paul Zille and the faculty who attended a seminar I gave at the University of Cape Town.

Special thanks go to the following, whose help went far beyond their comments on drafts. My sister Carole Lewis took time out of a very full schedule as Dean of Law at the University of the Witwatersrand to get information to me once I had returned to Canada. (And I draw attention to this familial relationship, since I quote approvingly from her submissions to the Hearing in Chapters 2 and 3.) Michelle Norton was responsible for that Cape Town conversation and then encouraged my tentative steps into the project as it developed. Jennifer Llewellyn, who through her own exciting work on the TRC has a particularly rich understanding of it, provided both research assistance and extensive comments on my drafts. Mike Taggart provided both initial encouragement and extensive commentary on my penultimate drafts. Cheryl Misak, as always, proved my most careful critic.

In Cheryl's regard, a word of explanation of the dedication is required. She became critically ill in April of 1998 and I would have left unfinished a project in which she had so intimately been involved had she not succeeded in fighting a deadly infection. Even at the worst times, the care she got over almost three weeks in the Intensive Care Unit of St. Michael's Hospital gave her family and many friends hope and, eventually, Cheryl herself the resources to pull through.

I also thank several members of the Truth and Reconciliation Commission who went out of their way to make material available to me: Yasmin Sooka, Tracy Stein, Hanif Vally, Willem Verwoerd and, especially, Melanie Lue.

The Connaught Foundation of the University of Toronto and the Social Sciences and Humanities Research Council of Canada made possible my stay in South Africa, as did the support of Ronald Daniels, Dean of my Law Faculty, Mark Thornton, Chair of my Philosophy Department, and Danie Visser, Dean of Law at the University of Cape Town. The first draft was written in the study of Dirk and Betine van Zyl Smit's beautiful house, and their generosity contributed greatly to the success of our stay in Cape Town. Irwin Manoim, editor of the *Mail and Guardian's* superb website, kindly gave me permission to quote from its archive. Tim du Plessis of *Beeld* kindly gave me permission to use his photograph of the swearing-in at the Legal Hearing of the Attorneys-General which appeared in the *Sunday Times* of 2 November 1997, p. 16, and Annie van Baart of the *Sunday Times* arranged its transmission to my publisher.

Last but not least, Alexander and Sophie, through their cheerful tolerance of the quirks of academic parents, helped in no small way.

In writing the book, I have relied on the written submissions to the Legal Hearing of the TRC and the Transcript of the oral proceedings. Since the Transcript is in poor condition in parts, due to technical problems with the recordings, I prefer to rely on written submissions where these formed the main part of the oral submission. I also rely on my own notes and on personal impressions over the three days of the Hearing, including informal conversations with Commissioners and participants. Some of the information and observations gleaned from the latter will be reported without direct attribution.

In the hope of easing the reader's journey through three crowded days, a Schedule of the Hearing is included at the end.

Since completion of the manuscript of this book, the 1998 *South African Law Journal* has published some of the submissions to the Hearing.

1

Truth, Memory and the Rule of Law

I listened to the Prosecutor and I saw that he did not have any ideas about us. He was ignorant of our ways and feelings. I looked at the Judge and the prosecutor and the thought came to me that they were ants and in engaging with them we were dwarfing ourselves. It is a curse to be a Judge when you believe that you hold the life of a person in your hand. Only God holds our lives in his hands. He gives it and He alone can take it.

Andrew Zondo, 19-year-old soldier of the African National Congress, after being sentenced to death for planting a mine in 1985 which killed five people in a South African shopping centre.[1]

1. Introduction

This book presents an account of three days at South Africa's Truth and Reconciliation Commission (TRC). It is an account of the Legal Hearing—South Africa's official inquiry into the legal order during the apartheid era and into those who sustained it.

The TRC is meant to form one of the principal building blocks in the "historic bridge" described in the "Post-amble" to South Africa's Interim Constitution of 1993—a bridge "between the past of a deeply divided society characterized by strife, conflict, untold suffering and injustice, and a future founded on the recognition of human rights, democracy and peaceful coexistence and development opportunities for all South Africans, irrespective of colour, race, class, belief or sex".[2]

The Post-amble suggested some of the essential features of the TRC by requiring that the South African Parliament would enact

---

[1] McBride Submission, 11.
[2] Constitution of the Republic of South Africa Act 1993, s. 232(4).

legislation to carry out the promise of the Constitution to lay "the secure foundation for the people of South Africa to transcend the divisions and strife of the past, which generated gross violations of human rights, the transgression of humanitarian principles in violent conflicts and a legacy of hatred, fear, guilt and revenge". The violations and transgressions, the Post-amble continued, could "now be addressed on the basis that there is a need for understanding but not for vengeance, a need for reparation but not for retaliation, a need for *ubuntu*[3] but not for victimisation".

The legislation itself had to put into effect the following scheme:

"In order to advance such reconciliation and reconstruction, amnesty shall be granted in respect of acts, omissions and offences associated with political objectives and committed in the course of the conflicts of the past. To this end, Parliament under this Constitution shall adopt a law determining a firm cut-off date, which shall be a date after 8 October 1990 and before 6 December 1993, and providing for the mechanisms, criteria and procedures, including tribunals, if any, through which such amnesty shall be dealt with at any time after the law has been passed".

The Post-amble concluded with the following ringing declaration:

"With this Constitution and these commitments we, the people of South Africa, open a new chapter in the history of our country.
    Nkosi sikelel' iAfrika. God seen Suid-Afrika. Morena boloka sechaba sa heso. May God bless our country. Mudzimu fhatutshedza Afrika. Hosi katekisa Afrika".

However, one should be aware from the outset that the Interim Constitution and its products like the TRC were the result of a compromise negotiated between the various political parties engaged in the process of designing a new order for South Africa. Since the handover of power was negotiated, it was not considered a realistic option to have Nuremberg-type criminal trials where perpetrators, or at least the main perpetrators, of human rights abuses would be punished for their crimes. Those who felt compromised by any kind of inquiry favoured an option of official amnesia about the past, a forgetting underpinned by a blanket amnesty. But this option was neither realistic nor morally acceptable. And so South Africans opted

---

[3] *Ubuntu* is a word which in this context means both "compassion" and "recognition of the humanity of the other"; see Kader Asmal, Louise Asmal, Ronald Suresh Roberts, *Reconciliation Through Truth: A Reckoning of Apartheid's Criminal Governance*, 2nd edn. (Cape Town: David Philip, 1997), p. 21.

for the truth commission model which had been developed in various forms within other systems of transitional justice, for example, in Chile, Argentina and El Salvador.

These commissions have in common only that they are official inquiries into the past which seek to present an account of the details of the repression inflicted by the old regime. The scope of such an inquiry, the powers given to the commission and the consequences that follow from it depend largely on the extent to which the old regime still holds power during the transition.[4]

As we will see, the TRC has vast powers and it goes well beyond any of its models in the degree to which it is open, driven by public participation, and able to craft and shape its inquiry. For the scope of its inquiry is wide, it has tools to enforce participation, and its reports are supposed to lead to institutional reform and reparations to victims.

The TRC's difference from other models is a result of its beginnings in a debate about how to manage the transition to democracy, and of the fact that it was designed by a parliament after public hearings, rather than by a presidential commission with its eye firmly on not rocking the boat. In addition, the appointment of Archbishop Desmond Tutu as Chair of the TRC resulted in a particular understanding of its role in reconciliation, one which was in no way suggested or required by the official statutory mandate. Under his direction, Commissioners go beyond the statutory mandate and actively seek professions of repentance from perpetrators of abuses and of forgiveness from their victims. The slogan adopted by the TRC—"Truth: the road to reconciliation"—indicates the seriousness with which the TRC takes the aspiration to reconciliation. Finally (and this was anounced early in 1998), once the TRC itself has formally been disbanded, its work will continue through a body known as the "Institute for Change, Memory and Reconciliation"

---

[4] In a useful comparative article, Priscilla B. Hayner notes the following four characteristics of a truth commission: "First, a truth commission focuses on the past. Second, a truth commission is not focused on a specific event, but attempts to paint an overall picture of certain human rights abuses, or violations of international humanitarian law, over a period of time. Third, a truth commission usually exists temporarily and for a predefined period of time, ceasing to exist with the submission of a report of its findings. Finally, a truth commission is always vested with some sort of authority, by way of its sponsor, that allows it greater access to information, greater security or protection to dig into sensitive issues, and a greater impact with its report": see "Fifteen Truth Commissions—1974 to 1994: A Comparative Study" (1994) 16 *Human Rights Quarterly* 597, 604.

which will focus on advanced research into the TRC's final report and participate in the global debate about the significance of the TRC for transitions in other countries.

The TRC was established in terms of the Promotion of National Unity and Reconciliation Act 1995. Section 3(1)(a) declares its task to be:

> "(a) Establishing as complete a picture as possible of the causes, nature and extent of the gross violations of human rights . . . including the antecedents, circumstances, factors and context of such violations, as well as the perspectives of the victims and the motives and perspectives of the persons responsible for the commission of the violations by conducting investigations and holding hearings".

Gross violations are defined in section 1(1)(xix) as:

> "the violation of human rights through—
> (a) the killing, abduction, torture or severe ill-treatment of any person; or
> (b) any attempt, conspiracy, incitement, instigation, command or procurement to commit an act referred to in paragraph (a),
>   which emanated from conflicts of the past and which was committed during the period 1 March 1960 to the cut-off date within or outside the Republic, and the commission of which was advised, planned, directed, commanded or ordered, by any person acting with a political motive".

The Commission is divided into three committees. The Committee on Human Rights Violations has the task of conferring victim status on individuals who claim to have been subject to human rights violations.[5] Those who have victim status conferred on them are eligible for government reparations. This committee has also taken it as part of its mandate (in terms of section 3(1)(a)) to hear

---

[5] 1995 Act, s. 1(1)(xix) defines "victim" as "(a) persons who, individually or together with one or more persons, suffered harm in the form of physical or mental injury, emotional suffering, pecuniary loss or a substantial impairment of human rights—(i) as a result of a gross violation of human rights; or (ii) as a result of an act associated with a political objective for which amnesty has been granted; (b) persons who, individually or together with one or more persons, suffered harm in the form of physical or mental injury, emotional suffering, pecuniary loss or a substantial impairment of human rights, as a result of such person intervening to assist persons contemplated in paragraph (a) who were in distress or to prevent victimization of such persons; and (c) such relatives or dependants of victims as may be prescribed".

Note that not all victims attend victims' hearings. The sheer number of victims results in the TRC selecting "representative" victims to tell their stories in a public forum.

testimony which will establish the "complete picture" of gross human rights violations; and, as we will see, it was a submission at such a hearing which eventually led to the TRC deciding that the Commission, rather than any specific committee, should hold an inquiry into the legal order.

The Committee on Amnesty hears applications for amnesty from those who have committed gross human rights violations. As long as the act fits the criteria set out in section 1(1)(ix) and as long as the applicant has made "full disclosure of all relevant facts",[6] amnesty will be granted. The grant of amnesty carries significant benefits, since it grants the applicant immunity from both criminal and civil liability.[7]

The Committee on Reparation and Rehabilitation has as its main task preparing a report to government which will form the basis for reparations to and rehabilitation of victims.[8] It also participates in one of the most important tasks of the TRC as a whole, the making of "recommendations to the President with regard to the creation of institutions conducive to a stable and fair society and the institutional, administrative and legislative measures which should be taken or introduced in order to prevent the commission of violations of human rights".[9]

In addition, the TRC has an investigating unit with police powers of search and seizure and the TRC itself has the authority to subpoena reluctant witnesses to appear before it.[10]

---

[6] 1995 Act, s. 20(1)(c). Amnesty can be granted for any politically motivated crime, but only gross human rights violations require an Amnesty Hearing.

[7] 1995 Act, s. 20(7)(a).

[8] 1995 Act, s. 25(1)(b)(i) permits the Committee to make recommendations on urgent interim measures.

[9] 1995 Act, s. 4(h) read with s. 25(1)(b)(ii).

[10] See chapter 6 of the 1995 Act. Section 31(i) provides: "Any person who is questioned by the Commission in the exercise of its powers in terms of this Act, or who has been subpoenaed to give evidence or to produce any article at a hearing of the Commission shall, subject to the provisions of subsections (2), (3) and (5), be compelled to produce any article or to answer any question put to him or her with regard to the subject-matter of the hearing notwithstanding the fact that the article or his or her answer may incriminate him or her.

(2) A person referred to in subsection (1) shall only be compelled to answer a question or to produce an article which may incriminate him or her if the Commission has issued an order to that effect, after the Commission—(a) has consulted with the attorney-general who has jurisdiction; (b) has satisfied itself that to require such information from such a person is reasonable, necessary and justifiable in an open and democratic society based on freedom and equality; and (c) has satisfied itself that such a person has refused or is likely to refuse to answer a question or produce an article on the grounds that such an answer or article might incriminate him or her".

The work of the TRC is thus threefold. First, it is supposed to bring to light the truth about how the edifice of apartheid was sustained, the truth about the inner workings of the apartheid machine between 1 March 1960 and 10 May 1994.[11] Secondly, it seeks to build a foundation for reconciliation through the illumination of truth. Criminal or retributive justice is put aside in the hope that truth will emerge through a process of collective inquiry aimed at promoting reconciliation. Thirdly, the insights gathered in that process, collected in the final report of the TRC, are supposed to assist in transforming the institutional framework of government. If the TRC's purpose is to do justice, the kind of justice at which it aims is best described as reconstructive—a mode of justice which seeks institutional transformation through an examination of the wrongs of the past.[12]

2. The Apartheid Divide

The ordinary day-to-day operation of the apartheid machine inflicted huge suffering on the majority of South Africa's population. In the cause of white supremacy, people were forcibly removed from their homes, their land was taken away from them, family members were separated from each other, they were stripped of their citizenship and consigned to dustbowls ruled by dictatorial puppets, and they were explicitly told that they should have just those rights and just that amount of education that would fit them into an economic system run for the exclusive benefit of the white minority.

Apartheid inflicted violence daily on all those who were the victims of its racist laws. That violence was "ordinary" only in that it was part of the fabric of daily existence. There was also the "extraordinary" violence of apartheid—the beatings, torture, and murder (sometimes amounting to massacre) which the security forces dealt out to political opponents of the ordinary violence.

---

[11] The 1995 Act has been amended once by Act 84 of 1995 to change the cut-off date from the original one of 10 December 1993 in order to include gross human rights abuses commmitted just prior to the elections of 1994.

[12] In an unpublished paper, Jennifer J. Llewellyn and Robert Howse argue that the justice with which the TRC is concerned is restorative: "Institutions for Restorative Justice: The South African Truth and Reconciliation Commission as a model for dealing with conflicts of the past". I address such an argument briefly in Chapter 4.

The focus of the TRC on "*gross* human rights abuses" and its start date for its inquiry of March of 1960 reflects its concern with the extraordinary rather than the ordinary violence of apartheid. For in March of 1960, police in Sharpeville—a black township not far from Johannesburg—opened fire on a group of blacks protesting South Africa's pass laws, killing 69 and injuring 180. The National Party government introduced a state of emergency and enacted legislation which permitted it to ban its main political opposition, the African National Congress (ANC) and the Pan African Congress. That banning in turn resolved both the ANC and the Pan African Congress to turn to armed struggle to bring about change in South Africa. The government's decision to outlaw the main agents of black opposition to apartheid and those agents' decision to resist by armed force began a process which ended formally with the first election on the basis of a universal franchise in 1994.

Legal opposition to this cruel and degrading regime was virtually closed off to blacks during the 1960s. Illegal opposition was met with the iron fist of the security forces and even those who chose legal oppposition often found themselves targeted by the police or the military.

The security forces enjoyed vast powers to detain for interrogation suspected opponents of the regime, and the statutes which empowered them defined the offences against the regime very broadly. However, the security forces and their political masters often, especially in the last years of the regime, found these powers "under law" insufficient. They commonly resorted to extra-legal methods—murder and torture—in a bid to get rid of opposition leaders and to cow the youth of South Africa's townships, who had taken the fight against apartheid to the streets.

The law under which the security forces operated made it very difficult to get proof of what happened in detention. Torture was inflicted by groups of men on one detainee at a time, and so it was the word of one against the lies of many. Those who died often died alone, whether in detention or in "hits" outside of detention, and the security forces were adept at "sweeping" the scenes of their crimes to get rid of evidence.

During apartheid all this was well known to those who did not choose to close their eyes and ears. The majority of whites did so choose, preferring to believe that tales of suffering, torture and murder were but communist propaganda, an important element in what was claimed by the security establishment to be a "total onslaught" against South Africa. It was, to be sure, necessary for them to hold this belief in order to avoid confronting the facts about the ordinary violence of apartheid.

Of the rest of the whites, a small minority knew and did something, either by trying to work against apartheid from within or by joining the liberation organisations. The other part of those in the know were whites who approved of what they knew, who knew but simply did not care, or who were actively and zealously involved in inflicting the suffering.

South Africa's black population, subjected as they were to the day-to-day violence of apartheid, had no trouble believing the tales of torture of those who came out of detention. And they did not have to be told that the deaths of leaders and others in and out of detention were the work of apartheid's soldiers.

Given that so many South Africans should now know, in broad outline, what went on during those years, the work of the TRC may seem gratuitous. But its work is clearly important.

The TRC brings to light the details of what happened and forces a public acknowledgment both of the general pattern of events and of specific acts. It is, for example, only through the public hearings of the TRC that white South Africans have been forced to acknowledge that the security forces systematically engaged in assassinating their opponents. It is also important to surviving victims and their families and friends to have publicly aired exactly what was done, and family and friends of those who were murdered, some of whom disappeared without trace, need to get a public account. By offering amnesty to those who fully confess to having committed gross human rights abuses in the cause of maintaining (or opposing) apartheid, the hope of the TRC is that the facts of who did what to whom and under whose orders will come to light. In addition, there is the hope that a full understanding of the past will promote construction of a better future. The hope of "never again"—that the inequities of the past will not be repeated—is thought to require a full confrontation with the past.[13]

---

[13] One should also note that the government, dominated by the African National Congress, has not shown itself to be entirely immune from the knee-jerk reactions of the old order. Its policy in regard to maximum security prisons and its proposed legislation on bail, both a reaction to public panic about uncontrolled crime, have been criticised by human rights activists as a return to the ways of the past.

Finally, what people should know does not of course equate to what they do or want to know and the TRC regards it as crucial to South Africa's future that white South Africans acknowledge their responsibility for the wrongs of the past. It is of course the case that South Africa's future depends in large part on the participation of white South Africans in building a new order, for white South Africans had what amounted to a legally enforced monopoly on skills under apartheid. This fact alone would have required that many of the officials of the old regime kept their jobs. But in any case it was agreed between the parties to negotiations about the shape of the new order that civil servants would keep their jobs until retirement if they did not opt to be pensioned off. And no less important than the commitment of white government officials to the new order is the commitment of whites in the private sector. So the TRC has seen one of its tasks to be the education both of white supporters of the old regime and of those, who while they might not have been active supporters, could not be categorised as resisters.

Since many whites fear or resent the TRC, there is deep resistance to its work. For example, on 3 November 1997, the *Cape Times* reported that Archbishop Tutu, Chairperson of the Truth Commission, had been denied the honour of the Freedom of Cape Town by City Council members from the old ruling party—the National Party—because they are resentful of his work on the TRC.[14] The very next day, the *Cape Times* reported that a witness who had come forward to implicate the head of the Commission's Investigative Unit, Dumisa Ntsebeza, in one of the worst massacres carried out by a liberation organisation, had confessed that his evidence was concocted by senior policemen.[15]

However, resistance to the TRC is by no means confined to whites. The TRC finds itself caught between those who desire official amnesia—a forgetting of the past in order to get on with things—and

---

[14] The Council relented after a week of intense public criticism, bestowing the honour unanimously on Archbishop Tutu.

[15] The Heidelberg massacre, carried out by the armed wing (APLA) of the Pan African Congress, took place shortly before the first democratic elections were held in South Africa. Armed men burst into a crowded bar (the Heidelberg Tavern) and indiscriminately fired on the patrons, killing four (three of whom were not as it happens white) and injuring others. Ntsebeza was accused by the witness, Bennett Sibaya, of providing a getaway car for the soldiers. Had the accusation not been convincingly disproved, the entire work of the Commission would have been put under a cloud of suspicion. (Though it must be noted that Sibaya has since put into doubt the evidence he gave to the Commission of Inquiry established to investigate his allegations.)

those who want the only kind of justice they consider appropriate—criminal or retributive justice.

At the least, the work of the TRC, even its very existence, evokes strong and conflicting emotions both in South Africans and in outside observers. Those who have participated in the hearings, or watched highlights on the news and in a weekly television programme devoted to analysing the work of the TRC, have mixed reactions. In Amnesty Hearings, few of the perpetrators seem ready to confess more than the bare minimum. Often they seem untouched by the process, either refusing to apologise or crafting their apologies in such a way as to avoid confronting their conduct. Moreover, the apologies are frequently tainted by exculpatory attempts to explain how the perpetrators were victims themselves of ideological brainwashing or how they were just following orders.[16]

Those at the pinnacle of the hierarchy, the cabinet ministers reponsible for the security forces, have consistently denied giving orders to torture and kill. They profess great surprise that their orders to "neutralise" and "eliminate" their opponents could have been so misinterpreted by their minions. They have no explanation of why they did not take action, given their professed commitment to the rule of law, when deaths followed such orders with great regularity.

The victims and their families thus often seem frustrated by the exercise—not enough comes to light and they find (a constant refrain) that the perpetrators have not bared their souls, or opened their hearts. And it is not only the victims of human rights abuses who might find repugnant the thought that even the worst perpetrator of such abuses can walk free as long as he fulfils the conditions for a successful amnesty application. Indeed, some families of victims brought a constitutional challenge—rejected by the Constitutional Court—to the amnesty provision in the statute, on the basis that the TRC had usurped the right entrenched in the Interim Constitution to have "justiciable issues settled by a court of law or, where appropriate, another independent or impartial forum".[17]

---

[16] Perhaps the most notorious example here is Winnie Madikizela Mandela, though it has to be said that Archbishop Tutu explicitly suggested to her an exculpatory form of apology; for a vivid account of the Hearing devoted to her activities, see Antjie Krog, *Country of My Skull* (Johannesburg: Random House South Africa, 1998), pp. 243–60.

[17] Interim Constitution, s. 20(7). See *Azanian Peoples Organisation (AZAPO) and Others* v. *President of RSA and Others* 1996 (8) BCLR 1015 (CC).

In addition, the thought is increasingly voiced in South Africa that the TRC's intention to be even handed is gravely misconceived in that it includes gross human rights abuses committed by the liberation organisations within the scope of its inquiry. The claim here is that this "impartiality" invites one to relativise the moral turpitude involved in maintaining apartheid by putting the gross human rights abuses involved on an equal moral footing with the acts of those who fought to overthrow an evil system. Here one encounters echoes of the famous *Historikerstreit*—battle of the historians—which broke out in Germany in the 1980s, when Ernest Nolte, a conservative political scientist, sought to explain the Holocaust as an understandable reaction to Bolshevism. The Holocaust here is portrayed as an "'Asiatic' deed" (one untypical of a European race) but one which has to be understood as an exceptional response to a prior and morally equivalent "Asiatic" terror inflicted by the Bolsheviks.[18] Similarly, in South Africa the concern is that an inquiry into human rights abuses on both sides invites whites to think of the extraordinary violence of apartheid as a justified response to the violence of anti-apartheid forces.

At the same time, the TRC is frequently accused of lacking the impartiality needed to command the respect of all South Africans because of the inevitable emphasis of the TRC on the abuses perpetrated by the security forces of the national government and on the sins of whites, together with the sympathy the Commissioners sometimes openly express for the general policy direction of the ANC government.[19] Given this range of feelings and reactions, no-one could write about the TRC dispassionately let alone impartially. Even those who are deeply sceptical of the good it can do are

[18] See Ernest Nolte, "The past that will not pass: A speech that could be written but not delivered", in Ernest Piper (ed.), *Forever in the Shadow of Hitler: Original Documents of the Historikerstreit, The Controversy Concerning the Singularity of the Holocaust*, James Knowlton and Truett Cates trans. (New Jersey: Humanities Press, 1993), p. 18, esp. at pp. 21–2. The original documents from this fascinating debate are collected in this volume.

[19] See for example, the opinion piece by Steven Friedman, Director of the Centre for Policy Studies, and a respected political commentator, in *Business Day* (website), 23 February 1998, "Commission's Impartiality under Fire". Friedman, responding to a call by Tutu for whites to apologise for apartheid and to accept the need for reconciliation, argues that the TRC, as it nears the end of its work, has "become more a source of division than of unity". He claims that the Commission's "promise of reconciliation was, from the outset doomed to failure" in part because the "religious imagery of its understanding of reconciliation" is "no more accidental than the prevalence of Christian priests and theologians in the truth commission: the desire of anti-apartheid politicians for a moral reckoning with the system was melded onto a particular religious view of reconciliation".

required by their scepticism to reflect on their place in both the old apartheid order and the new democratic order.

This fact is, I think, especially true of white South Africans, who, unless they were involved in the work of the liberation movements or in legal opposition to apartheid, were all to some extent complicit in sustaining apartheid. The TRC attempts to force white South Africans to judge themselves even as they try to form judgments about those who were on the front line of enforcing apartheid, whether these are the assassins and torturers of the regime or the judges who applied the laws under whose cover the assassins and torturers operated.

There can be no doubt, in my view, that the TRC goes about as far as one can to forcing South Africans, particularly white South Africans, to confront the institutionalised divide of apartheid South Africa—the divide between black South Africans who could not help but know of the ordinary and extraordinary violence of apartheid and the whites who refused to acknowledge or care enough about what was going on or who found the violence justified.[20] A public process of revealing the extraordinary violence of apartheid opens up the possibility of confronting one's role in passively standing by or actively participating in the ordinary violence.

Put differently, the direct benefit of the ordinary violence of apartheid to all whites was a "cushy" lifestyle, some (including myself) living in luxury virtually unmatched in the rest of the world. But that benefit could be sustained only by the extraordinary violence of apartheid and so the TRC should open whites' eyes to both the moral awfulness of apartheid and their responsibility for the way in which it was sustained. The TRC thus attempts to force white South Africans to ask themselves how they could have been complicit in such an evil ideology, and how they could have ignored or justified for so long the sufferings of the majority of South Africans.

It is worth noting here that the principal basis for the Constitutional Court's rejection of the legal challenge to the amnesty provisions in the TRC's statute was that the truth commission model is essential in contexts like the South African one to the development

---

[20] And the situation was made even more complex by the fact that the apartheid machine constructed a racial hierarchy with whites at the top, then South Africans of Chinese descent, then South Africans of East Asian descent, then, "coloureds" or South Africans of mixed black and white descent, with blacks at the bottom. This hierarchy gave to groups other than black South Africans a real incentive to participate in maintaining apartheid.

of democracy. The Court reasoned that not only had a policy of amnesty been mandated by South Africa's Interim Constitution, but the harm to a few who might have got more in the way of retributive justice through the criminal justice system, or more in the way of monetary compensation through the civil justice system, was outweighed by the benefits of the truth and reconciliation process, not only to victims in general, but to all South Africans. Here the Court offered two main reasons.

First, the Court said that the information which the TRC was likely to disinter would otherwise remain hidden. That would leave both "the victims and the culprits who walk on the 'historic bridge' described" by the Post-amble to "hobble more than walk to the future with heavy and dragged steps delaying and impeding a rapid and enthusiatic transition to the new society at the end of the bridge, which is the vision that informs the epilogue [Post-amble]".[21]

Secondly, the Court said that "even more crucially, but for a mechanism providing for amnesty, the 'historic bridge' itself might never have been erected":

> "For a successfully negotiated transition, the terms of the transition required not only the agreement of those victimized by abuse but also those threatened by the transition to a 'democratic society based on freedom and equality'.[22] If the Constitution kept alive the prospect of continuous retaliation and revenge, the agreement of those threatened by its implementation might never have been forthcoming, and, if it had, the bridge itself would have remained wobbly and insecure, threatened by fear from some and anger from others. It was for this reason that those who negotiated the Constitution made a deliberate choice, preferring understanding over vengeance, reparation over retaliation, *ubuntu* over victimisation".[23]

But, as we will now see, resistance to the work of the TRC can come from a different source than victims or perpetrators or those who feel that they will be lumped together with the perpetators; it also comes from those who for purely pragmatic reasons wish to limit an inquiry into the past for fear of disruption of progress.

[21] *Azanian Peoples Organisation (AZAPO) and Others* v. *President of RSA and Others* 1996 (8) BCLR 1015 (CC), Deputy President Mahomed, speaking for the majority of the Court. Justice Didcott concurred in the result but offered narrower reasons on some issues.

[22] Phrasing taken from ss. 33(1)(a)(ii) and 35(1) of the Interim Constitution.

[23] *Azanian Peoples Organisation* v. *President of RSA*, n. 21 above, at 1028–9, some footnotes omitted.

3. The Politics of the Rule of Law and the Politics of Memory

A statement by a man who has become the most important jurist of the new South African order, Arthur Chaskalson, the first President of South Africa's Constitutional Court, haunted the Legal Hearing and hovers over this book as a constant rebuke.

From the early 1960s, Chaskalson had played a role in representing accused in political trials which made him one of the two leading "political" or human rights advocates at the South African Bar. The other was Sidney Kentridge, and their influence is evidenced by the frequency with which their names dominate an account like mine. Chaskalson went on to became the first director of the Legal Resources Centre, which from 1979 moved political lawyering from a defensive and reactive stance to active challenges to apartheid legislation.[24]

In a speech in 1989, "Law in a Changing Society", to mark the tenth anniversary of the Centre, Chaskalson contemplated, though not with great confidence, the possibility of the dismantling of apartheid and the creation of a democratic society.[25] Although one could not, at this time, predict the end of apartheid, Chaskalson thought it important to set out a vision of the positive role law could play in establishing a democratic order.

Here he had to contend with the fact that law had been used as the instrument of apartheid. Unlike the new South Africa where the Final Constitution—successor to the Interim Constitution—explicitly requires that statutes are consistent with constitutional values, the Parliament of apartheid South Africa was supreme, unlimited by any constraints on its legislative power other than constraints to do with the "manner and form" of its legislation. In other words, statutes had to comply with various formal steps culminating in signature by the head of state in order to be recognised as valid; but it was taken for granted that there were no substantive limits on legislation, limits on the content of statutes. Hence, judges seemed under a

---

[24] Kentridge had towards the end of the apartheid era increasingly made the London Bar the focus of his legal work. He did accept a brief appointment as an acting justice of the Constitutional Court.

[25] Arthur Chaskalson, "Law in a Changing Society" (1989) 5 *South African Journal on Human Rights* 293.

duty to interpret clearly expressed legislation as the Legislature had indicated it should be interpreted, no matter how morally repugnant they might themselves find the legislation.

But, said Chaskalson, this created an "almost schizophrenic approach by courts" to interpretation of apartheid law. For the common law heritage of the judges required them to interpret statute law, in so far as this was possible, in the light of principles developed by judges in their decisions which "deny all forms of discrimination" and which seek "to protect fundamental rights and freedoms":[26] "They were at one and the same time being asked to articulate and give effect to equitable common law principles, and to uphold and enforce discriminatory laws: at one and the same time to be an instrument of justice and at another to be an instrument of oppression".[27]

Here Chaskalson is referring to the fact that the South African legal order is part of the family of common law legal orders, one in which judicial decisions on the interpretation of the law lay down binding precedents for the future. And, as we will see in Chapter 2, the common law heritage of South Africa includes principles derived from Roman-Dutch law, the legacy of the first white settlers.[28] In other words, judicial decisions over time are a source of law; together they make up the common law. And embedded in the South African common law were judicially crafted presumptions, which had their roots both in the English common law tradition and in the Roman-Dutch sources. Examples are the presumption that statutes should be interpreted so as to give maximum effect to individual liberty and the presumption that statutes should be interpreted so as to give maximum effect to a principle of equality of all individuals before the law. However, Chaskalson's claim that judges were under a duty to resort to common law in a legal order where Parliament is supreme and under the control of a government determined to use the law to implement an evil ideology is not unproblematic.

[26] Ibid., 294.

[27] Ibid., 294.

[28] The place of Roman-Dutch law has been a subject of academic controversy, in particular whether the old authorities on Roman-Dutch law are just part of the common law or in some way a superior source of law. Such controversy is often tinged by nationalism, by Afrikaner versus British national sentiments. However, since the Roman-Dutch authorities endorsed roughly the same set of principles as the common law ones to which Chaskalson referred, this controversy does not affect the rule of law issue canvassed in the text. Indeed, in the heyday of apartheid, Afrikaner nationalism favoured the plain fact approach described below, one which marginalised both the Roman-Dutch authorities and the common law.

He clearly acknowledges one problem—because statute law takes precedence over the common law, it seems that the particular common law presumptions will not apply as long as the government takes care to enact through Parliament clearly stated policy which is inconsistent with the presumption. Another problem follows hard on the heels of the first; even if judges were to use such presumptions when they could, their interpretations would always be subject to statutory countermand, a likely prospect if the government is sufficiently determined to get its policy implemented unchecked by the presumptions.

Most important is that Chaskalson's suggestion that judges are under a duty to resort to common law presumptions in cases of alleged ambiguity in statutory language is controversial. Even when statutes are not clear, so that one can make a case that there is an ambiguity in the statutory language which common law presumptions might clarify, judges have to be predisposed towards using such presumptions before the presumptions will have any effect. They have to adopt a view of the rule of law and of the judicial role in upholding the rule of law which requires judges whenever possible to interpret statute law so as to make it consistent with fundamental principles of the common law *because* of the moral importance of these principles.

In short, Chaskalson's view of the rule of law is controversial because many judges are hostile to any idea that their moral sensibilities should have any impact on interpretation. As they understand it, their duty as judges is to interpret the law as it was in fact intended by the legislators to be interpreted.

In my previous work on judges during the apartheid era, I characterised this alternative interpretative approach, one which was adhered to by the majority of South African judges, as a "plain fact approach".[29] Plain fact judges hold that the judicial duty when interpreting a statute is always to look to those parts of the public record that make it clear what the legislators as a matter of fact intended. In this way, the judges merely determine the law as it is, without permitting their substantive convictions about justice to interfere. And in South Africa, the facts of the public record—both the deeds and the policy of those charged with implementing apartheid—were

---

[29] David Dyzenhaus, *Hard Cases in Wicked Legal Systems: South African Law in the Perspective of Legal Philosophy* (Oxford: Clarendon Press, 1991), p. 57. The term was coined by Ronald Dworkin, *Law's Empire* (London: Fontana Press, 1986), pp. 6–11.

very clear as to what the National Party majority in Parliament wanted. Indeed, judges knew from the record that judicial decisions which imposed legal constraints on the implementation of apartheid statutes would usually be overruled by legislative amendments to make the government's intention plain. Thus in cases where arguably a statutory provision seemed ambiguous, such judges reasoned that their duty as judge required them to clear up the ambiguity, not by reference to a common law presumption, but by reference to the public facts of the matter about how the Legislature would have wanted the statute interpreted. And that understanding of duty was rooted in a particular conception of the rule of law. That conception has it that the role of judges in upholding the rule of law largely involves judges' seeing to it that the officials who implement a statute do so in accordance with the law as it was, as a matter of plain fact, intended to be implemented.

An example will help to clarify this issue. In the late 1950s, the common law presumption of equality was invoked to challenge the validity of a proclamation made under the Group Areas Act 1957. This Act clearly contemplated differentiation between racial groups in the sense that it provided that areas would be reserved for the exclusive ownership and/or occupation of a particular group; but there was no statement of its object which indicated or implied that the differentiation might be unequal.

In *Minister of the Interior* v. *Lockhat*[30] (1961), the Appellate Division, South Africa's highest court of appeal during apartheid, was faced with a challenge to the validity of a proclamation dividing the city of Durban into group areas on the ground that whites had been given the best areas while only the poorer areas were available to Indians and that suitable accomodation in this areas would not be available for some time. Lockhat, an Indian, argued that the effect of the division was to discriminate to a substantial and therefore unreasonable degree against Indians and such unreasonable discrimination had to be expressly authorised by the enabling legislation to be valid.

In the court which first heard this challenge,[31] Judge Henochsberg acknowledged that the Act did contemplate some degree of "differentiation". But he said that he could find no express authorisation in the statute of discrimination coupled with partiality and inequality to

---

[30] 1961 (2) SA 587 (A).
[31] *Lockhat* v. *Minister of the Interior* 1960 (3) SA 765 (D).

a substantial degree. He thus upheld the challenge because, in the absence of specific authority in the statute to the contrary, common law presumptions must prevail. He said that "the exercise of a power to proclaim group areas can and should . . . be exercised without the inevitable result that members of different races are treated on a footing of partiality and inequality to a substantial degree".[32]

Henochsberg's decision was taken on appeal to the Appellate Division. Judge Holmes, in delivering the unanimous decision of the Appellate Division, rejected the challenge. He accepted that the power to discriminate unreasonably had to be given expressly or by necessary implication. But though the power to discriminate unreasonably was not expressly given in the Act, he thought that it was "clearly implied":

> "The Group Areas Act represents a colossal social experiment and a long term policy. It necessarily involves the movement out of Group Areas of numbers of people throughout the country. Parliament must have envisaged that compulsory shifts of persons occupying certain areas would inevitably cause disruption and, within the foreseeable future, substantial inequalities. Whether all this will prove to be for the common weal of all the inhabitants is not for the Court to decide . . . The question before this Court is the purely legal one whether this piece of legislation impliedly authorises, towards the attainment of its goal, the more immediate and foreseeable discriminatory results complained of in this case. In my view, for the reason which I have given, it manifestly does".[33]

It is a rule of South African judicial practice that judges must not look to the parliamentary record—what was actually said in parliamentary debates—for evidence of legislative intention. But had Holmes looked there he would have found that in the debates leading up to the enactment of the statute, Nationalist politicians had emphasised that it was not to apply unequally.[34] So the question is, given the fact that he did not attempt to show that any part of the Act indicated this necessarily implicit authorisation, and given that Henochsberg could find no such indications, where did Holmes find it?

I suggest that the implicit authorisation resides in the public record revealed by the general design and implementation of apartheid policy. Whatever was said in parliamentary debates in 1950 when the Group Areas Act was first enacted, no adult South African

---

[32] Ibid., 786.
[33] *Minister of the Interior* v. *Lockhat*, n. 30 above, 602.
[34] 1950 House of Assembly Debates, cols. 7810, 7827.

would have doubted in 1960 that the Nationalist government and its executive administration intended to implement what Albert Luthuli, former president of the African National Congress, described in his Nobel Peace Prize Address in 1961 as "surely the most terrible dream in the world"[35]—a policy of total racial segregation designed to leave whites in a vastly superior position to blacks in every possible dimension of social and political life, including the ownership and occupation of land. Nor could there be any doubt that this policy was going to be implemented whatever the cost in suffering and humiliation to racial groups other than the whites.

Moreover, it is clear that Holmes thought of himself as duty-bound to come to that conclusion. He was anxious to point out both that the question he faced was a "purely legal one", to be resolved by statutory interpretation, and that it is not the court's role to decide on whether the statute serves the "common weal". Such remarks clearly indicate that the judge supposed himself to be legally required to decide a controversial case of statutory interpretation in accordance with the intentions which in fact explained the statute, whatever his personal moral views about the statute. And this understanding of judicial duty is ultimately based in a political theory about the relationship between judiciary and legislature. That theory says that judges act appropriately when they defer to certain facts of the matter about legislative intention and thus they should adopt interpretative tests which seek to find such facts before resorting to other sources of legal authority, most notably the common law.

Chaskalson, then, in depicting the dilemma of South African judges caught between the "facts" about the intention of apartheid statutes and the pull of common law principles neglects that class of judges who did not find themselves in that dilemma. And, as we have just seen, they did not find themselves in that dilemma because their understanding of their duty did not take them beyond what they took to be facts of the matter about legislative intention.

Chaskalson did note that in "reviewing the history of the courts of this country some writers have criticized the way in which South African judges have discharged their duties over the years". But he clearly thought it unwise to dwell on judicial failings and it is at this point that he made the statement I referred to earlier:

[35] Thomas Karis and Gwendolen M. Carter (eds.), *From Protest to Challenge: A Documentary History of African Politics in South Africa* (Stanford, California: Hoover Institution Press, 1987), vol. 2, p. 710.

"That they could have done better than they did is I think now clear. But that is true of all of us, and little is to be gained by lamenting the past. What is important is the future, and it is here I believe that we will come to appreciate that we owe much to our judges, and a great deal to some of them. For despite all the paradoxes they have somehow held to the infrastructure and have kept alive the principles of freedom and justice which permeate the common law. True, at times no more than lip service has been paid to these principles, and there have been landmark cases where opportunities to give substance to and uphold fundamental rights have been allowed to pass without even an expression of discomfort, let alone a vindication of the right. Yet the notion that freedom and fairness are inherent qualities of law lives on, and if not reflected in all of the decisions, is nonetheless acknowledged and reinforced in numerous judgments of the courts. That is an important legacy and one which deserves neither to be diminished nor squandered".[36]

Chaskalson's suggestion that, in the event that South Africa could implement a true democracy the past ought not to be lamented, must be taken seriously. He rightly enjoys the personal authority of a lawyer who dedicated his professional life to the oppressed, an authority now greatly enhanced by his Presidency of the Constitutional Court. Thus, his statement was frequently quoted at the Hearing. And one might think he was proved right given the issue which I mentioned in the Preface—that the truth which the Hearing seemed to unleash was like a wrecking ball, demolishing on all sides.

The question has to do here with the politics of memory. Is it healthier to leave a traumatic past largely behind, dwelling only on its positive moments, in order to go forward into a healthy future? Clearly, those who established the TRC answered "no" to this question and so the "no use in lamenting the past" stance may seem in direct conflict with the rationale for establishing the TRC.

The conflict has to be described, at least initially, in somewhat tentative terms because of a special problem which a TRC-type hearing encounters when it inquires into a legal order, especially into the role of judges. One might think that a TRC-type inquiry is justified as long as it confines its inquiry to investigations of perpetrators and victims, but that an investigation of judges risks politicising the judiciary in a way which compromises their role for the future.

One can note here that even in those transitions where it was

---

[36] Chaskalson, "Law in a Changing Society", n. 25 above, 295.

deemed fit to adopt a policy of lustration or of purging officials compromised by the past, judges have been seen to present a special case for exemption from lustration. The problem is well summed up by Neil Kritz, senior scholar on the rule of law at the United States Institute of Peace: "[T]he rule of law requires an independent judiciary insulated from political pressures. This generally means that judges are not removable from their posts. Even if judges were easily purged, it might take years to train a qualified class of new lawyers and judges to replace them on the bench".[37] On the other hand, as Kritz notes, there is a dilemma here:

"[I]n most cases of transition from totalitarian or authoritarian regimes, the judiciary was severely compromised and was very much part of the old system, implementing the repressive policies and wrapping them in the mantle of the rule of law. In post-war Germany, when victims of the Nazi persecution were authorised to file claims for damages, some of them were stunned to find their claims asigned to the very same judge who had sentenced the claimants or their relatives in the first place. In order to enhance the power and independence of the judiciary as part of the democratization process in post-communist Poland, a law was enacted establishing the irremovability of judges. One consequence, subsequently recognized, was that many tainted communist judges thereby became entrenched in the 'new' court system. An effort followed to create a system for the verification of judges based on their past activity, and apply that system to both prospective new judges and those already in office".[38]

However, it is important to see that the brief account of the rule of law and adjudication just given throws into question Kritz's understanding of the rule of law in much the same way as it throws into question Chaskalson's account of the dilemma faced by South African judges. Both Kritz and Chaskalson suggest that an idea of the rule of law as antipolitics is worth preserving during a transitional process, where a nation is moving away from a period during which one of the problems was that a repressive regime used the law as an instrument of oppression, thus inevitably politicising the role of judges.[39] They suggest, in other words, that the rule of law should be

---

[37] Neil Kritz, "The Dilemmas of Transitional Justice", in Kritz (ed.), *Transitional Justice: How Emerging Democracies Reckon with Former Regimes* (Washington, DC: United States Institute of Peace, 1995, 3 vols.) vol. I, p. xix at pp. xxv–xxvi.

[38] Ibid.

[39] Here I draw on Ruti Teitel, "Transitional Jurisprudence: The Role of Law in Political Transformation" (1997) 106 *Yale Law Journal* 2009, esp. at 2029 ff.

conceived as neutrally as possible so that judges can be seen to stand above the political fray of a transition, accountable only to the law.

The idea that the rule of law can be conceived as antipolitics is then thrown into question because the choice of conceptions of the rule of law for South African judges during apartheid was so obviously a political one. One cannot argue that the problem is that judges adopted a politicised understanding of the rule of law when no apolitical one was available.

Indeed, I will argue later both that the conception of the rule of law as antipolitics makes sense only within a plain fact approach to interpretation and that, in any case, the antipolitical stance of the conception is driven by politics, by the argument that it is politically appropriate that judges adopt that conception.

Moreover, while the politics of the different understandings of legal duty at play in adjudication might have been largely implicit for South African judges during apartheid, if an apolitical understanding of the rule of law was not available to them then, there is no reason to suppose that it will become available during a transition. Indeed, as we will see, implicit politics become wholly explicit if one does not choose amnesia or partial amnesia as the way to settle the issue of memory. The politics of the rule of law get obscured by a politics of memory which opts for total or partial amnesia.

Once one sees that the politics of the rule of law and the politics of memory are connected in the context of transitional justice, one is better placed to understand the kind of costs of amnesia which Kritz traces in the last part of the quoted passage. As the German post-war example shows, the grave damage to the institutions of law and justice that resulted from permitting compromised individuals to remain in legal office, whether as judge, other legal official, or academic, was not solely due to facts about their personalities. It was also due to the fact that their legal philosophies—their understanding of legal duty and the rule of law—continued unchallenged.[40]

In sum, in the South African transition where lustration or purging of officials was ruled out by negotiations, the option remained of bringing compromised legal officials to account for their doings. And that option could not be ruled out by a judgment about

---

[40] See Ingo Müller, *Hitler's Justice: The Courts of the Third Reich*, Deborah Lucas Schneider trans. (Cambridge, Mass.: Harvard University Press, 1991) and Michael Stolleis, *The Law Under the Swastika: Studies on Legal History in Nazi Germany*, Thomas Dunlap trans. (Chicago: University of Chicago Press, 1998).

the politics of memory which depended on a conception of the rule of law as antipolitics. Just as remembering the past will reveal the politics of the different understandings of the rule of law, so a policy of forgetting the past (however noble its motivation) will obscure such politics, perhaps permitting the bad old politics to exercise a hold on the future.

The complexity of the issues at stake here was best addressed by Friedrich Nietzsche in his 1874 essay "On the uses and disadvantages of history for life".[41] There he argued that we need history, but only to the "extent that history serves life".[42] He thus decried those who study history as a purely "antiquarian" pursuit, because that attitude treats history as a repository of dead memories—memories which contain no lesson for the present, providing at most a measure of comfort for those who wish to escape the present into the past.

Nietzsche also identified the "monumental" and the "critical" attitudes to history. The former looks to history to find an unbroken chain of great events which together provide the basis for going forward into a glorious future. But that attitude, he says, harms not only the past but also contains great risks for the future. In distorting our past in the fashion monumental history requires, we distort the product of that past—the present—and so lose sight of the present. We identify only those moments which seem positive stepping stones to greatness and ignore those on which a critical history—a "tribunal" "which judges and condemns"—would fasten.[43]

But Nietzsche does not think that critical history is without its problems. For one thing, "every past is worthy of being condemned"; "it is in the nature of human things [that] human violence and human weakness have always played a mighty role in them".[44] Put differently, given that all of us have pasts which are vulnerable to damaging scrutiny, opening up "the past" to scrutiny will implicate each of us, and not always in a productive fashion. For another, to get on with life sometimes requires forgetting in order not to be weighed down by the burdens of the past. An obsession with the past is like a state of perpetually imposed sleeplessness—it cripples action here and now.[45] And finally, critical history is "always dangerous" because in its nature it risks becoming self-serving. We do it to identify the "aberrations" of the past in order to free ourselves of them, and that

---

[41] In Friedrich Nietzsche, *Untimely Meditations*, R.J. Hollingdale trans., intro. by J.P. Stern (Cambridge: Cambridge University Press, 1997), p. 57.
[42] Ibid.   [43] Ibid., pp. 70–2.   [44] Ibid., p. 76.   [45] Ibid., p. 62.

amounts to an attempt to give ourselves "as it were *a posteriori* [retrospectively], a past in which one would like to originate rather than the one in which one did originate".[46] In other words, critical history risks deteriorating into monumental history, as the victors in the process of recollection construct the past which they wish to take forward.

Nevertheless, Nietzsche deems critical history worthy of the risk, perhaps because the forgotten or distorted past still encumbers the present as a "dark, invisible burden".[47] One therefore has to take care in setting the limit to forgetfulness.

> "To determine this degree, and therewith the boundary at which the past is to be forgotten if it is not to become the gravedigger of the present, one would have to know exactly how great the *plastic power* of a man, a people, a culture is: I mean by plastic power the capacity to develop out of oneself in one's own way, to transform and incorporate into oneself what is past and foreign, to heal wounds, to replace what has been lost, to recreate broken moulds".[48]

Here Nietzsche seems to suggest that only a strong people, culture, or individual can cope with serious critical history. And perhaps Chaskalson's statement might then be interpreted not as a general stricture against lamenting the past, but as an anticipation of the dangers of lamenting the past when the bonds that unite those doing the lamenting are not only fragile, but in the process of being forged. But if this is Nietzsche's point—if it is the case that only one who risks nothing can afford to examine the past critically—then it seems that critical history becomes a luxury, an indulgence for those who can afford it not unlike the indulgence of history in the monumental mode.

The beauty of Nietzsche's analysis is that it alerts us to the dangers of both doing and avoiding critical history. It seems that we have to do it, but we have to find some way of setting a limit. And whatever way the limit is set will involve an unsatisfactory choice between conflicting considerations, unsatisfactory because there is no neat way of settling the conflict. Put differently, wherever the limit is set, some legitimate consideration will resist setting it there.[49]

---

[46] Ibid., pp. 76–7.   [47] Ibid., p. 61.   [48] Ibid., p. 62, his emphasis.

[49] And here I can rely on the authority of the Constitutional Court in *Azanian Peoples Organisation (AZAPO) and Others* v. *President of RSA and Others*, n. 21 above, where Deputy President Mahomed said (at 1029): "The result [of the general structure of the TRC] is a difficult, sensitive, perhaps even agonising, balancing act between the need for

I will in what follows grapple with the issue of limit-setting. The complexity of the task in this context might well seem to undermine my own efforts, and indeed I hope to provide enough material for my analysis to be vulnerable to a critique from within. But there is one conclusion which I believe to be on firm ground. The severe limit which Chaskalson thought necessary and which we will see was argued for at times at the Hearing was highly inappropriate. Some of his fears proved real – the Hearing failed to stay wholly on the side of productive investigation since it at times degenerated into the clamour of special interests, weakly governed by Commissioners who could seem both sanctimonious and partisan. Nevertheless, the Hearing succeeded in renewing and focusing a process of inquiry into law which can only serve South Africa well.[50]

4. The Legal Hearing

It is against this background that I wish to examine the TRC's Legal Hearing. This was but one of the hearings into the role of the professions and institutions of apartheid, the others included hearings into

justice to victims of past abuse and the need for reconciliation and rapid transition to a new future; between encouragement to wrongdoers to help in the discovery of truth and the need for reparations for the victims of that truth; between a correction in the old and the creation of a new. It is an exercise of immense difficulty interacting in a vast network of political, emotional, ethical and logistical considerations. It is an act calling for a judgment falling substantially within the domain of those entrusted with lawmaking in the era preceding and during the transition period. The results may well often be imperfect and the pursuit of the truth might inherently support the message of Kant that 'out of the crooked timber of humanity no straight thing was ever made' [Immanuel Kant paraphrased in Isaiah Berlin's essay on "Two Concepts of Liberty" in *Four Essays on Liberty* (Oxford: Oxford University Press, 1969) at p. 170]".

Though note that Mahomed went on to say that there "can be legitimate debate about the methods and the mechanisms chosen by the lawmaker to give effect to the difficult duty entrusted upon it in terms of the epilogue. We are not concerned with that debate or the wisdom of its choice of mechanisms but only with its constitutionality" (1029–30).

[50] Antjie Krog, Afrikaner poet and journalist, has this to say about the TRC after two years of in-depth reporting on its Hearings: "With all [the TRC's] mistakes, its arrogance, its racism, its sanctimony, its incompetence, the lying, the failure to get an interim reparation policy off the ground after two years, the showing off—with all of this—it has been so brave, so naively brave in the winds of deceit, rancour and hate. Against a flood crashing with the weight of a brutalizing past on to new usurping politics, the Commission has kept alive the idea of a common humanity. Painstakingly it has chiselled a way beyond racism and made space for all of our voices. For all its failures, it carries a flame of hope that makes me proud to be from here, of here": Antjie Krog, *Country of My Skull*, n.16 above, p. 278.

the role of the media, the medical profession, business, political parties, and the churches. These hearings were set up by the TRC in terms of its understanding of its broad mandate to establish "as complete a picture as possible of the causes, nature and extent of the gross violations of human rights . . . including the antecedents, circumstances, factors and context of such violations".

What makes these professional and institutional hearings different is that their purpose is not to establish who is a victim or who may get amnesty. Rather, they are meant to be inquiries into how professions and institutions which on the face of it seemed no different than their counterparts in Europe or North America, were deeply implicated in apartheid.

Archbishop Desmond Tutu said in his opening address to the Legal Hearing that it was the "most important of the professional hearings", almost as important as the "victim/survivor hearings". His reason was similar to the one contained in the paradox we saw Chaskalson sketch above; law was used as the instrument of apartheid but also seemed to hold out some promise of curbing its worst excesses.[51]

Indeed, one can say that even the illegal acts of the security forces were "under the cover of the law", since the law made it so difficult to get evidence of what was happening. Even more important, though, is that the Legal Hearing forced the connection to be made between what I have called the ordinary and the extraordinary violence of apartheid. By examining together the administration of statutes which set out the programme of apartheid and the statutes which set up the framework for suppressing opposition to apartheid, the Hearing revealed the continuum between ordinary and extraordinary violence.

In his address, Archbishop Tutu told of what it was like to grow up as a black child in a world of daily humiliation, not only of oneself but, inevitably more painful, of one's parents. That humiliation, he pointed out, was enshrined in the law of the land, laws whose violation demanded the sanctions of the criminal law, branding as criminals people attempting to exercise basic human rights.[52]

---

[51] "You see, in dealing with human rights violations, you are really concerned with justice, law, order, the disposition of power and authority and how these are regulated within conventional parameters so that they are not abused"; Transcript, p. 2.

[52] Transcript, pp. 3–7. Note that Tutu quoted extensively from Judge Pius Langa's submission, including the extracts reproduced below in Chapter 2, text to n. 59.

Judges and magistrates upheld those laws, even interpreted them so as to give maximum effect to their policy. The Attorneys-General—the civil servants in each province who controlled prosecutions—saw to the prosecution of violations of apartheid law. The legal profession, divided between the Bar of advocates who enjoyed an exclusive right of audience before the Supreme Court and the side-Bar of attorneys whose extra-curial work included instructing the advocates, by and large participated in sustaining apartheid law or did their best to ignore it. And the legal academy managed for the most part to educate their students and to write about the law as if apartheid did not exist.

In other words, the law was not self-executing under apartheid. It required administration, application and interpretation by judges, magistrates, prosecutors, officials of the Departments of Justice and Law and Order, and lawyers, both in the academy and the legal profession. Apartheid law was in large part the statutes enacted by the National Party-controlled Parliament, which enjoyed a legislative supremacy unchecked by any written constitution. But it was also the law that arose out of decisions made by civil servants, the judiciary, and the legal profession. And the great majority of lawyers had a legal education which failed to make apartheid and its law part of the curriculum, and also did not generally give students critical tools for understanding their society.

So at the Legal Hearing two not unrelated questions were put to those who staffed the legal order. How was it that you implemented without protest, and often with zeal, laws that were so manifestly unjust? And how was it that when you had some discretion as to how to interpret or apply the law, you consistently decided in a way that assisted the government and the security forces? And to those whose skills could have been used to resist—if only by criticising—apartheid law, the question was put of why they stood passively by or actively supported the regime.

These questions had a special poignancy for all except the ordinary civil servants in the government ministries who were subject to a rigid sytem of command from above. The judges and magistrates who interpreted the law, the Attorneys-General who directed prosecutions, the advocates and attorneys who argued cases, and the legal academics who trained lawyers and expounded the law, all had in common the following characteristics. They subscribed to the view that the administration of the law is also the administration of justice.

And they jealously wished to maintain the independence of their role from political interference under the new order by claiming that they had maintained independence under the old. The special poignancy comes about in that they seemed to think that their role during the apartheid era had an element of justice to it and that their commitment to independence of role was displayed in the public record of their deeds under apartheid. And, as we will see, the situation of the judges was the most poignant of the group who would not and could not claim that they were just following orders.

5. Trial or Inquiry?

The TRC invited all who had played a role in the apartheid legal order to present written submissions in answer to a set of questions on their role during apartheid. It expected that the most important of these submissions would then be summarised orally before the Commission during the Hearing, so that specific questions could be put to the presenters. At the end of each of the three days, a panel discussion was scheduled, in which representatives of different organisations who had not made an oral submission that day would debate the day's proceedings.

The TRC hoped to construct a different atmosphere from the one that prevailed at a victim or amnesty hearing. No-one would be applying for amnesty in a bid to escape a criminal prosecution, and no-one would be seeking to find out about the details of torture or assassination. No-one would need to be subpoenaed in order to get his or her evidence. Representatives of different parts of the old legal order would come forward to present their views in an atmosphere of inquiry rather than confrontation.

The TRC was thus anxious to assure those whom it invited that it was not concerned with findings of guilt or even with making judgements about what particular individuals or officers or organisations had done. The issue was not about putting a legal order, or any person or organisation, "on trial".[53] But these assurances, while

---

[53] For example, the letter sent to judges included the following paragraph: "The Commission would like to stress that as it is not the purpose of the hearing to establish guilt or hold individuals responsible, the hearing will not be of a judicial or quasi-judicial nature. The hearing is an attempt to understand the role the legal system played in contributing to the violation and/or protection of human rights and to identify institu-

sincere, proved unfounded. The atmosphere at the Hearing was more often than not confrontational and accusatory, more like a trial than an inquiry.

The stage was set for confrontation before the Hearing started. The magistrates, public servants who staffed the lower courts, and who had done most of the work of judicial administration of the apartheid laws, with one exception simply refused to make written submissions or to come to the Hearing.[54] The General Council of the Bar, the governing body for the different Bars of advocates in South Africa, nearly declined to make a written submission but in the end presented a three volume written submission and participated fully

tional changes required to prevent those abuses which occurred from happening again. We urge all judges both serving and retired to present their views as part of the process of moving forward".

Questions posed varied slightly according to the audience, but the following list of issues put to the judges is indicative of the general scope of the inquiry:

"(a) the relationship between law and justice.
(b) the principles and standards by which to evaluate the legal system;
(c) what informed judicial policy;
(d) what, if any, attempts were made by the Executive or other organisations/individuals to undermine the independence of the Judiciary;
(e) the relationship between the Judiciary and the State i.e.
   (i) the State Security Council;
   (ii) political Parties or organisations;
(f) the role of the judiciary in applying security legislation;
(g) the appointment of members of the Judiciary;
(h) the role of Commissions of Inquiry and the appointment of Judges to serve on these Commissions;
(i) the relationship between the South African Judiciary, legal profession and law schools;
(j) the exercise of judicial discretion;
(k) racial and gender discrimination in the Judiciary, legal profession and law schools;
(l) the role of other functionaries namely:
   (i)   the Minister of Justice;
   (ii)   the Department of Justice, including line functions and the Justice College;
   (iii) magistrates;
   (iv)   Attorneys-General;
   (v)   legal Profession: Bar Council, Association of Law Societies, Para-Legal Association;
   (vi)   lay assessors;
   (vii) interpreters; and
   (viii) the homelands (self-governing territories and independent states).
* Recommendations on how the legal system can be transformed to reflect a human rights culture and a respect for the rule of law, and which will address the perception that justice is the privileged domain of few in our society."

[54] The Regional Court President of Pretoria, Mr G. Travers, was the exception. In the end, Travers persuaded two magistrates to make submissions, but too late for them to be heard.

in the Hearing. Some Law Faculties made written submissions, but few sent representatives to participate. And we will see that some showed complete indifference towards the work of the TRC.

Several judges did in the end make written submissions. Others indicated contempt. For example, C.F. Eloff, Judge President or most senior judge of the Transvaal Provincial Division, said that that the content of the letter of invitation to participate left him with the "impression that what you plan to do on October 1997 will be a meaningless exercise".[55] Judge David Curlewis, who enjoyed a reputation during the apartheid era as a "hanging judge" and as impervious to arguments about the need for judges to uphold the rule of law, dismissed the invitation as "three pages of waffle".[56] He then proceeded to spark a public outcry by his remarks on sentencing a serial killer to thousands of years of imprisonment. For he expressed his great regret that the death penalty is no longer available in South Africa and condemned politicians for interfering with judicial work by abolishing the death penalty, when in fact it was the Constitutional Court which, in its first decision, found the death penalty in violation of South Africa's Constitution.

No judge was willing to participate in person in the Hearing despite the best persuasive efforts of Archbishop Tutu. Their absence was the most conspicuous feature of the three days of the Hearings. Their presence was perceived to be crucial, so much so that the draft programme issued on 22 October still had them scheduled to appear on 27 October, the first day. It was their failure to appear, combined with the non-appearance or reluctance to appear of others, which set the stage for the confrontational tone of the proceedings.

That tone was cemented by the Hearing itself. Archbishop Tutu, in his opening address, excoriated the judges. Judges, he said, were faced with moral choices under apartheid and generally they had made the wrong one. They had been faced with another choice—whether to appear before the TRC, and again they had made the wrong choice. This showed, he said, that they "had not yet changed a mindset that properly belongs to the old dispensation.".[57]

Four of the five oral submissions which immediately followed his address attacked the judges for failing to be there to account for their

---

[55]   Letter of 10 September 1997.

[56]   See the report by Carmel Rickard, *Sunday Times*, 2 November 1997, p. 16.

[57]   Transcript, pp. 8–9.

role. In the first, I argued that the judges of the old order should be present to answer a charge of dereliction of duty.

The second, given by Professor Lennox S. Hinds of Rutgers University on behalf of the International Association of Democratic Lawyers, put forward the case for regarding apartheid law as violating international human right standards to the point where apartheid law constituted a gross abuse of human rights. By implication, this case made the judges complicit in gross abuse of human rights, and Professor Hinds suggested, in answer to questions put by Hanif Vally, chief legal officer of the Commission who had the task of leading evidence during the Legal Hearing, that a good technical case could be made for arraigning judges on a charge of complicity in such abuse.[58]

In the third, Ms Paula McBride, a human rights activist, delivered a stinging indictment of the judiciary's role in meting out the death penalty. In the fourth, Ms Liza Key, a documentary film-maker, uncovered an unknown part of South Africa's legal history—the political biography of Dimitrio Tsafendas, assassin of Prime Minister and architect of apartheid Hendrik Verwoerd—which spoke volumes about the phenomenon of apartheid's institutionalised divide. In the fifth, four members of NADEL, the National Association of Democratic Lawyers, provided an account of the apartheid legal order as a whole in which the role of judges in sustaining the order figured prominently.

In all of these submissions, the depth of the critique of judges of the old order was matched by expressions of outrage that the judges of that order considered themselves above the TRC's process of inquiry into truth and attempts at reconciliation. And this issue did not go away. The Minister of Justice, Dullah Omar, pointedly began his oral submission by saying how pleased he was to accept the invitation to submit himself to the TRC's inquiry; even President Mandela, he said, would not be above accepting such an invitation.[59]

All oral submissions took the general form of submissions before the TRC, that is, of an oath or affirmation about the truth of one's testimony, followed by the submission, and then questions from the Commissioners, though the bulk of questions were put by Hanif Vally. The feeling of giving evidence in a court of law also no doubt contributed to the confrontational atmosphere.

[58] Transcript, pp. 47–8.
[59] Transcript, pp. 133–4.

Finally, the sense of confrontation was heightened by the nature of the submissions. Some, like those mentioned above, were deliberately confrontational, attacking judges or other officials. Some others adopted the classic pattern of perpetrators of human rights abuses— rote apologies coupled with exculpatory claims. Thus, just as in the Amnesty Hearings, the Commissioners would sometimes exhort those giving evidence to open their hearts, bare their souls.[60] Little new came to light in these submissions, except from that of the Director-General of Justice, where the officials had clearly been instructed by Minister Omar—a human rights lawyer and former detainee who had escaped one security force assassination attempt— to answer frankly any questions about their administration of security law.[61]

In addition, the Association of Law Societies—that is, of attorneys' associations—made full written submissions and participated fully, as did various groups of lawyers who have formed independent associations because of their dissatisfaction with the conservatism of the professions, most prominently NADEL, and the BLA or Black Lawyers' Association. Some "non-lawyers" made submissions. As we will see, these were among the most powerful of the Hearings. Several Attorneys-General made both written and oral submissions as did some individual practitioners and academics, a group of law students from the University of Natal, a representative of Amnesty International, and the Legal Resources Centre, the non-governmental organisation founded in the late 1970s to mount human rights challenges to apartheid legislation.

Like any trial, however, the bulk of the proceedings were in fact quite tedious. Perhaps as a result of the latitude the TRC had become used to giving victims to tell their story, the presiding Commissioners, Archbishop Tutu on day one, and Ms Yasmin Sooka on days two and three, made little effort to confine the oral submissions to the scheduled times.[62]

But there were electric moments on each day; on day one, the critique of the absent judges; on day two, the presentation by the General Council of the Bar; and on day three, the appearance of the

---

[60] See, for example, the Transcript, at pp. 472 and 497–8.

[61] The Department revealed the operation of an Internal Board which reviewed detentions. The officials were unable to give a satisfactory account of the workings of the Board, but significant was that some judges participated in its decisions; Transcript, pp. 607–36.

[62] And sometimes an oral submission consisted of largely irrelevant ramblings.

Attorneys-General. It was in those moments that the drama of law's relationship with justice was played out on a live stage. But before we launch into the account of the Hearing itself, it is important to raise one last question about both this work and the Hearing, one which, like the others raised so far, can be addressed fully only at the end.

6. Focusing on Judges

There is a legitimate question about both the Hearing's and my own focus on judges. After all, judges are but a small part of any legal order; indeed, they are a small part of any legal order's judicial system if we conceive such a system as including all those officials charged with making authoritative determinations of the legal rights of those subject to the law. The cutting edge of any legal order—the place where subject meets the law—is going for the most part to be in the enforcement of the law by the police and in the adjudication of disputes about the law by magistrates. For this reason, some thought that the focus on judges at the Hearing distracted the TRC's inquiry from more important issues.

However, I believe such a focus to be both inevitable and productive. Robert Cover, an American Professor of Law, showed why this is the case in his pioneering work on a group of judges in antebellum America who, despite their commitment to the abolitionist cause, almost relentlessly interpreted laws enforcing slavery in such a way as to shore up the institution of slavery.[63]

Cover pointed out that studies of the relationship between law and justice—a relationship highlighted when one studies the role of law in implementing and sustaining injustice—for the most part accepted "the perspective of the established order".[64] For such studies took the drama of the "disobedient" as exemplary of the problem—the stories of those who appeal to a "juster justice" beyond the law to justify disobedience.[65]

The disobedients, and any study which makes them exemplary of the relationship between law and justice, take the perspective of the established order because they assume that the law is what the

---

[63] Robert Cover, *Justice Accused: Antislavery and the Judicial Process* (New Haven, Conn.: Yale University Press, 1975).
[64] Ibid., p. 1.   [65] Ibid.

powerful in that order suppose it to be. Disobedients make their moral stand on the basis of the utter injustice of the law, an injustice created by the arbitrary will of a powerful and unjust ruler. And they therefore exclude the possibility that the law is more than the static embodiment of some ruler's will, determinable (as the plain fact approach suggests) as a matter of fact.

It is important, Cover thought, that a study of law and justice canvass that excluded possibility by asking whether the law provides opportunities to do justice which rulers, no matter how powerful they are, cannot completely control. Only that possibility allows that the relationship between law and justice might be an intrinsic one, one which creates tensions within the law when the powerful use the law as an instrument of oppression.

We have already seen that the central figure in the South African legal order, President of the Constitutional Court Arthur Chaskalson, and the central figure in the TRC, Archbishop Tutu, hold the view that the relationship between law and justice is to some extent intrinsic. And, as Cover argues, it is adjudication by judges which best manifests the tensions which arise out of that intrinsic relationship when law is put in the service of injustice. For judges everywhere claim that their duty is not simply to administer the law, but to administer justice. Indeed, the oath of office which South African judges swore during apartheid stated that they would "administer justice to all persons alike without without fear, favour or prejudice, and, as the circumstances of any particular case may require, in accordance with the law and customs of the Republic of South Africa".[66]

As I pointed out in my submission to the TRC, one can adopt the view that the justice of the law mentioned in the oath is simply the conception of justice which, as a matter of fact, the powerful have used the law to implement.[67] Alternatively, one can read some significance into the word justice, for example, by noting that the oath would look rather odd if one substituted for "justice" the phrase "ideology of the powerful".

Encapsulated in these two ways of viewing the relationship between law and justice is the age-old debate in the philosophy of law between legal positivists and natural law theory. Positivists argue that the relationship between law and "juster justice" or true justice is

[66] Supreme Court Act 1959, s. 10(2)(a).
[67] Dyzenhaus Submission, p. 1.

purely contingent on political circumstance, while the natural lawyers argue that there is some intrinsic relationship. The complexity of that debate, especially in its more technical aspects, goes well beyond the confines of this book.[68]

But an important, and I would argue the principal, aspect of that debate is illuminated by a focus on the role of judges at the TRC, even though their role was confined to some written submissions. For if we are concerned with the relationship between law and justice, then, as Cover says, we cannot study that relationship without maintaining the possibility that it is an intrinsic one. The relationship has to be instrinsic if law is to provide a place where those subject to it can contest it when it is used as an instrument of brute and arbitrary power. Only if the relationship is intrinsic can law provide the basis for judges to be more than the ants whom young Andrew Zondo encountered in the trial which culminated in his judicially-ordered death.

It is not that I think that the question of the relationship between justice and the law can be settled by three days of hearings before the TRC. But just as we hope to catch intimations of the answer to that question in the predicament of abolitionist judges in northern states in antebellum America, who sent escaped slaves back to slavery under the Fugitive Slave Laws, in the trial of judges at Nuremberg, or as people around the world struggle with the idea of how to do justice during periods of transition from one political order to another, so the TRC's Legal Hearing should echo beyond South Africa's borders. The three days in October 1997 when an entire legal order was in effect put on trial in Johannesburg provide a rare opportunity to reexamine the relationship between law and justice.[69]

---

[68] I deal with the technical aspects of the debate more fully in *Hard Cases in Wicked Legal Systems: South African Law in the Perspective of Legal Philosophy*, n. 29 above.

[69] The Hearing took place on 27, 28, and 29 October 1997.

2

Judicial Dilemmas: Tales of (Dis)empowerment

In our view, the judiciary is certainly not free from blame for the role it played during the period under review but that does not warrant attempts to denigrate its very substantial contribution to society during a contentious and troubled era in the life of the country.

Judges Smalberger, Howie, Marais and Scott of South Africa's Supreme Court of Appeal, concluding their written submission to the TRC.[1]

I am quite satisfied that during my term of office in Transkei the Judges there did everything in their power to protect the individual against the Executive and to uphold human rights.

Judge C.S. White, of the Transkei High Court, written submission to the TRC.[2]

Even the "liberal" apartheid judges gritted their teeth and got on with the job. In doing so, they sealed the fate of the oppressed. They stamped the respectability of their learning and the unassailability of their robes on the devious and cruel designs of the apartheid politicians and policemen. In many senses it could be argued that what they did was far worse than what the apartheid police did—they were educated enough to have known better.

Paula McBride, human rights activist, written and oral submission to the TRC.[3]

1. To Go or Not To Go?

In late 1996, Krish Govender, a human rights lawyer, made a submission at a Victim Hearing. Using the TRC's standard form, he filled in under "Victim" "The South African People", and under "Nature of Violation" "Injustice under the Apartheid Judiciary". It was this

[1] Smalberger *et al.* Submission, p. 17.
[2] White Submission, p. 1.
[3] McBride Submission, p. 2.

submission which began the debate which led to the decision to hold a Legal Hearing.

The TRC invited Michael Corbett, at that time Chief Justice of South Africa, to respond, which he did, saying that although he did not have a mandate to speak on behalf of the "judiciary as a whole", he had circulated his memorandum "among the present members of the Appellate Division" and that "it bears their endorsement".[4]

In his memorandum, Corbett defended the judicial record under apartheid and objected on practical and constitutional grounds to Govender's suggestion that judges who had held office prior to 1994 should be held accountable for their conduct before the TRC. This memorandum was the principal document in the debate leading up to the Hearing. It also exemplified a pattern in the responses to the TRC's inquiry into the judicial record and, as we will see, these responses reveal much about the predicaments of the apartheid judiciary. In particular, we will see that (contrary to Corbett's own view) the two main parts of his memorandum are connected—the force of the independence objection depends on the merits of his defence of the record.

Corbett's practical objection to judges being called to account before the TRC was that this was not "feasible":

In order to determine whether Judge X has allowed justice to be subverted in some alleged manner in a particular case, the TRC would in effect have to retry the case: read the record of the proceedings (often very long) and determine, often without the benefit of counsel's argument, whether or not Judge X came to the correct conclusion or not, and, if not, whether this was due to some improper factor or reason. The mind boggles at what all of this would involve. The impracticality of it all is manifest.[5]

Corbett went on:

But there is a more important, a more fundamental, objection to this suggestion. This has to do with the principle of judicial independence, an important facet of the constitutional separation of powers. In order to be true to his judicial oath and to administer justice to all persons alike "without fear, favour or prejudice" a judge must enjoy independence from the legislature, from the executive, from any body or authority which could be tempted to influence his decisions. Various constitutional provisions

---

[4] Corbett Memorandum, p. 1.
[5] Ibid., p. 11.

underpin such independence: e.g. the appointment of judges for life (subject to a statutory "retirement" age); a prohibition on the reduction of their salaries; security of tenure of office, subject only to a process of Parliamentary impeachment on grounds of misbehaviour, incapacity or incompetence. This does not mean that a judge is not accountable or above the law. He is accountable to a superior court of appeal; he performs his duties openly and in public and is thus subject to daily scrutiny and criticism; and in the last resort there is impeachment. Outside these parameters, however, a judge may not be called to account for his or her judgments or to debate and justify before, for instance, governmental bodies or commissions.[6]

His stance could only be consistent, however, if judges made no submission at all, which is why, at least initially, the judges seemed disinclined to respond in any way to the TRC's invitation. That some of their number in the end made written submissions, and that Corbett's successor as Chief Justice, Ismail Mahomed, stated that judges were free to appear, indicates that independence was not the only or even the most important issue.

The other reasons were well known, and they reveal much about the complexity of the new South Africa. From early on in the apartheid era, the National Party government packed the bench either with political appointments or with lawyers who had no history of opposition to apartheid. During this time, there was a small minority of "liberal" judges who consistently maintained their independence by deciding their cases, where possible, in the light of what they considered to be fundamental values of the rule of law. Since the majority of judges currently serving are still "old order" judges (judges appointed under the old order) judges from the minority group, as well as "new order" (newly appointed) judges, feared that a judicial debate about the old order would rupture the fragile collegiality which now exists and which they regard as necessary to make the new order workable. Put differently, collegiality in this context is not just a matter of judges getting along together but of judges committing themselves to the values of the new constitutional order.

The danger of rupture is no doubt real. And this was especially so if South Africa's two most senior judges were to appear. Here I refer

---

[6] Ibid., pp. 11–12.

to Ismail Mahomed, who presides over the Supreme Court of Appeal—the renamed Appellate Division which is now the final court of appeal on all except constitutional matters—and to Arthur Chaskalson, President of the Constitutional Court, the final court of appeal on constitutional matters.[7] They were both distinguished human rights advocates during the apartheid era and the public perception of the role of judges in the new order will depend in large measure on their leadership.

Mahomed, who is of Indian or East Asian descent, would not have been offered, nor would he have accepted an offer, of appointment to the bench until the end of apartheid was in clear sight. Indeed, he has recently told of his humiliation at the Pretoria Bar, which openly embraced racial segregation; and of how, after moving to the more liberal Johannesburg Bar, he was still precluded by apartheid legislation from having an office in Chambers, from using the courts' robing roooms, even from using the Bar's common room, so that he sometimes ended up eating his lunch in the toilets. He has also described the humiliation inflicted when, in appearing before the court over which he now presides, he had to leave the province in which it is situated at nightfall each day since that province—the Orange Free State—precluded by law people of his race from being within its boundaries after dark.[8]

And Chaskalson also could not have served, nor would he have been invited to serve, as a judge under apartheid. He had been part of Nelson Mandela's defence team in the trial which ended in Mandela's life imprisonment, and, as we saw in Chapter 1, had founded and pioneered the work of the Legal Resources Centre, an organisation devoted to human rights law. Indeed, it was revealed during the Hearing that he and other human rights lawyers had been targeted for special attention by the security services.[9]

For either of them to criticise judges of the old order would risk much. This would be particularly so in the case of Mahomed, since it is well known that his appointment as Chief Justice was formally opposed by most of the old order judges still serving on the Supreme

[7] The court also has *de novo* jurisdiction over certain constitutional issues in terms of the Final Constitution of 1996, s. 167.

[8] "Address by the Honourable Mr Justice Ismail Mahomed at a dinner given by the Johannesburg Bar on 25 June 1997 to celebrate his appointment as Chief Justice of the Supreme Court of Appeal" (1997) 114 *South African Law Journal* 604, at 604–5.

[9] See Transcript, p. 404, oral submission of the Legal Resources Centre.

Court of Appeal. One of them, Judge Joos Hefer, whose record of diligence during apartheid in keeping the law from being an obstacle to security force action was second to none, publicly called on Mahomed to do the "honourable" thing and withdraw his nomination.[10] Chaskalson, in contrast, presides over a Court created and appointed under the new dispensation. Its present members are mostly drawn from a short list compiled by a Judicial Services Commission, which conducts public interviews after a process of nomination; the final selection from the shortlist is made by the country's President.[11]

As we will see, one can gather from the written submission Chaskalson and four other judges made that his view is that the institutional legitimacy which he and the other judges of the Constitutional Court are in the process of building requires collegiality between the judges of all courts. Morever, for both Chaskalson and Mahomed, as well as for less senior new order judges, it must have been significant that it would appear odd for a judge appointed to the new order bench because of his or her credentials as an advocate for human rights to continue such advocacy against fellow judges before the TRC.

Given the tensions in the air, the best hope was for an appearance by a retired judge of the old order with good rule of law credentials, and those criteria pointed to Corbett. He had been appointed Chief Justice a couple of years before the end of apartheid and was one of the few judges of the old era, and one of a small minority in the old order Appellate Division, who had consistently displayed his genuine commitment to the rule of law.

Such was his commitment, that Pierre Rabie, Chief Justice during the period of severe repression of the 1980s, had kept Corbett off the "emergency team". Rabie, as Chief Justice, controlled the composition of particular benches, and when it came to deciding cases which challenged the validity of executive action to control opposition to apartheid, he generally selected judges he thought could be trusted to reject challenges to repression.[12]

---

[10] See Mungo Soggot, "Battle Lines Drawn Over Chief Justice", *Electronic Mail and Guardian*, 20 September 1996. Hefer's call earned him a public rebuke from Corbett.

[11] This method of open appointment applies to all appointments to the bench in the new order.

[12] See Edwin Cameron, "Nude Monarchy: The Case of South Africa's Judges" (1987) 3 *South African Journal on Human Rights* 338; John Dugard, "*Omar*—Support for Wacks's Ideas on the Judicial Process?" (1987) 3 *South African Journal on Human Rights* 295 and

In the absence of a "new order" judge of Mahomed's or Chaskalson's stature, or an "old order" judge like Corbett, it was almost inevitable that no judge who had enthusiastically served the old order would come forward. Since, as we have already seen in Chapter 1, one can safely venture that many of those judges feel they have nothing to apologise for, they would have attended only if an oral submission threatened to make a compelling case for their attendance.

Yet another reason for judicial absence must be aired, one which comes across in all of the written judicial submissions. Judges of the old order, even those who had a reputation for commitment to the rule of law, were deeply unwilling to confront their past. This unwillingness was in part due to the phenomenon of the institutionalised divide mentioned earlier, which created different worlds for white and black South Africans. And this phenomenon combines with the all too human desire of judges to regard themselves as having done their duty, where duty means not just carrying out the technical requirements of a role, but having been morally upstanding occupants of that role. As we will see, this desire is nowhere better illustrated than in that part of Corbett's memorandum where he objected strenuously to two issues taken up in Govender's submission.

One issue concerned the imposition of a death penalty on Andrew Zondo, whose words after his sentence to die by hanging are reproduced at the beginning of Chapter 1. Zondo had been found guilty in 1986 of planting a limpet mine in 1985 which killed five civilians. He was 19 years old at the time, 20 when he was hanged.

The judge who condemned Zondo to hang was Raymon Leon, widely regarded as one of the most liberal judges of the most liberal bench in the country, the Natal bench. While the death sentence was mandatory for acts like Zondo's, it was in the discretion of a judge, sitting with two assessors, to find extenuating circumstances; and Leon had found none. He recognised Zondo's youth as a potential factor in a finding of extenuating circumstances but found that, in the circumstances, it was not a compelling factor.

"The Judiciary and National Security" (1982) 99 *South African Law Journal* 655; and Geoffrey Bindman, *South Africa and the Rule of Law* (London: Pinter Publishing (International Commission of Jurists), 1988). For a sensitive treatment of the issue, see Stephen Ellman, *In a Time of Trouble: Law and Liberty in South Africa's State of Emergency* (Oxford: Clarendon Press, 1992), ch. 3.

Govender had this to say:

Amongst the extenuating circumstances advanced before sentence, was the factor of [Zondo's] youth. This alone ought to have spared him his life, as it would have, in any other civilised Court of law in the world. This was rejected.

This case in particular was steamrolled from trial to conviction to appeal, petition and finally execution, at an unusually rapid pace, to satisfy the apartheid cries for revenge. The task of the defence lawyers and expert witnesses who were called was made difficult in a highly charged atmosphere of great hostility. Even during a short recess in Court Mr Zondo was assaulted by a member of the public as he sat in the dock.[13]

Here is Corbett's response:

At the time when this case was decided (1986) the law imposed a mandatory death sentence upon a person eighteen years of age or older convicted of murder where no extenuating circumstances were found to be present. The Court had no choice in the matter *[emphasis added]. The onus of establishing extenuating circumstances rested on the accused. In deciding the issue of extenuating circumstances the Court (comprising the Judge and two assessors) had to assess the accused's moral blameworthiness, taking into account* all *[original emphasis] the circumstances, including the personality of the accused and the nature of the murder and the manner of its commission.*

The trial Judge was an experienced and highly respected member of the Natal Bench. The Court gave careful and anxious consideration to the question of extenuation and took into account the fact that the accused was a little over nineteen and a half years of age when the crime was committed. The circumstances of the case were that the accused planted an armed limpet mine at Amamzimtoti on 23 December 1985, two days before Christmas. It was timed to detonate at 11h00, which it did. Five people, including two children, were killed and scores were injured. The Court found on the evidence that this was a deliberate, pre-meditated killing and that the accused had afterwards expressed to his accomplice his dissatisfaction with the fact that "only four people" had been killed. It appears that in 1982, at the age of sixteen (and then in his Matric class at school) the accused was recruited by the African National Congress and sent to neighbouring countries, where he joined Umkhonto we Sizwe [the military wing of the African National Congress]. He spent about two

---

[13] Govender Submission, p. 2.

years in Angola, during which time he learned to handle explosives and fire-arms. In 1985 he returned to South Africa, where he taught others (some of them older men) what he had learned in Angola. The Court concluded that although the accused's youth was a factor, it was not a compelling factor; and that taking all the circumstances into account a finding of no extenuating circumstances should be made.

After judgment the trial Judge refused an application for leave to appeal to the Appellate Division on the issue of extenuating circumstances. The accused petitioned the Chief Justice and the petition was considered by three Judges of the Appellate Division, who refused leave to appeal. Leave could be granted only if there were reasonable prospects of success; and the appeal could only succeed if the Court was shown to have materially misdirected itself or committed an irregularity or if the finding on extenuation was one which no reasonable court could have made. No such grounds were established.

The allegation that this case was "steamrolled" is, in my view, without foundation. The crime was committed on 23 December 1985. The accused appears to have been arrested shortly thereafter for on 4 January 1986 he made a statement about the event to a magistrate. His trial took place . . . at the beginning of April, 1986. He was represented by experienced counsel. There is no suggestion that the accused was not given adequate opportunity to present his case . . . I am [not] able to comment on the averments of a "highly charged atmosphere of great hostility" and of an assault on the accused by a member of the public, save to say that such trials are conducted in open court and that the nature of the crime was such as to evoke strong public reaction, at least in certain segments of the community.[14]

The other issue which aroused Corbett's indignation was Govender's suggestion that the TRC should investigate the case of Demitrio Tsafendas. In 1969 Tsafendas had assassinated Dr Hendrik Verwoerd, Prime Minister of South Africa and architect of grand apartheid. He used his office as a parliamentary messenger to get close enough to Verwoerd to stab him. At his trial, Tsafendas had been found unfit to plead because he was mentally disordered. He was thus ordered to be detained "at the State President's pleasure" and he is still alive in a South African mental hospital. Govender referred to Tsafendas as a "victim of apartheid" and suggested that the failure to try him had to be investigated.[15]

[14] Corbett Memorandum, pp. 2–4.
[15] Govender Submission, p. 6.

Corbett's response was that Tsafendas had been adequately represented before the Judge President of the Cape Provincial Division,
Judge A.B. Beyers. The medical evidence was that he was a schizophrenic, and he thought that his life was ruled by a tape worm.
Corbett added that the "suggestion that the case should be 'reviewed
and investigated' is, with respect, pointless and absurd. To describe
him as a 'victim of apartheid' is, in my view, bizarre".[16]

Once he had responded to the specific examples Govender had
adduced, Corbett proceeded to "correct certain misinformed asump-
tions which appear to underlie his presentation".[17] His "correction"
emphasised the difference in the judicial oaths of office under the old
order and under the new. Under the old, judges swore to "administer
justice to all persons alike, without fear, favour or prejudice and . . .
in accordance with the law and customs of South Africa", whereas
under South Africa's Interim Constitution of 1993, they swore to
"uphold and protect the Constitution of the Republic and the fundamental rights entrenched therein and in doing so to administer
justice to all persons alike without fear, favour or prejudice, in accordance with the Constitution and the Law of the Republic". Corbett
emphasised, that is, the fact that in the old order, "Parliament was
supreme":

*For practical purposes [Parliament] could pass any law it liked; and it
did so. The courts had no power to question the validity of the laws
Parliament made. Still less could they declare them invalid. The court
had no option but to apply the law as they found it, however unjust it
might appear to be. Of course, often the statute passed by Parliament was
unclear and in such cases, when required to interpret it, the court was
presented with a choice between an interpretation which produced
inequity and one which did not. In such cases the courts were in a
position to make the latter choice in the process of construing the will of
Parliament; and they often did so. In this they were legitimately
applying the principles of Roman-Dutch law relating to statutory interpretation, which included the presumption that the Legislature did not
intend to oust the jurisdiction of a court of law, or to interfere with the
common law more than was plainly and unambiguously indicated;[18] the
presumption against retrospectivity; the presumption that the Legislature*

---

[16] Corbett Memorandum, pp. 12–13.
[17] Ibid., p. 7.
[18] For the relationship between Roman-Dutch and common law, see Chapter 1, n. 28.

did not intend an inequitable, unjustifiable or unreasonable result; the restrictive interpretation given to penal provisions and the presumption in favorem libertatis *[in favour of liberty]; and so on. I could quote many examples illustrative of the application of this approach to statutory interpretation in the so-called "apartheid years", but this would unduly protract this presentation. Thus, generally speaking, our courts did by a process of interpretation ameliorate in many instances the effect of harsh laws. It would be foolish for me to contend that they always did so; or to seek to defend every decision in the human rights field; or to claim that the courts did all that they could have done. But the broad picture is, in my estimation, a favourable one and very different from that portrayed by Mr. Govender.*

The judge then seemed to hesitate for a moment in his praise for the judiciary, realising that "[i]t might perhaps be said that I, having served on the Bench since 1963, have been too close to the action to make an objective assessment". But he hesitated only a moment:

Let me, therefore, quote what Mr. Sidney Kentridge QC had to say on the topic in an article published in the September/October 1994 number of "Counsel" under the heading "The Independent Bar in South Africa": "During the apartheid years in South Africa many people helped keep alive the idea that the individual has rights and liberties which the state is not entitled to infringe. But there are not many organised institutions of which this could be said. Among them were certainly the Bar and the Supreme Court".

After referring to certain political appointments made by the then South African government, Mr. Kentridge proceeds: "It had an undoubted and serious effect on the standards and standing of the court. Nonetheless, throughout the period the South African Supreme Court as a whole remained an independent court which in an appreciable number of cases provided some protection against the excesses of the executive . . . Government hopes that their appointees would take their side were frequently disappointed".

Corbett then quoted the passage from Chaskalson's 1989 address, in which Chaskalson had said that "we owe much to our judges, and a great deal to some of them" and that "little was to be gained by lamenting the past"[19]

In sum, Corbett's arguments were that it was impracticable to call

---

[19] Ibid., pp. 7–10, and for Chaskalson, see Chapter 1, text to n. 36.

judges to account, that the principle of judicial independence precluded judges from appearing before the TRC, and that, in any case, there was no basis for summoning them since their record had been for the most part good. In addition, he suggested that insofar as the record had some bad spots, one had to understand that in a legal order where Parliament is supreme, judges are bound to interpret the law as they find it. Finally, he allied himself with the claim that there was little to be gained by lamenting the past.

It is important to note that Corbett presented his arguments as if the principle of judicial independence is a free-standing principle, that is, it would preclude judges being held accountable even if their record had been bad and even if it were practicable to call them to account. As we will now see, the presentations at the Hearing fundamentally challenged each of his arguments and, in so doing, demonstrated their interdependence. Indeed, we will see that Corbett dug the grave for his argument that the judges should not submit themselves to the TRC by his account of the record, in particular his account of the Zondo and Tsafendas matters.

2. Corbett Under the Spotlight

Both parts of Corbett's argument about why judges should not appear before the TRC were thrown into doubt by the written submission presented by Dean Carole Lewis of the Law Faculty of the University of the Witwatersrand.[20]

In her submission, she pointed out that Corbett's practical objection to judges' appearing before the TRC rested on the claim that the exercise of reexamining specific cases would be both unproductive and time-consuming. But, she noted, at the same time as making this objection, Corbett had said that an examination of the record showed that it had been favourable. She continued:

His estimation is an important one and the facts upon which it is based might usefully be made the subject of investigation and analysis by the Commission. Judge Corbett in effect recognizes that judgment can be pronounced without the interminable process he envisages, but in effect is saying that it is for the judiciary to pass judgment on itself. This runs

---

[20] Dean Lewis points out that there had not been time to consult the faculty as a whole so she presented the submission in her personal capacity.

counter to the basic tenets of justice and, more to the point, to the terms of the legislation, which entrusts the task to the Commission.[21]

In short, Corbett had created a severe tension in his argument that one could not go into particular cases both by defending the judiciary in the two specific matters and by making a broad claim about the general record.

In response to Corbett's constitutional argument about judicial independence, Lewis explained that:

[h]ad Parliament considered that the judiciary should be exempt from the duty to testify, moral and legal, that rests on every other member of our society who has something that ought to be told and made public, it would surely have said so. By taking the stance that they have no such duty, judges place themselves, however unintentionally, above the law. In itself this is obviously wrong, but it is all the more undesirable in a society such as ours in which the legitimacy of our new constitutional order, which gives judges the power to override the democratic will, is by no means established.[22]

She recognised that there was a danger that "the dignity of the judiciary might be compromised by impertinent or inappropriate questioning"; but judges, she said, had the experience to handle such questioning and the TRC could ensure that "impropriety is kept to a minimum". Further, against this danger "must be set the good it would do to the reputation of the bench were testimony to be given; a measured assessment of the role of the legal profession and, in particular, the judiciary would do much to improve its standing in the eyes of a still-disillusioned public".[23]

Notice that this point is one which also has to be put into the balance against the value of sustaining collegiality, mentioned in the last section as a major though not publicly articulated obstacle which judges perceived lay in the way of judicial appearance at the TRC. Moreover, whatever the tensions that would have been created by the appearance of one of the new order judges, or of the old order liberal judges, one has to take into account the possibility that the kind of collegiality bought at the expense of an open and honest debate about the substance of judicial independence might be a very shallow one, unlikely to sustain a judiciary which carries the burden of huge expectations.

---

[21] Lewis Submission, p. 3.   [22] Ibid.   [23] Ibid.

Two of the oral submissions on the first day of the Hearing revealed the flaws in Corbett's defence of the judiciary in the Zondo and the Tsafendas matters. Paula McBride dealt with Zondo, highlighting the following details of the case: the mine was planted in retaliation for a South African Defence Force raid into Lesotho, a country landlocked by South Africa, in which nine refugees were killed; Zondo's accomplice in planting the mine, 35-year-old Mr X, turned state's evidence, and thereby got full indemnity; Zondo had claimed to have attempted a warning phonecall to get the shopping centre evacuated, but Raymon Leon, the trial judge, chose rather to believe Mr X, who had every reason to play down his role while playing up Zondo's in order to try to earn indemnity from the judge against prosecution. Indeed, Leon described X as an excellent witness. He discredited Zondo's testimony on the basis that Zondo, during the first few days of his detention, had lied to the police to protect X at a time when Zondo was unaware that X had already been captured.[24]

McBride also noted that after the Zondo matter Leon had been converted to abolition, but only (on Leon's own description) after sending someone to the gallows in "at least twelve" and "possibly as many as twenty" cases and that he knew of one judge who had never passed the death sentence. This was her comment:

Judge Leon was converted to abolition only after sentencing between "twelve and twenty" people to death—most people who have deliberately caused the deaths of others remember how many people they have killed. Judge Leon and others like him had the luxury of passing on the job of death to the others. Judge Leon never went into the execution chamber, he did not pull the lever that opened the trap door, he never watched the "dance macabre" or washed the bloodied white hoods worn by the condemned. It was not Judge Leon that had to teargas prisoners out of their cells and drag them up the steps to the gallows. It was not his job to go outside the walls of the prison and inform mothers and fathers of the death of their children. If he had done this, his memory would have served him better.[25]

Perhaps even more telling than Leon's failure of moral imagination—his failure to connect "violence and the word"[26]—is his failure

---

[24] McBride Submission, pp. 7–8.   [25] Ibid., p. 6.
[26] See Robert Cover, "Violence and the Word", in Martha Minow, Michael Ryan, and Austin Sarat (eds.), *Narrative, Violence, and the Law: The Essays of Robert Cover* (Ann Arbor, Michigan: Michigan University Press, 1995), p. 203.

of political imagination. This second failure was highlighted by McBride in her quotation from Professor John Milton's dissent as an assessor in a case later that year in Natal, again on the question whether there were extenuating circumstances in a murderous attack by the African National Congress:

How am I to assess the morality of this act? . . . In a normally ordered society where every citizen enjoys the full range of civil liberties and equal access to the political process, to resort to an act of political protest of this sort would be a totally senseless act and in my view without the slightest justification. What then of a society where a citizen does not enjoy equal access to the political process, where he is denied certain rights and liberties by reason of his race? [27]

The way that Corbett chose to tell Zondo's story—from one side of South Africa's divide—and his claim that Leon "had no choice"— an attempt to disempower the court—convicts him too of a failure of both moral and political imagination. It was true that a judge, as Corbett said, had "no choice" but to impose the death penalty if no extenuating circumstances were to be found. But there is the fact that not only did some judges always find extenuating circumstances, but that Zondo's age and the political circumstances of the case made such a finding relatively easy, if a judge could resist being swayed by the sentiments of white South Africans.

And while it is always the case that if one is not present at the trial or does not read the entire record, it is difficult to second-guess the trial judge's finding as to the credibility of witnesses, Corbett moves too quickly to Leon's defence. Indeed, the stress that Corbett lays on the fact that Leon refused leave to appeal and that the Appellate Division rejected Zondo's petition suggests that he agrees that Leon had no choice in regard to the finding of no extenuating circumstances.

It is Leon's suggestion of his own infallibility in this matter through his refusal of leave to appeal which most angered McBride and which is the strongest evidence of failure of moral imagination.[28] Corbett carries forward this failing, though in his case it is

[27] McBride Submission, p. 9. The death sentence was passed on the perpetrator of the attack—Robert McBride, who married Paula McBride on death row. Robert McBride survived his sentence as he fell within the scope of a moratorium on the death penalty.

[28] "Judge Leon in his arrogance, presumed no other court would reach a different decision, and he refused Andrew leave to appeal"; McBride Submission, p. 11.

compounded by the fact that it takes place in 1996, two years after the inauguration of the new political and legal order. He unwittingly portrays the judges as the ants—the powerless creatures—whom Zondo thought unfitting for engagement.

That same conclusion follows from Corbett's depiction of Tsafendas and his dismissal of the description of Tsafendas as a "victim of apartheid" as bizarre. Liza Key, who is producing a documentary on Tsafendas's life, shattered the white South African myth that Tsafendas was a demented white of Greek extraction who murdered Verwoerd only because a tape worm he imagined dominated him had given him the order to kill.[29]

Tsafendas, we now know from Key, was a "coloured"—a person of mixed racial descent. At his white boarding school in South Africa, he was called "Blackie", a derogatory reference to his dark skin colour. He had been a paid up member of the Communist Party in the 1930s and three days before he killed Verwoerd had applied under South Africa's absurd laws for "reclassification" from privileged white to "coloured". In his interrogation after the murder, he said that he "was so disgusted with [Verwoerd's] racial policy" that he went through with his "plan to kill the Prime Minister".

None of this came out at the time, because Tsafendas did not stand trial. The judge, Beyers, said of him that "I can as little try a man who has not at least the makings of a rational mind as I could try a dog or an inert implement . . . He is a meaningless creature". But as Key points out, Tsafendas was a highly intelligent man, who spoke several languages and had travelled the world. She admits that he was seriously disturbed at the time of the murder, and is now clinically mad; though she stresses that one cannot say how much his present state of mind is due to the fact that he was imprisoned for almost 25 years on death row, where, in addition to the torture of being subjected to the noises of condemned and the dying, the warders regularly beat him up and urinated in his food.

She also asks how one should evaluate his state of mind at the time of the murder against the mind of Verwoerd, architect of the madness of apartheid, who was well known to believe that he was in personal communication with, and under the personal protection of, the Almighty. Moreover, Key argues, Tsafendas's act was not without

---

[29] Key's oral submission was published in full by the *Mail and Guardian*, 31 October–6 November 1997, pp. 23–5. I rely on this rather than the often faulty Transcript.

meaning. He himself said after the murder that history would judge the rightness of his act, and Key points out the moral of the tale:

It is a matter of record that Verwoerd was succeeded by John Vorster—a Prime Minister who, whatever his other sins, began the process of reform in South Africa which was carried on, however falteringly, by P.W. Botha[30] and brought to fruition, however unintentionally, by F.W. de Klerk.[31] Whatever the motivation, when that hand stilled the heart of the Hollander[32] it can be said to have set in motion the retreat from ideological racism and set the country on the road which led directly to that moment, more than quarter of a century later, when Nelson Mandela walked out of the gates of Victor Verster Prison to the adulation of an adoring world. Meaningless he was not, in the historical sense.[33]

Not only, then, is there much "point" and no "absurdity" in reopening Tsafendas's case but what is bizarre is not the claim that he was a victim of apartheid, but that Corbett in 1996 still has so much trouble seeing over the apartheid divide. Once again he adopts the tactic of disempowering the judges—Beyers had no choice in the light of the evidence. It appears, in the light of Key's evidence, that the better description is that Beyers could not at this moment see the madness of apartheid; indeed, that he was blinded by that madness to the complexity of the man before him.[34]

The ultimate move in disempowerment though came at that point in Corbett's memorandum where, as we saw, he "correct[ed] certain misinformed assumptions which appear to underlie [Govender's] presentation". In these passages, the move of disempowerment is clear—judges generally had no choice because of parliamentary supremacy. Then we see the move of empowerment—when statutes were ambiguous or unclear judges could—indeed, were under a duty—to decide cases in terms of common law presumptions which promoted equity. Then, there is the claim—also one of empowerment—that the record generally displays that judges did their duty in both respects; they upheld the law when it was clear and interpreted the law so as to promote equity when it was not. And in support of this last claim, Corbett could cite two of the most eminent

---

[30] Second last President of apartheid South Africa.
[31] Last President of apartheid South Africa.
[32] Verwoerd was born in Holland.
[33] Key Submission, p. 23.
[34] Though the same judge resisted racial segregation in the courtroom.

human rights advocates in South Africa, Chaskalson and Kentridge.

However, notice that there is a distinction between, on the one hand, Corbett's claim that the record of judicial decisions was "generally" good, and, on the other, Kentridge's suggestion that there were an "appreciable number" of good decisions. And while Chaskalson's talk of "numerous" good decisions in his "no use in lamenting the past" address[35] is closer in spirit to Corbett's description, one can have lots of good decisions and still a record that is not "generally" good because there are even more bad decisions.

One must also take into account the clearly expressed desire on the part of both advocates to present as good a picture of the past as possible for the sake of the future; indeed, as I have noted, Chaskalson's suggestion that there is no point in lamenting the past indicates a desire to avoid the kind of scrutiny which the TRC was appointed to bring about. While one might think that South Africans—security police, politicians, the military, judges, etc.— would have been better off forgetting about their past in order to go forward into the future, that thought is a challenge to the purpose of the TRC and not relevant to argument before it. In addition, there is an issue, which I shall deal with in the next chapter, of the very close links between Bench and Bar which makes advocates in South Africa leery of critique of the Bench.

Most important of all in assessing the record, and ignored by Corbett in his submission, is that the record of the judiciary under apartheid was a product of a judicial hierarchy, in which the Appellate Division had the last judicial say. Apart from Corbett and a couple of other Appellate Division judges, the judges to whom the new legal order owes a great deal were a handful of judges who sat on the Provincial Benches, especially the Natal Bench. And the cases which Chaskalson in his address described as landmarks of judicial failure to give any substance to fundamental rights were landmarks precisely because the Appellate Division, the highest court of the land, overruled lower courts' decisions upholding fundamental rights. Indeed, when the Judge President of Natal, Judge Milne, was appointed to the Appellate Division in the late 1980s, it was rumoured that the appointment of this liberal judge to a highly illiberal court was made in order to deprive the Natal Bench of his leadership while subjecting him to the leadership of Rabie, who

---

[35] See Chapter 1, text to n. 36.

could keep Milne along with Corbett off the emergency team.

That the record was not only spotty but generally bad was admitted in the written submission of Judge Gerald Friedman, now Judge President of the Cape, and one of the old order judges who had done much to uphold the rule of law. He gave this summation of the work of the courts: "the courts' record as an upholder of the rights of the individual in the application of security legislation, cannot, with obvious exceptions, be defended".[36] He also said that "[e]xamples of judgments of the Appellate Division during the states of emergency during the 1980s in which decisions given in the provincial division in favour of the subject were reversed and findings made in favour of the executive are legendary and do not bear quoting".[37]

Corbett, in other words, had converted the exceptions into the rule and then failed to acknowledge the role of his own court—the Appellate Division—during the height of repression in ensuring that the exceptions had little effect beyond demonstrating the potential for judges to do otherwise.

Indeed, it was on Chief Justice Rabie's leadership of South African judges which had prompted the charge in my own submission of judicial dereliction of duty. For the Appellate Division was in the late 1980s accused of being collaborators in a "war against law",[38] of conniving in the "lawless" exercise of state power,[39] and of "a betrayal of the principles to which it owes its existence".[40] Judges, I submitted to the TRC, are accused in these terms not of a failure to understand the scope of their duty, but of acting outside of that scope—of forsaking or abandoning their duty altogether.[41] My argument to the TRC, which I will elaborate in Chapter 4, was that judges were estopped from claiming that they should be held accountable only to the law if their decisions showed that they had not been faithful to the fundamental principles of their legal order.

Rabie had also displayed his lack of regard for these principles—

---

[36] Friedman Submission, p.15.

[37] Ibid., p.14.

[38] Nicholas Haysom and Clive Plasket, "The War Against Law: Judicial Activism and the Appellate Division" (1988) 4 *South African Journal on Human Rights* 303.

[39] Geoffrey Budlender, "Law and Lawlessness in South Africa" (1988) 4 *South African Journal on Human Rights* 139, at 139–40.

[40] Etienne Mureinik, "Pursuing Principle: The Appellate Division and Review under the State of Emergency" (1989) 1 *South African Journal on Human Rights* 60, at 62–3, commenting on *Omar* v. *Minister of Law and Order* 1987 (3) SA 589 (A) and *Staatspresident* v. *Release Mandela Campaign* 1988 (4) SA 903 (A).

[41] Dyzenhaus Submission, pp. 7–8.

the principles of the rule of law—in areas beyond the executive-minded judgments of his security team. He had prepared the way for such judgments in a report—the Rabie Commission Report—which endorsed government security policy. And, as was revealed during the oral submission made by the Legal Resources Centre to the TRC, in 1986 Rabie had privately instructed the Judges President—the most senior judge in each province—to order judges who sat on the Board of the Legal Resources Centre to resign. He advised them that the Centre was a subversive organisation which was about to be banned and that some of its staff members were about to be detained. The Centre also revealed that Rabie personally contacted one of the judges on the Board as the Judge President of that province was on holiday at the time.[42] The National Party government estimated Rabie's value to its repression of opposition so highly that at the end of his term of office he was kept on for a while as Acting Chief Justice, a title which had no legal warrant and which was arguably unconstitutionally bestowed.[43]

But the Corbett-Rabie confrontation, which would have done much to shed light on judicial service to apartheid, did not happen, because Corbett would not initiate it. More significantly, Corbett's refusal to initiate that confrontation required him not so much to draw a curtain over the past, but to present a very contentious claim on behalf of the judiciary. Since that claim required him to evaluate the judicial record both in particular cases and in general, he undermined his own claim that such evaluation was impracticable. And since what made his evaluation contentious is judicial decisions of his own Court which arguably betrayed the rule of law, his constitutional claim about judicial independence was on very shaky ground. One cannot easily argue that judges' independence will be compromised by asking them to account for their conduct when they are called to account because of conduct which compromised their independence. As we will now see, the tensions in Corbett's memorandum plagued most of the judicial submissions discussed in this chapter.

[42] Only one judge succumbed to this pressure; see Legal Resources Centre Submission I, p. 3. The representative of Legal Resources Centre went on to say, "In my view, the security establishment had managed to get through to the judiciary by convincing the Chief Justice to serve as its agent to weaken the LRC. That the executive could use the judiciary at all is extraordinary and highlights the fact that the power of the state had become so unbridled that it was beginning to affect and corrode the independence of the judiciary" (ibid.).

[43] See Cameron, "Nude Monarchy: The Case of South Africa's Judges", n. 12 above.

3. Evaluating the Record

Judicial reluctance to give a frank appraisal of the record tarnished nearly all the other judicial submissions, even that which Chaskalson, Mahomed, P. Langa (Deputy President of the Constitutional Court), H.J.O. van Heerden (Deputy Chief Justice of the Supreme Court of Appeal), and Corbett jointly wrote.

There is much to admire in this submission. It unequivocally condemns apartheid and acknowledges both that law sustained apartheid and that judges often opted to give maximum effect to apartheid law. It also publicly commits the South African judiciary to a culture of constitutionalism and human rights and to accepting the importance of continuing judicial education in order to sustain such a culture. However, the submission also bears the mark of a judicial opinion crafted by judges of widely different views who can only agree at the cost of skirting controversy.

We already have encountered most of these personalities. It helps to know that Langa is a black judge, who submitted a highly personal separate submission, in which he told of the hardship and humiliation he encountered in his own progress from a destitute background to advocate at the Natal Bar. Van Heerden, a respected though conservative member of the old order Appellate Division, who had dissented twice when he found himself on Rabie's emergency team, would in the normal course of events have been Corbett's successor as Chief Justice.[44] He was not, as it happens, one of the judges who opposed Mahomed's move from Judge of the Constitutional Court to Chief Justice of the Supreme Court of Appeal. But to have his name on the submission gave it legitimacy with the old order judges who opposed Mahomed's appointment.

It is no surprise then that the Chaskalson *et al.* submission, while deeply critical of apartheid and its laws, avoids contention on several occasions. It does not so much "lament" the judicial past as dwell on the exceptions as indicative of the record and as the basis for the progress into the constitutional future. Further, the submission

---

[44] See Ellman, *In a Time of Trouble: Law and Liberty in South Africa's State of Emergency*, n. 12 above, p.65, commenting that "when judges from outside the team dissented from emergency decisions—and even in one case where the judge did not dissent but rather concurred in the result on quite different grounds—they never sat on another emergency case during Rabie's tenure in office".

declined to deal with the issue of whether lawyers should have accepted appointments to the bench during apartheid. Instead, the judges quoted excerpts from an academic debate of the early 1980s about this issue, commenting only that the excerpts illustrated the issue's "complexity".[45]

That debate began when a law professor, Raymond Wacks, argued in a lecture in 1983 that liberal judges should resign because the net effect of their remaining on the bench was to legitimise an illegitimate system.[46] Wacks's argument was novel because he relied on an account of adjudication put forward by Ronald Dworkin, at that time Professor of Jurisprudence in Oxford, which was designed to support the opposite conclusion from the one which Wacks reached.

Dworkin sought to show, against the claims of contemporary legal positivists, that legal duty and moral duty must to some extent coincide. His account of the way judges decide "hard" or controversial cases about the interpretation of law suggests that the best way to understand judicial interpretation is by a two stage process.[47] At the first stage, the judge must ask what answers to the question posed by the case "fit" or plausibly explain all the relevant legal material. Given that the case is hard, the judge will find more than one answer, and so must proceed to choose between them by asking which answer best justifies the relevant legal material, showing it in its "best light". At this stage, the stage of soundness or justification, the judge is duty-bound to say what the answer is to the question posed by the case in terms of what he or she takes to be the "soundest theory of the law". Since a judgment at this stage is one about what justifies the law of a particular political community, it is an inherently moral justification.

Dworkin thus claims that the judicial obligation of fidelity to the law is both legal and moral. Judges are accountable to the law. But in cases where at issue is the interpretation of the law, their duty is not, as the plain fact approach I described in Chapter 1 would have it, to find an answer determined by alleged facts about the public record. Rather, judges must work out the moral basis for the law relevant to the question before them and then decide that question in the light of that basis. It should follow from Dworkin's account that in any

---

[45] Chaskalson *et al.* Submission, p. 19.

[46] Raymond Wacks, "Judges and Injustice" (1984) 101 *South African Law Journal* 266.

[47] See Ronald Dworkin, *Taking Rights Seriously* (London: Duckworth, 1978 (new impression)) and *Law's Empire* (London: Fontana, 1986).

legal order judges are able to make sense of a duty which is moral as well as legal.

Wacks, however, argued that a Dworkinian account of adjudication in the South African legal context showed that legal duty and moral duty were in contradiction. Apartheid ideology had so permeated the legal order that judges were, on the best interpretation of South African law, under a legal duty to decide their cases in the light of the apartheid "morality" which best explained the law of South Africa. They could lie about what the law required, but that was a severely limited strategy, or they could protest, but that strategy was likely to be a futile one. Hence, the only course open to them was to resign.[48]

Professor John Dugard, South Africa's foremost academic critic of the apartheid legal order, responded that Wacks underestimated the room for creative interpretation still open to judges.[49] He challenged the claim about the net effect of liberal judges remaining on the bench and pointed out that other participants in the legal order, lawyers and academics, also legitimated it. Finally, Dugard relied on the observation made by Etienne Mureinik, also an academic human rights lawyer, which Chaskalson *et al.* quote in their submission, calling it "powerful": "If we . . . argue that moral judges should resign, we can no longer pray, when we go into court as defence counsel, or even as the accused, that we find a moral judge on the Bench".[50]

In another jointly written submission, four old order judges of the Appellate Division, who still serve on the same court, Judges Smalberger, Howie, Marais and Scott, allied themselves with the "no use in lamenting the past" view and with the claim that the record was generally a good one.[51] This submission, unlike the Chaskalson

[48] Wacks, "Judges and Injustice", n. 46 above.

[49] John Dugard, "Should Judges Resign? A Reply to Professor Wacks" (1984) 101 *South African Law Journal* 286.

[50] Etienne Mureinik, *Sunday Tribune*, 3 April 1983, reproduced in *Lawyers for Human Rights: Bulletin No. 3*, January 1984 (Johannesburg) 19. See Chaskalson *et al.* Submission, p. 19.

[51] Recall that Corbett, in his response to Govender, said that he had circulated it among the members of the Appellate Division and that "it bears their endorsement"; Corbett Memorandum, p. 1. There is a significant shift in tone from that memorandum to the Chaskalson *et al.* Submission, though it was widely suspected that Corbett's participation in the content of the Chaskalson *et al.* Submission made it much more conservative than it would otherwise have been. However, that change in tone was thought sufficiently radical to prompt Smalberger *et al.* into restating Corbett's original position. Judge Pius Langa's independent submission is understood to be an oblique comment on the conservative elements of the Chaskalson *et al.* Submission.

et al. submission, did deal at some length with the issue of accepting a judicial appointment under apartheid.

Smalberger *et al.* claimed that courts were so essential in "so racially polarised and divided a society" that the reasons for having them were "utterly compelling". "A society without courts cannot continue to function in a civilised manner and must descend ultimately into a state of social anarchy". They said that if advocates had refused appointment, judges would have been appointed from the civil service, with the result that courts would have been "ultimately composed entirely of political puppets". And they suggested that they could anticipate on appointment that "more than 95% of the judicial work . . . would not involve us in 'political' cases and . . . there was a great need for properly qualified and experienced people to perform that vital function in the interests of all in society". Finally, they claimed at several points that the "overwhelming majority" of citizens wanted them at their posts, even that "South African lawyers and the public at large, irrespective of colour, were at one in requiring courts and in requiring them to be, and to remain, independent". "Without courts, society would have to resort to self-help. That would mean that the less powerful in society would be at the mercy of the more powerful. Courts which were not independent were arguably worse than no courts".[52]

Smalberger *et al.*'s treatment of the issue of legitimacy is riven with tension. They wish, on the one hand, to empower themselves. Not only, they say, did we judges have to hold society together—to maintain civilisation when the alternative was chaos—but we prevented the powerless from being further oppressed. So important was our role that no South African could have thought that we should do otherwise. On the other hand, at many other places in their submission they disempower themselves. Yes, they say, we were independent, but "Parliament was supreme". "The courts had no option but to apply the law as they found it, however unjust it might appear to be".[53]

The last words of the sentence just quoted are revealing. The judges do not say "however unjust the law was", but that apartheid law *might* have *appeared* unjust. Contrast this sentence with a passage from the Chaskalson *et al.* submission:

---

[52] Smalberger *et al.* Submission, pp. 3–6.
[53] Ibid., p. 9.

Apartheid was defined by law and enforced by law. It is necessary, therefore, to acknowledge the role of the legal system in upholding and maintaining apartheid, and the injustices associated with it. There can be no half-measures about this. Apartheid caused poverty, degradation and suffering on a massive scale . . . Apartheid, in itself, and in the way it was implemented, constituted a gross abuse of human rights.[54]

In the light of this contrast, the need of Smalberger *et al.*to maintain their sense of themselves as having been pivotal agents in maintaining "civilisation" leads them, in 1997, as still serving judges of the old order, to fudge the issue of apartheid's injustice. They do say in paragraph 1 of the submission that South Africa was "afflicted with many offensive and unjust laws made by Parliament", but they change their tone when it comes to discussing their role in applying such laws.

Indeed, in paragraph 4 of their submission, when they give their "blunt" appraisal of apartheid, they say that white domination was at first "understandable" since whites just happened to have resources which blacks lacked, and that it was only when blacks' "aspirations" changed, as they became "more educated", that "white political domination" was an "obstacle".[55] This crude colonial version of South Africa's past whitewashes a cruel history of pillage, violence, and institutionalised racism in just the way that the history textbooks of the apartheid regime attempted.

They cannot therefore bring themselves to see that for most blacks, but also for many whites, there was no question but that the legal order they faithfully served was illegitimate. They still do not see that most blacks' encounters with the law were in the apartheid enforcement machine managed by the magistracy which relentlessly churned out convictions for unrepresented black people accused of violating apartheid's laws.

Reflect here on the contrast between their description and Deputy President of the Constitutional Court, Pius Langa's account of his experience as a black South African under apartheid law. Langa tells in his submission how he made his way from court clerk in the Department of Justice, to court interpreter, to public prosecutor, to magistrate, before he became an advocate at the Durban Bar in 1977.[56] In other words, he had not only seen the apartheid legal

---

[54] Chaskalson *et al.* Submission, p. 4.
[55] Smalberger *et al.* Submission, p. 3.
[56] Langa Submission, p. 2.

machine from the inside but had been involved in the enforcement of its law. He then said:

I am making this submission because I believe that the judiciary occupies, and will continue to occupy, a crucial position in our democracy. The relationship which it has with the rest of the community is therefore important. It should be regarded as an integral part of the community it serves and it can only function properly if it enjoys the complete trust and confidence of that community. I believe that that confidence was severely damaged in the past. In order for it to be completely restored and its maintenance guaranteed, I believe that there should be a common under-standing of the role of the judiciary and the courts, as well as how the former perceive their functions and responsibilities towards society. The divisions and conflicts of our apartheid past have distorted the relation-ship between, on the one hand, institutions involved in the administration of justice, including the judiciary and, on the other, significant sections of the South African community. This has to be set right now in order to ensure and to maintain a healthy democracy, which fully espouses the values of the new constitutional dispensation. I make the submission in the hope that the story of some of the personal experiences, perceptions and observations, shared as they are by thousands of other citizens of this country who were similarly placed, might assist in bringing about a greater appreciation of how others were affected by the operation of the legal system during the period under review. I make this submission also because of my belief that the correction of this distortion, the restoration of complete trust, is not something which should simply be assumed because the country now has a new Constitution. A process needs to take place, a process which will not only liberate those members of the judiciary who have felt the alienation, but which will also reassure the formerly oppressed about the judiciary's rededication to justice for all.[57]

Langa then described the apartheid legal machine from the perspective of one who had been subject to its ordinary violence, in this case South Africa's pass and influx control laws—the laws which controlled the supply of black labour to the urban centres.

The whole process at the influx control offices was painful and degrading and particular aspects of it inflicted deep humiliation on the tens of thousands who were on the receiving end of these regulations. For example, we had to stand in a queue in a large hall for medical examina-

[57] Ibid., p. 3.

tion. *As a 17 year old, I remember having to avert my eyes from the nakedness of grown men in a futile attempt to salvage some dignity for them in those queues where we had to expose ourselves to facilitate the degrading examination. To anyone who failed to find work during the currency of their permits loomed the very real threat of being declared "an idle or undesirable Bantu"* [58] *[section 29(1) of the Urban Areas Act 1945] by the Commissioner's court and being subject to be sent to a farm colony. Scores of people were processed through those courts and sentenced on charges such as failing to produce a reference book on demand. To watch was a soul destroying exercise. In my opinion, no one who has been subjected to the experience of the harsh implementation of the pass laws and the influx control regulations can ever forget the experience. I have no doubt that the role of the courts in the implementation of the pass laws contributed to a diminishing of the esteem which ordinary people might have had for institutions set up to administer justice. It was one thing, however, having the overtly discriminatory and repressive laws in the statute book. Their ugliness was exacerbated to a large degree by the crude, cruel and unfeeling way in which many of the officials, black and white, put them into operation. There was a culture of hostility and intimidation against those who came to be processed or for assistance. The face presented by authority, in general, was of a war against people who were unenfranchised and human dignity was the major casualty. In general, whatever intervention there was by the legal profession would have been on a client basis, with too few people involved to make an impact. The role of the judicial system at this level was to put the stamp of legality on a legal framework structured to perpetuate disadvantage and inequality.* [59]

In the light of the above contrast, and of the peroration to Smalberger *et al.*'s submission, quoted at the beginning of this chapter, we can see why it was so important for the judges to account for their conduct before the TRC.

Note that none of the judges involved in drafting the Smalberger *et al.* submission had been part of Rabie's emergency team. And the judges thus far criticised have been judges, like Corbett and Leon, who had distinguished themselves as liberal judges. It was a puzzling feature of the Hearing that at times it seemed as if it was the judges

[58] Government terminology for black South Africans changed from time to time; "native", "Bantu" and even "plural" were used at different times.

[59] Langa Submission, pp. 4–6.

who were not stalwarts of apartheid, and even known to be deeply opposed to it, who were most under the spotlight of the TRC.

It may seem harsh, for example, to judge Leon on the basis of one judgment, whatever the merits of his decision that there were no extenuating circumstances in the Zondo case. Indeed, Malcolm Wallis, S.C.,[60] of the Natal Bar, during the panel at the end of day one pointed out that advocates like himself, who were willing to take on matters like the Zondo matter *pro deo* [without charge], heaved "a sigh of relief" when they saw that Leon was the presiding judge.[61]

One reason for this focus on judges whom one might have predicted to survive the Hearing unscathed or at least relatively unscathed was simply that only such judges were prepared to make submissions. But there is a more important reason, one which Smalberger *et al.* evaded by suggesting that the issue which faced those considering judicial appointment was the choice between chaos and civilisation and which Chaskalson *et al.* mentioned but declined to take on. When Wacks challenged judges to resign, his challenge was not to all judges, but only to judges who fell into the minority group of liberal judges—those for whom apartheid was abhorrent.

Of the old order judges, only Friedman dealt fully with this issue in his submission:

Some judges accepted appointment without qualms about applying the apartheid laws. Others who felt that there was still room for the advancement of human rights, accepted appointment to the Bench during the apartheid years and, having done so, decided not to resign. They were motivated by the feeling that if they refused appointment or resigned, as the case may be, their positions would be filled with practitioners who were supporters of the government policy and therefore likely to be less sensitive to the necessity for a human rights approach on the Bench than they were. Those judges who did not relish having to apply the apartheid laws were aware that their presence on the Bench tended to lend legitimacy to the unjust system of apartheid. But weighing all the arguments for and against, those judges did so in the belief that the contribution which they might be able to make, would advance rather than retard the cause of justice and that they would be in a position to apply the unjust apartheid laws as humanely as possible within the parameters of their judicial oath.[62]

---

[60] S.C. stands for Senior Counsel, and Q.C. for Queen's Counsel. These titles reflect the advocate's appointment to the most senior rank of the profession.

[61] Transcript, p. 166.

[62] Friedman Submission, pp. 5–6.

In sum, the issue was not how South Africa would manage without courts but the legitimising effect of the participation by liberal judges in a highly oppressive legal order.

But even a liberal old order judge like Friedman was tempted to underestimate the scope for judges to have done better. In his submission he dealt with the vexed issue of judicial admission of confessions in evidence when those confessions had been extracted from the accused when detained in solitary confinement under one or other piece of security legislation. For example, section 6 of the Terrorism Act 1967, which dealt with "Detention of terrorists and certain other persons for interrogation", stated:

> "(1) Notwithstanding anything to the contrary in any law contained,[63] any commissioned officer as defined in section 1 of the Police Act, 1958 (Act No. 7 of 1958), of or above the rank of Lieutenant-Colonel may, if he has reason to believe that any person who happens to be at any place in the Republic, is a terrorist or is withholding from the South African Police any information relating to terrorists or to offences under this Act, arrest such person or cause him to be arrested, without warrant and detain or cause such person to be detained for interrogation at such place in the Republic and subject to such conditions as the Commissioner may, subject to the directions of the Minister, from time to time determine, until the Commissioner orders his release when satisfied that he has satisfactorily replied to all questions at the said interrogation or that no useful purpose will be served by his further detention . . .
>
> (5) No court of law shall pronounce upon the validity of any action taken under this section, or order the release of any detainee.
>
> (6) No person, other than the Minister or an officer in the service of the State acting in the performance of his official duties, shall have access to any detainee, or shall be entitled to any official information relating to or obtained from any detainee".

Friedman said that such provisions created a "dilemma" for the courts:

The detainee would testify how he was assaulted. The police or security force members, on the other hand, would go into the witness box and deny these allegations. In this they would be corroborated by the district surgeon who would testify that no evidence of any assault was found on the detainee. One knows now from the evidence which has emerged at

---

[63] This peculiar phrasing was meant to tell courts that the Terrorism Act should not be read as subject to any law which might mitigate its operation, for example, common law presumptions.

hearings of the Commission that many of these witnesses were prepared to lie to the Court. Despite cross-examination it was very often impossible to find that their testimony was untruthful since the court has, in each case, to make its findings on the evidence which is placed before it. That evidence included the testimony of the magistrate or police official who took down the confession, that the person making it had no visible signs of recent injuries.

It must, however, be pointed out that in a number of cases evidence of a confession was in fact rejected.

The fact that it was commonplace for detainees to allege that they had been tortured, did not entitle the court, in any particular instance, to depart from the principle that each case must be decided on its own facts.[64]

However, while section 6 and its counterparts were on their face draconian, Friedman's description of the judicial dilemma does not fully confront the history surrounding such provisions.

In 1971, Barend van Niekerk, a professor of law at Natal University and a particularly outspoken critic of apartheid, had made a speech at a public meeting held to protest the death of a detainee held under section 6 of the Terrorism Act. In his speech, he offered a simple solution to judges for dealing with the dilemma described by Friedman: since it was widely accepted that solitary confinement for a long period is in itself torture, judges could simply refuse to accept any evidence procured in confinement.[65]

At the time Van Niekerk made this suggestion, a judge in Natal was trying a much publicised "terrorism" case in which the accused and several state witnesses had been detained for lengthy periods under the Terrorism Act. The defence counsel in the case alleged that there had been torture. Van Niekerk had personally extended an invitation to them to attend the meeting, though they did not in fact do so.

Van Niekerk was subsequently charged with contempt of court and with attempting to defeat or obstruct the ends of justice. The trial judge, Fannin, acquitted him of the second charge but convicted him of the first, sentencing him to a R100 fine with the alternative of one month's imprisonment. Van Niekerk appealed and the Appellate Division confirmed the finding of guilt on the contempt charge and

---

[64] Friedman Submission, pp. 11–12.
[65] For a general account, see John Dugard, *Human Rights and the South African Legal Order* (Princeton, N.J.: Princeton University Press, 1978) pp. 293–302.

also held, contrary to Fannin, that as a matter of law Van Niekerk had had the requisite intent to support the charge of attempting to defeat or obstruct the course of justice.[66]

In the course of his judgment for the Court, Chief Justice Ogilvie Thompson quoted at length from Van Niekerk's speech. In one of the quoted extracts, Van Niekerk made it clear that he regarded his call to judges (and lawyers in general) as one which asked them to pay heed to their duty to uphold the rule of law:

"The Terrorism Act, as I have said, is a negation of what any true lawyer would ever call justice. And yet our lawyers, the guardians of our nation's legal heritage, have done so very little to mitigate its crudities. What then can our lawyers do? In the very first place our lawyers, all our lawyers from Judges downward, can make their voices heard about an institution which they must surely know to be an abdication of decency and justice. No doubt, they will tell you, it is not their function to criticise the law but to apply it. This is the very understandable retort of our Judges to the demand sometimes made upon them to have their influential voices heard when the rule of law is trampled into the dust. But we must surely ask these lawyers, when will a point ever be reached when their protests become justified? Will they still make their excuse for abject inactivity if it is decreed that public flogging be introduced for traffic offences, the burning at the stake for immorality and decapitation for the use of abusive language? Surely we have reached the stage that we are no longer merely dealing with a nicety of jurisprudence but with the essential quality and survival of justice itself. Surely also lawyers should realise that by remaining silent at the helm of their clinging cash registers they are not only perpetuating these palpable injustices but that they are indeed also lending them the aura of respectability. Above all, they should realise that by remaining silent in the face of what they know to be inherently unjust, cruel and primitive they are indeed sullying themselves and the reputation of their profession. Cannot our Judiciary even go further and in effect kill one aspect of the usefulness of the Terrorism Act for our authorities? They can do so by denying, on account of the built-in intimidatory effect of solitary confinement, practically all creditworthiness to evidence procured under those detention conditions".[67]

[66] *S* v. *Van Niekerk* (1972) 3 SA 711 (A). The Attorney-General of Natal had exercised a right in terms of a statutory provision to ask the trial court judge to reserve a question of law for the appeal court to decide. That is, the appeal court would decide whether, as a matter of law, the facts found to be proved by the trial court could, contrary to that court's finding, support a conviction on the charge of attempting to defeat or obstruct the course of justice. If the appeal court's answer was in the affirmative, it was then open to it to make an order or merely to state its finding. The Appellate Division chose the second option.

[67] Quoted ibid., at 716–17.

A second extract from Van Niekerk's speech alluded to a Minister's answer to a parliamentary question about deaths in detention under the Terrorism Act, that "an unknown detainee had died of an unknown cause at an unknown place at an unknown date". Van Niekerk said:

> "By taking an unequivocal stand now on this momentous question, at the very least by adding their prestigious and informed voice to our demand for an open judicial enquiry into possible abuses under the Terrorism Act, our Judiciary will indeed also be laying a symbolical wreath on the unknown grave of that unknown man; by doing just that they may in fact avoid the laying of wreath one day to a concept which, through their and our inactivity, dies an unknown death on an unknown day—a wreath to justice itself".[68]

The common thread in these passages is, then, that judges and other lawyers were neglecting their duty to uphold the rule of law. But Ogilvie Thompson did not deal with this issue, nor with the point raised by Van Niekerk's counsel that legal authority in other jurisdictions would regard evidence procured under conditions of solitary confinement as evidence procured by torture, and hence as inherently unreliable.[69]

---

[68] Ibid., 719.

[69] Counsel for Van Niekerk relied on *Blackburn* v. *Alabama* (1960) 361 US 199 4 L ed. 2d, at 247, 248 and *Miranda* v. *Arizona* (1966) 384 US 16 L ed. 2d, at 708–9, 714; see the Heads of Argument preceeding the decision at 712–13. Both of these decisions provided firm ground for a claim that in the USA such evidence would be excluded by the courts.

In particular in *Miranda*, Chief Justice Warren for the majority of the Supreme Court held that the circumstances of incommunicado interrogation are such that even if the police exert no physical brutality on the detainee, the mental intimidation involved is "equally destructive of human dignity" and exerts a pressure which vitiates voluntariness; see 439–58. Had Ogilvie Thompson condescended to deal with this issue, he would no doubt have found that the authority had no force in South Africa, because the Supreme Court's analysis was bound up with the Fifth Amendment, the constitutionally entrenched guarantee against self-incrimination, and there was no such guarantee in South Africa. For in a speech in the same year, he argued that the South African legal order, unlike the system in the USA, required that a judge interpret the law not as he "perhaps would like it to be, or as he might consider it ought to be, but as set out in the relevant statutory provisions so interpreted". Criticism of the judges, he said, had not always accorded "full recognition to the circumstance that, once a judge has determined what he conceives to be the intention of the legislature, he must perforce give effect to the intention so determined": N. Ogilvie Thompson, "Speech on the Centenary Celebrations of the Northern Cape Division", (1972) 89 *South African Law Journal* 30, 33–4.

But it is not clear that the Supreme Court's decision depended on this constitutional peg; it would only have thus depended had there been specific statutory authorisation for incommunicado interrogation. Moreover, in a case decided in the same year as *S* v. *Van Niekerk*, the English Court of Appeal held, on basic common law grounds, that a confes-

Instead, Ogilvie Thompson noted that the public could not help but associate Van Niekerk's claims with the terrorism trial and therefore as designed to influence the Court, even if in fact the Court was not influenced. Since the claims, if acted upon by the Court, would require it to ignore detainee-evidence, "irrespective of the instrinsic merits of that evidence", Van Niekerk was asking the Court to engage in conduct which would "manifestly be a gross dereliction of duty". For he was asking judges to act "contrary to their obvious duty to consider all evidence on its merits".[70] Hence Van Niekerk was guilty of contempt of court. Ogilvie Thompson also held that the general scope of Van Niekerk's speech—the fact that it was addressed to the "Judiciary generally"—put it "foursquare witin the ambit of the crime of attempting to defeat or obstruct the course of justice".[71]

It is hardly surprising that Ogilvie Thompson came to these conclusions. In 1964 he had given the judgment of the Court in the Appellate Division decision which set the course for that Court's generally supine attitude towards security law, *Rossouw* v. *Sachs*.[72] This case arose out of the detention in terms of section 17 of the "90-day law"[73]

---

sion is not voluntary when it was obtained by "oppression", where "oppressive questioning" is questioning which "by its nature, duration or other attendant circumstances (including the fact of custody) excites hopes (such as the hope of release) or fears, or so affects the mind of the suspect that his will crumbles and he speaks when otherwise he would have remained silent". See the Headnote to *R* v. *Prager* [1972] 1 All ER 1114 (CA), at 1114, summarising Lord Justice Edmund Davies's reasoning at 1117.

[70] *S* v. *Van Niekerk*, n. 66 above, 725.

[71] Ibid., 725–6.

[72] 1964 (2) SA 551 (A).

[73] The "90-day detention law" was the name given to s. 17 of Act 37 of 1963, which was enacted to assist the government in countering the underground activities of the African National Congress and the Pan African Congress. Section 17(1) provided that "Notwithstanding anything to the contrary in any law contained, any commissioned officer . . . may . . . without warrant arrest . . . any person whom he suspects upon reasonable grounds of having commmitted or intending . . . to commit any offence under the Suppression of Communism Act . . . or the Unlawful Organizations Act . . . or the offence of sabotage, or who in his opinion is in possession of information relating to the commission of such offence . . . and detain such person . . . for interrogation . . . until such person has in the opinion of the Commissioner of Police replied satisfactorily to all questions at the said interrogation, but no such person shall be so detained for more than ninety days on any particular occasion when he is so arrested".

Section 17(2) provided that no person was to "have access" to the detainee except with the consent of the Minister of Justice or a commissioned officer, though the person had to be visited not less than once a week by a magistrate. Section 17(3) provided that "No court shall have jurisdiction to order the release from custody of any person so detained". The section was effective for 12 months and thereafter was subject to annual renewal by proclamation of the State President.

(a predecessor of section 6) of Albie Sachs, an advocate deeply involved in the extraparliamentary opposition.[74]

Sachs's lawyers asked for a declaratory order against Rossouw, a senior security policeman, who was responsible for Sach's arrest and detention. The order sought declared, first, that Rossouw was not entitled to deprive Sachs of "any of his rights and liberties save to detain him for interrogation and save to deprive him of access to other persons". Secondly, it declared that Sachs was "entitled to at least the same rights and liberties while in custody as are enjoyed by awaiting-trial prisoners or other non-convicted persons who are being detained under the provisions of some other law". More particularly, he was to be allowed out of his cell for reasonable and adequate exercise and recreation and to be permitted to receive an adequate supply of reading and writing materials, subject to the scrutiny of those detaining him. The statute did not deal with these issues.

Two judges of the Cape Provincial Division had granted the order in an unreported judgment. They held that a detainee had the right both to exercise and to an adequate supply of reading matter and writing materials. The judges said that to deprive a detainee of that right amounted "in effect to punishment" and that it would be "surprising to find that the Legislature intended punishment to be meted out to an unconvicted prisoner". They concluded that the decision of the official in charge of detainees "is not come to in the exercise of any discretion conferred on him in law. His decision is at all times subject to correction in a court of law".[75]

Ogilvie Thompson overruled this decision in giving the unanimous judgment of the Court.[76] First, he pointed out that the offences covered by the statute were predominantly designed to dislocate the public order or directed against the safety of the state itself. Secondly, section 17 introduced a procedure which was both "novel and drastic". A person was expected in its terms to incriminate himself under interrogation, which ran counter to the general principles of South African criminal law. And the detainee was

---

[74] Sachs is now a Judge of the Constitutional Court.

[75] Quoted by Ogilvie Thompson in *Rossouw* v. *Sachs*, n. 72 above, at 564, 556–7.

[76] It is worth noting that prior to this decision the Appellate Division had overruled a decision of the Natal Provincial Division in which it had been held that a person could not be arrested more than once in terms of s. 17, because this would render the limit of 90 days illusory. See *Loza* v. *Police Commander, Durbanville* 1964 (2) SA 545 (A), overruling *Mbele* v. *Minister of Justice* 1964 (4) SA 606 (N).

precluded from having access to his legal adviser which was contrary to the "generally accepted principles of our law". He said that although the section "in terms only excludes the jurisdiction of the Court in relation to ordering the release of the detainee, the inability of the latter to have access (save with the consent of the Minister or a commissioned officer) to his legal adviser is likely in practice effectively to preclude any resort to the Court during the period of his detention".[77]

This last factor seemed to the judge to be specially significant in regard to his finding that the section did in fact authorise "psychological compulsion". It led him to override his initial unwillingness, in determining what he called the "true purpose" of section 17, to attribute an intention to Parliament of authorising such compulsion.

In Ogilvie Thompson's view, Parliament could not have intended that the detainee should be subjected to any form of assault, nor that his health or resistance should be impaired by inadequate food or living conditions. "Third degree methods" were clearly not authorised. The government had in fact conceded all of this but submitted that the purpose of detention was to imprison or "punish" the detainee while he declined to speak. Sachs submitted that detention was merely for the purposes of "recurrent interrogation". Ogilvie Thompson held that neither submission was "entirely correct". The purpose was "to induce the detainee to speak"—to reply satisfactorily, in the opinion of the Commissioner, to all questions.

But the judge was still left, as he saw it, with a choice between two options as to the purpose of the statute. Parliament, in authorising such a detention, could have intended that the detainee should continue to enjoy all his ordinary rights and privileges, saving only such as were necessarily impaired either by the very fact of detention itself or by the other express provisions of the section. Or Parliament could have intended that, in furtherance of the object of inducing the detainee to speak, the continued detention should be as effective as possible, "subject only to considerations of humanity as generally accepted in a civilised country".[78]

After examining the relevant legal materials, Ogilvie Thompson came to the conclusion that the second was the true purpose despite his own acknowledgment that "for detainees who may broadly be

---

[77] *Roussouw* v. *Sachs*, n. 72 above, 558–9.
[78] Ibid., 560–1.

classed as intellectuals, the deprivation of reading matter or writing materials during their detention may approximate to the application of a form of that very 'psychological compulsion' so emphatically repudiated by counsel for appellant".[79]

In short, since Ogilvie Thompson had in 1964 read the purpose of psychological compulsion into a statutory provision which did not explicitly state this to be its purpose, he clearly regarded such compulsion as legitimate given the context of governmental concerns about security which led to the enactment of the statute.

Thus it was hardly surprising that in the 1970s he ignored both of Van Niekerk's arguments; first, that if the purpose was psychological compulsion, confessions produced under such compulsion were irredeemably tainted by involuntariness, and, secondly, that the way in which such detention provisions were shielded from judicial supervision meant that they endangered the rule of law which judges are duty-bound to uphold. For one of the pillars of the rule of law in the common law tradition is that judges must ensure that when public officials act, especially when they exercise police powers, that they act in accordance with the law.[80]

In other words, the fact that judges were prevented by such provisions from ensuring that detainees were treated lawfully in detention meant that judges had a legitimate ground for complaint that the law to which they were supposed to hold public officials to account had been rendered unenforceable by the Legislature. Since the conditions of detention made it difficult if not impossible for a court to ensure that a detainee was not subject to unlawful treatment, and since there was a plausible case to be made for the claim that solitary confinement is a kind of torture, the map of judicial duty was not as clearly drawn as Ogilvie Thompson tried to convey.

It is perfectly consistent, that is, to argue that a judge has a duty to

---

[79] Ibid., 565.

[80] This requirement of the rule of law was the occasion for challenges which sought to persuade judges to assert some control over detention, when information suggested that a detainee was being unlawfully treated. In *Schermbrucker* v. *Klindt* 1965 (4) SA 606 (A), the majority of the Appellate Division, following *Rossouw* v. *Sachs*, refused to make an order to bring a detainee to court so that the court could investigate evidence, smuggled out of detention, that a particular detainee was being tortured. In *Nxasana* v. *Minister of Justice* 1976 (3) SA 745 (D), Judge Didcott managed to find a way around the holding in *Schermbrucker*, despite the fact that the Appellate Division had seemed to build an impregnable wall around detention. See David Dyzenhaus, *Hard Cases in Wicked Legal Systems: South African Law in the Perspective of Legal Philosophy* (Oxford: Clarendon Press, 1991), pp. 112–20, and pp. 132–42, for detailed analysis.

consider all the evidence on its merits but that in certain circumstances it is appropriate for a judge to refuse to consider the evidence. If the evidence is obtained by torture or by placing the witness in circumstances of extreme psychological compulsion, judges may well find that a more fundamental duty—one to uphold rule of law requirements—preempts the duty to consider evidence on its merits.

Notice that Ogilvie Thompson went further than merely lending judicial blessing to the practice of extracting evidence from detainees in solitary confinement. As John Dugard pointed out, he attempted to stifle academic criticism of the judicial role in serving apartheid.[81]

In his judgment in *S* v. *Van Niekerk*, Ogilvie Thompson anticipated the charge of judicial censorship. He said:

> "The Terrorism Act undoubtedly contains many stringent provisions, not least of which are those relating to detention in solitary confinement and the virtual exclusion of all resort to the courts in relation to such detention. Criticism of these, and other provisions of the Act is readily understandable and, provided it be expressed within legitimate bounds, constitutes no contravention of the criminal law. Nor are either individual Judges or the Judiciary above all criticism. A radical distinction, however, exists between, on the one hand, legitimate criticism and, on the other hand, the generic crime of defeating or obstructing (or attempting to defeat or obstruct) the course of justice and the species of that crime designated contempt of court".[82]

However, he also noted an "increasing tendency" "[f]or some years past on the part of certain academic lawyers to criticise the Judiciary from time to time for failing to comment adversely upon certain statutory provisions". And he noted that the previous Chief Justice, L.C. Steyn, and he himself had commented adversely on this tendency in speeches they had delivered at various functions.[83]

But the Appellate Division's decision in *S* v. *Van Niekerk*, whatever Ogilvie Thompson said, not only punished a particular

---

[81] Dugard, *Human Rights and the South African Legal Order*, n. 65 above, pp. 301–2.

[82] *S* v. *Van Niekerk*, n. 66 above, 719–20.

[83] Ibid., 720. See L.C. Steyn, "Regsbank en Regsfakulteit" (1967) 30 *Tydskrif vir Hedendaagse Romeinse-Hollandse Reg* 101. Steyn clearly had in his sights an article which severely criticised Ogilvie Thompson's judgment in *Rossow* v. *Sachs*: A.S. Mathews and R.C. Albino, "The Permanence of the Temporary—An Examination of the 90- and 180-Day Detention Laws" (1966) 83 *South African Law Journal* 16. For Ogilvie Thompson's speech, see N. Ogilvie Thompson, "Speech on the Centenary Celebrations of the Northern Cape Division", note 69 above.

academic critic for criticising the judges, but punished him for drawing their attention to a conception of the rule of law to which they were arguably beholden. Further, the main difference between section 6 of the Terrorism Act and the 90-day law was that the former made a permanent feature of South Africa's legal landscape what had in the 90-day law been regarded as temporary, since the law had annually to be renewed by proclamation of the State President.[84] Ogilvie Thompson had concluded that Van Niekerk was as a matter of law guilty of obstructing the course of justice. It therefore followed that any "general" critique of judges which urged them to follow their duty in particular cases under a different conception of the rule of law than a plain fact one was in risk of a charge of obstructing the course of justice.

In sum, Friedman's description of the dilemma which judges faced when evaluating detainee evidence is hardly different from Ogilvie Thompson's description in *S* v. *Van Niekerk*. Both see a problem which has to be treated case by case, rather than a dilemma of duties, one of which is arguably more fundamental because it pertains to the judge's duty under the rule of law.

Of course, mine and Van Niekerk's sense of that fundamental duty is controversial and one that is rejected by a plain fact conception. And, I am sure, it was Ogilvie Thompson's allegiance to a plain fact conception of legal duty under the rule of law which led him, via his decision in *Roussouw* v. *Sachs*, to his conclusions in *S* v. *Van Niekerk*. But the question for Friedman is why he adopted a description of the judicial dilemma dependent on a view of the rule of law which as a liberal judge he clearly rejected.

And here one can note that at the Hearing, the National Association of Democratic Lawyers (NADEL) revealed in their oral submission that in 1985 Judge Friedman had resigned from the Board of the Institute of Criminology at the University of Cape Town, in order to avoid association with the report *Detention and Torture in South Africa: Psychological, legal, and historical studies*.[85] This report was put together in full awarness of the judicial punishment meted out to Van Niekerk. So it very carefully evaluated evidence about the effects of solitary confinement in the absence of physical torture on detainees and the evidence for torture during

---

[84] See n. 73 above.
[85] Don Foster, with Dennis Davis and Diane Sandler, *Detention and Torture in South Africa* (London: James Currey, 1987). See the Transcript at p. 102.

detention in South Africa, which it found to sustain a finding that torture was commonplace.

The obvious inference from this story is not that judges were disempowered by the lies of the security police and others, nor by the statutes which explicitly authorised solitary confinement and impliedly authorised torture. Rather, they disempowered themselves by punishing Professor van Niekerk for having challenged them to do better, and thus they had trouble facing up to evidence of the effects of the practice they had in effect condoned.[86]

The tactic employed by the judges here attempts to deal with their cognitive dissonance—their psychological reaction to the uncomfortable gap betwen the injustice in which they were complicit and their sense of justice—by suppressing the factors which cause discomfort. And such tactics are present to a greater or lesser extent in all of the submissions in which old order judges participated. Robert Cover, in his pioneering work on the topic of judicial cognitive dissonance, deals with various "judicial response patterns".[87] The one which we have just seen Friedman resort to Cover calls "ascription of responsibility elsewhere".[88]

Another response pattern Cover discusses is "elevation of the formal stakes":

"For a judge who believed himself to have chosen fidelity to law over a personal, moral impulse . . . the choice became an easier one as the underlying justification for adherence to formal obligation was raised to the highest possible level. Assuming the initial decision to have been a hard one, the judge might, therefore, begin to perceive the chosen formal values as more important than before or the not-chosen moral values as less important. Thus, we will expect that either in the course of making his decision or as an immediate consequence of it, the judge will come to

---

[86] This story is told in part in the Chaskalson *et al.* Submission, at pp. 9–10. However, it is told blandly without any indication of the judges' sense of what the courts should have done both in respect of the issue of detainees' statements and of Van Niekerk's speech. Of course, the inference is—the section heading is "Role of law in stifling political dissent"— that the Court should not have found Van Niekerk guilty and, perhaps, that the courts should have taken seriously his argument about excluding statements. But it seems that the compromise reached between the judges making the submission requires leaving the inference to the reader.

[87] See Robert Cover, *Justice Accused: Antislavery and the Judicial Process* (New Haven, Conn.: Yale University Press, 1975), pp. 226–9. As we saw in Chapter 1, Cover explores these issues as they arose through responses by abolitionist judges required to interpret statutes which enforced slavery in nineteenth-century USA.

[88] Ibid., pp. 236–8.

enlarge the initially small gap between the desirability of the moral and formal choices".[89]

This response pattern is in fact the most pervasive in the judicial submissions and it is articulated in all the judges' discussions of parliamentary supremacy and the disempowerment of judges in the face of such supremacy.

In this respect, two passages from judgments of the past were frequently quoted by judges and others. The first was from a judgment by Judge Mervyn King, in explanation of his failure to come to the assistance of an appellant who had raised a common law defence of necessity to a charge under the Group Areas Act of unlawfully residing in a "white" area. As explained in Chapter 1, the Act empowered the government to reserve residential areas for particular racial groups, and had been implemented in a fashion which benefited whites while causing great hardship to others, often involving the forced removal of thousands of people from their homes to be dumped in barren areas outside of the "white" urban centres. King said of his failure:

> "An Act of Parliament creates law but not necessarily equity. As a judge in a court of law I am obliged to give effect to the provisions of an Act of Parliament. Speaking for myself and if I were sitting as a court of equity, I would have come to the assistance of the appellant. Unfortunately, and on an intellectually honest approach, I am compelled to conclude that the appeal must fail".[90]

The other passage is from *In re Dube*, a 1979 judgment by Judge John Didcott, perhaps the most innovative of the liberal old order judges, now a member of the Constitutional Court:

> "Parliament has the power to pass the statutes it likes, and there is nothing the courts can do about that. The result is law. But that is not always the same as justice. The only way Parliament can ever make legislation just, is by making just legislation".[91]

As the NADEL submission showed, these quotations, once properly contextualised, do not do the exculpatory work they are supposed to.[92] King's claim followed the judgment of the Appellate

---

[89] Ibid., pp. 229–30.
[90] *S* v. *Adams* 1979 (4) SA 793 (T) at 801.
[91] *In re Dube* 1979 (3) SA 820 (N) at 821.
[92] NADEL Submission, pp. 7–13.

Division in 1961 in *Minister of the Interior* v. *Lockhat*,[93] discussed in Chapter 1, a decision which held that executive steps to implement the Group Areas Act could not be challenged on the administrative law ground that the Act did not expressly permit unreasonable means of implementation. The Appellate Division said there that Parliament, when it designed the "colossal social experiment" involved in the policy of dividing up the country, must have envisaged that there would be "substantial inequalities".[94] In short, the courts had disempowered themselves by refusing to apply ordinary common law presumptions of statutory interpretation.

Further, there was a real question as to the extent of this self-disempowerment. In 1986, Judge Richard Goldstone, now a judge of the Constitutional Court, put "a spanner in the work" of implementing the Group Areas Act by holding that a magistrate could not order ejectment following a conviction under the Act unless he had first inquired into the personal hardship the ejectment would cause and the availability of alternative accommodation.[95]

Finally, as NADEL pointed out, Didcott in *Dube* had explicitly condemned the statutory provision with which he was dealing, the "idle and undesirable" clause of the Bantu (Urban Areas) Act, which we encountered in Pius Langa's submission. This clause permitted a "commissioner", a magistrate, to declare someone to be "idle and undesirable" if he had been unemployed for 122 days or more in the past year, thus rendering that person subject to removal from the "white" area and to detention if the commissioner saw fit.[96]

The case was before Didcott because, in terms of the Act, the papers on the matter had to go from the commissioner to a judge for review. The judge had then to certify that what had happened had been "in accordance with justice". Dube, a 24-year-old epileptic who lived with his mother, had been sentenced to detention at a farm colony if he did not find work within 30 days or leave Durban, where his mother lived. Didcott's comment on the phrase "in accordance with justice" immediately preceded the extract quoted by NADEL from *Dube*:

"The trouble is [the commissioner's certification] was not ['in accordance with justice']. It may have been in accordance with the legislation and,

[93] 1961 (2) SA 587 (A).
[94] Ibid., 599–60.
[95] *S* v. *Govender* 1986 (3) SA 969 (T).
[96] NADEL did not supply the detail that follows in the next paragraphs.

because what appears in legislation is the law, in accordance with that too. But it can hardly have been said to be 'in accordance with justice' ".

And he then went on to find that Dube could not fall within the scope of the "idle and undesirable" section since that section applied only to those "capable of being employed" and Dube's epilepsy rendered him "not capable of being employed in the ordinary sense". Thus Didcott set aside the commissioner's certification and said that "on this occasion at least, it is possible to apply the Act and do justice simultaneously".[97]

This was not a major victory against apartheid. But it showed that a judge who did pay attention, as his oath required, to the fact that he was supposed to administer justice in the circumstances of the particular case had significant room for interpretative manoeuvre. But to be capable of doing that, the judge had to see more than the substantive injustice of the law he was called upon to administer. It was clear, as NADEL pointed out, that an old order judge had also to be able to see that the law was made by an illegitimate legislature before he would be generally inclined to adopt such a creative approach to interpretation.[98]

Two submissions on day one of the Hearing, NADEL's and my own, dealt with the issue of the "defence of parliamentary supremacy". It seemed curious to us that old order judges who have kept their jobs in the new order would in 1997 invoke the supremacy of the apartheid legislature in defence of their record as if they were civil servants or security force personnel who could say that they were following orders. Zunaid Husain, one of NADEL's representatives, expressed his frustration with the continued resort to the defence at the Hearing: what you call a parliament, he said, "was merely a chamber for legitimising oppression".[99] This kind of positivism, as Husain termed it, however appropriate in a context where all citizens are represented in Parliament, was completely inappropriate in South Africa.[100]

Husain's point about positivism suggests, rightly in my view, that the issue was not just one about parliamentary supremacy; rather, it was about the understanding of parliamentary supremacy embedded within the plain fact approach. In my own submission, I outlined the

[97] *In re Dube*, n. 91 above, 821–2.
[98] NADEL Submission, pp. 51–2.
[99] Transcript, p. 86.
[100] Ibid.

main characteristics of the plain fact approach adopted by the majority of old order judges in their interpretation of apartheid statutes.[101] As we have seen, plain fact judges hold that the judicial duty when interpreting a statute is always to look to those parts of the public record that make it clear what the legislators as a matter of fact intended. In this way, judges attempt to determine the law as it is, without permitting their substantive convictions about justice to interfere. And in South Africa, the facts of the public record were very clear as to what the National Party majority in Parliament wanted. Indeed, judges knew from the record that judicial decisions which imposed legal constraints on the implementation of apartheid statutes would likely be overruled by legislative amendments to make the government's intention plain.

One reason that judges and others persisted in their view that the plain fact approach is appropriate is that they wished to make the following point: if you want us faithfully to carry out the intention of the Legislature in the new legal and political order, you cannot object to the fact that this is what we did under apartheid.

However, that explanation is again an attempt at disempowering exculpation. The plain fact approach is itself part of a judicial response pattern, one identified by Cover as a "retreat to a mechanistic formalism".[102] It avoids confronting the question about what the law is to which judges are to be faithful by stipulating that it is certain facts in the public record which determine the law. Judges who rejected the plain fact approach thought that other values— certain legal principles—were also law and that the virtue of independence lay in part in that it enabled judicial fidelity to such values. Arguably, the new legal order differs from the old mainly in that it entrenches the rights of those subject to the law in a written constitution, thus making it very explicit that fidelity to law is also fidelity to such values.

In sum, the plain fact view of independence was highly controversial and, as NADEL and I pointed out, had no substantive justification. Indeed, some of the submissions show how elevation of the formal stakes and retreat to mechanistic formalism work together— one had to do the former in order to feel comfortable with adopting the latter.

---

[101] Dyzenhaus Submission, pp. 11–12.
[102] Cover, *Justice Accused: Antislavery and the Judicial Process*, n. 87 above, p.232.

For example, Smalberger *et al.* implicitly support Wacks's argument for judicial resignation by claiming that there are "only two honest courses open to a judge" who finds that his "credo" conflicts with his oath of office—"either resign or comply with the oath of office".[103] But this way of staking out the terrain is highly contentious; a judge could try to reflect on what his oath of office commits him to, and is surely duty-bound to do so, if his credo includes the rule of law and it seems that the Legislature is engaged in undermining the rule of law.

Another example is to be found in an essay written by Pierre J.J. Olivier, an old order judge now serving on the Supreme Court of Appeal, which the TRC included with the judicial submissions. In this essay—"The Judiciary: Executive-Mindedness and Independence"— Olivier dealt at some length with work by critics[104] of the apartheid judiciary who had argued that judges should not adopt a plain fact approach but dismissed that work as follows:

> "In spite of my admiration for the industriousness of these commentators, I fail to be convinced that their suggestions, if implemented, could have made any difference to the quandary in which judges found themselves. The record shows that the legislator deliberately meant to subvert human freedom and dignity, or the traditional values of Roman Dutch law. It did so in precise, unambiguous language; any ambiguity, affording judges a *pro libertate* [in favour of liberty] interpretation, was soon enough closed by shrewd and effective statutory enactments.
>
> It was also argued . . . that the courts ought to have applied the international human rights law or international customs. The very case in which King J lamented his dilemma went on appeal to the Appellate Division, where the argument just mentioned was raised. An interesting argument, said the Appellate Division, but irrelevant. By our law, as I think in most other systems, a clear and unambiguous Act of Parliament overrules international law and customs".[105]

The same argument is to be found in other judicial submissions, including that made by Judge L.W.H. Ackermann of the Constitutional Court, whose sensitive and heartfelt personal account contrasts strongly with Olivier's supercilious tone.

As Ackermann tells us, he had been a judge of the Transvaal

---

[103] Smalberger *et al.* Submission, p. 7.

[104] Dennis Davis, John Dugard, Edwin Cameron, and myself.

[105] Pierre J.J. Olivier, "The Judiciary: Executive-Mindedness and Independence", (unpublished essay), pp. 18–19.

Provincial Division in 1980, but resigned to take up a Chair of Human Rights Law at the University of Stellenbosch in 1987. His resignation was prompted, he said, not only by his "general ethical and jurisprudential" objections to apartheid, but also by his belief that "the whole structure was irreconcilably at odds with my religious conviction that all humans are created equal in the image of god and indefeasibly equal in their fundamental dignity".[106]

Ackermann mentions that John Dugard had a "considerable impact" on his thinking though he clearly saw no room at the time of his resignation for the judicial creativity in the cause of human rights which critics like Dugard were advocating:

I cannot recall any particular judgment which I gave as a judge of the Transvaal Provincial Division, the result of which would have been substantially different had I applied to it the deeper insights I now have regarding human rights and their implementation. I do believe, however, that there were opportunities for all judges to have commented critically on apartheid and its legal consequences in their judgments, even though they considered themselves bound to apply the law as they found it.[107]

Ackermann says of his resignation that he regarded it, and still does so, "as an exclusively personal matter of conscience".[108] Indeed, his statement on resigning mentions his reasons for resignation in a very tangential fashion:

I wish to announce my resignation as a Judge of the Supreme Court with effect from 1 September 1987. The University of Stellenbosch has invited me to to accept the newly established chair in Human Rights Law. I believe that the effective protection of human rights in this country is the most important issue facing lawyers in the short, medium and long term. It is an issue which has addressed me, as a lawyer, ever more strongly over the past number of years. The human rights chair at Stellenbosch affords me a unique opportunity to devote all my time and energy to this task. In order to accept this invitation from Stellenbosch I approached the State President to consent, in terms of section 2(c) of the Judges' Pension Act, No. 90 of 1978, to my retirement from the Bench. Such request was, however, refused. I have accordingly decided to resign from the Bench in order to take up the Stellenbosch Chair.[109]

---

[106] Ackermann Submission, p. 4.   [107] Ibid., p. 3.   [108] Ibid., p. 5.
[109] Ibid., pp. 4–5. The option in terms of s. 2(c) of the 1978 Act would have permitted the judge to retire rather than resign.

In short, he understood his personal sense of moral duty to be in conflict with his duty as a judge, and therefore took the option which Wacks had advocated, though carefully avoiding any hint that his resignation had implications for other judges.

The difference between Ackermann, on the one hand, and Didcott and Friedman, on the other, is revealing of the predicament of judges under apartheid. Liberal judges were not simply judges who had liberal views, like Ackermann. For Ackermann, as we have seen, thought that apartheid was morally wrong but that his duty to some supreme legal norm required that apartheid legislation should be implemented as the plain fact approach required. He adopted the perspective which we saw Robert Cover describe in Chapter 1 as the perspective of the "disobedient", one who assumes that the content of the law is what the powerful take it to be and finds that content in deep conflict with his personal sense of morality.[110]

One can note here that Ackermann ended his submission with a powerful call to all judicial officers to embrace the Constitution— "the supreme legal norm overriding all else and which from now on informs all law and judicial conduct".[111] However, the contrast he implies between the old and the new legal orders suggests misleadingly, as Corbett did in his memorandum, that it was clear what the judicial duty was under the old.

Ackermann, then, shares with Smalberger *et al.*, the desire to avoid confronting the dilemmas which faced old order judges *as judges*. The difference between him, on the one hand, and Smalberger *et al.* and Olivier, on the other, is only that he heightens the sense of dissonance between his personal moral duty as citizen and his moral duty as judge.

Liberal judges, in contrast, were judges who thought that their legal duty—the duty they undertook to administer the law—was one which had to be informed by their moral values. Those moral values condemned not only the substantive injustice of particular apartheid statutes but also their illegitimate provenance. Such liberal judges sought to impose the rule of law on a government which attempted quite successfully to evade its constraints because the government had the help of a bench composed mostly of plain fact judges. And in order to see the need to impose the rule of law, such liberal judges

---

[110] See Chapter 1, text to n. 65.
[111] Ackermann Submission, p. 6.

had first to accept the illegitimacy of the Parliament whose statutes they were interpreting.

Very much the same point was made by Chaskalson *et al.*, when they said that the doctrine of parliamentary sovereignty was "debased" in "the absence of a democratic legislature" and that that debasement "should have led to a greater scrutiny by courts of legislative provisions invasive of the rights of the majority".[112] Indeed, they seemed to give qualified approval to John Dugard's view that legal education in South Africa was designed to produce lawyers who would unquestioningly follow what they took to be the intention of the Legislature, understood in the way the plain fact approach requires. For they quoted Dugard's claim that such an approach— one which Dugard identified with legal positivism—had not served South Africa well, since it had "prevented judges from fully perceiving that the judicial function is essentially an exercise of choice in the penumbral area of legal uncertainty. And it has discouraged lawyers from playing a more active role in the protection of those principles which make up the country's legal heritage".[113] Chaskalson *et al.* then comment:

Although positivism need not necessarily be as impoverished a jurisprudential doctrine as Professor Dugard suggests it was in South Africa, there can be no doubt that his observation that the form of positivism espoused by many South African lawyers and judges was a major factor contributing to the violation of human rights is correct. Lawyers in South Africa were not generally trained in an analytical or jurisprudential tradition which led them to question the content or purpose of laws and the judicial function. Until the late 1970s, most law schools provided students with a monotonous diet of black-letter law. What is more the primary emphasis in most law degrees was on private law, in particular Roman-Dutch law and its development. Without doubt these law schools produced technically competent lawyers, but their education lacked an important component.[114]

It is useful here to contrast Smalberger *et al.*, for they commented disparagingly on academic lawyers who had sought to explain the prevalence of the plain fact approach in terms of the education in

---

[112] Chaskalson *et al.* Submission, at p. 15.
[113] Dugard, *Human Rights and the South African Legal Order*, n. 65 above, p. 393.
[114] Chaskalson *et al.* Submission, p. 16.

South African law schools. Although they do not name names, it is clear that they have John Dugard's work in their sights:

> *There are those who attribute what they perceive to be the failure of the South African judiciary to safeguard civil liberties and mitigate the rigours of apartheid to that judiciary's alleged affection for "positivism" and Austinian theories of sovereignty and, somewhat patronisingly, to a deficient legal education at the universities, and a consequent inability to understand their true role. If the implication is that judges were free to ignore even the plainly expressed meaning of a statute because it was enacted by a parliament which was not elected by the majority of the country's citizens, it is a quite untenable proposition. And a moment's reflection should show how much worse the position would have been if the judiciary had adopted the oft-advocated "purposive" approach to the interpretation of offensive statutes enacted by the previous government.*[115]

In their bid to retreat to the high ground of mechanistic formalism, Smalberger *et al.* miss the main point completely. For the main point is not that the illegitimacy of the South Africa Parliament gave judges a lever, lacking in other jurisdictions, which entitled them to overrule Parliament when they had no constitutional warrant to do so. The point is that the illegitimacy of that Parliament should have alerted the judges to the fact that an approach to the interpretation of statutes whose justification depends on the existence of a democratically elected Parliament has no purchase in the absence of democracy. However, there is one insight that can be gleaned from this passage, though it needs a bit of preparatory work.

Dugard argued, as we have just seen, that judges should understand that they generally have a choice when it comes to deciding difficult matters of statutory interpretation. He then suggested that judges should adopt a "purposive" approach in deciding on their choice, one which looked beyond the text of the statute to important social values.

Now Dugard argued further that the social values which judges should opt for are those expressed in common law or Roman-Dutch law presumptions of liberty, equality, and so on.[116] Smalberger *et al.*'s retort at the end of the passage is that, on such an approach,

---

[115] Smalberger *et al.* Submission, pp. 10–11.
[116] Dugard, *Human Rights and the South African Legal Order*, n. 65 above, pp. 397–402.

judges would have found that the purposes of the statutes were best understood in the light of the social values of the powerful.

In other words, their implicit argument is, as I have already suggested, very much the same as the argument Wacks put forward to support the conclusion that liberal judges should resign because the best explanation of any apartheid statute was one in terms of the goals of apartheid, including the goal of ruthlessly stamping out political opposition. If judges had a choice, but had to exercise it to advance purposes or goals, then Dugard's favoured option of interpretation in terms of common law presumptions seemed illusory. However, if the denial of choice gives rise to the plain fact approach, as Dugard and Chaskalson *et al.* claim, then it seems that however one describes the situation, judges were compelled to come to the conclusions which the majority of judges in fact reached.

Smalberger *et al.* do in fact want to claim that such conclusions were inevitable. But their argument is a little more complex, and it is in line with the suggestion by Chaskalson *et al.* that "positivism need not necessarily be" so "impoverished a jurisprudential doctrine". For it was the case that from time to time even as diehard a plain fact judge as Rabie would give a judgment favouring the liberty of the individual rather than the purposes of the regime, as these would be identified by a plain fact approach. Indeed, in the leading study of the emergency team, Stephen Ellman notes that three decisions of the Rabie court "unmistakably and ... inventively protected the rights of emergency detainees", that is, of those detainees detained under the states of emergency during the 1980s.[117]

Among the reasons Ellman suggests for these anomalies are the Appellate Division's desire to preserve some meaningful role for itself in the South African legal order, which in turn required that legal order itself be preserved as providing some constraints on government. There had to be some boundaries beyond which the court would not permit government to go.[118] Ellman argues that Rabie and his like-minded colleagues shared here a general desire on the part of white South Africans to believe that they lived in a legitimate political and legal order, one in which the idea of the rule of law

[117] Ellman, *In a Time of Trouble: Law and Liberty In South Africa's State of Emergency*, n. 12 above, p. 115, referring to *Nkwentsha* v. *Minister of Law and Order* 1988 (3) SA 99 (A); *Apleni* v. *Minister of Law and Order* 1989 (1) SA 195 (A); *Minister of Law and Order* v. *Swart* 1989 (1) SA 95 (A).

[118] Ellman, *In a Time of Trouble: Law and Liberty In South Africa's State of Emergency*, n. 12 above, pp. 135–8.

was at least to some extent observed.[119] And he concludes that legal positivism was at times a real help to conservative judges who wished to constrain politics through law. If, that is, the decision that favoured human rights could be justified by reference to the letter of the statute, judges could give that decision without seeming to impose their own moral and political values on the law.[120]

Put differently, in each of the three cases in which the Rabie team did not deliver a plain fact result, there was in the statutory provision at issue some explicit element onto which a plain fact judge could fasten as an indication of actual legislative intent that the executive should observe the rule of law in its implementation of the security laws.[121] Thus, a plain fact judge could give a judgment upholding the rule of law, the one which common law presumptions would favour, but the explicit element in the statute permitted him to do so without having to rely on such presumptions. In contrast, if Dugard's purposive method were adopted in such cases, the judge would not be able to rely on a "fact of the matter" derived from the explicit statutory element. Rather, he would have to presume that he had a choice, one to be exercised in the light of Dugard's "purposes". And since the purposes in evidence in the public record were hostile to the constraints of the rule of law, the result would be the opposite of the one which Dugard's purposive approach was meant to reach.

The insight of Smalberger *et al.*, then, is that judicial choice does not take place at a moment when the law runs out of answers, so that a judge has to decide unconstrained by the law. But what they refuse to see is that judges had a choice under apartheid about how to understand the idea of law to which judges hold themselves accountable. And that choice was a political and moral one about the principles that should inform judicial fidelity to law. It is in denying that they had such a choice that Smalberger *et al.* seek to deny their moral responsibility as judges under the old order.

Moreover, that a plain fact approach could at times lead to the same results as an approach which relied on common law presumptions lends it no support. As I have argued elsewhere, if the reasons for wanting the rule of law pertain to the moral and political benefits of legal order, and if judges have a central role in upholding such order, then it is important for judges to articulate the principles

[119] Ibid., pp. 185–6.
[120] Ibid., pp. 232–3, 242–4.
[121] See, in addition, *Minister of Law and Order* v. *Hurley* 1986 (3) SA 568 (A).

which in their view are fundamental to the rule of law.[122] For judges to have upheld such principles only because they wish to preserve some sense of legitimacy, and only on those occasions when they did not need to state their commitment to the principles, shows of course that they had no real commitment to the rule of law. They helped to legitimate the extraordinary violence of apartheid by occasionally checking its exercise.

It is easy to judge harshly judges who adopted the plain fact approach, especially those who adopted it in tandem with their support for apartheid. And one should judge such judges harshly not only because they made themselves instruments of the morally abhorrent system of apartheid but also because, as judges, they were supposed to be more than civil servants.

But it may also seem to be the case that liberal judges, those judges who sought to uphold the rule of law, if anything did more than plain fact judges to legitimate the legal order of apartheid. We have seen that in order to interpret statutes so as to subject them to the rule of law, liberal judges had also to assume that the South African Parliament was at least to some extent legitimate, or at least that it aspired to legitimacy. For they assumed that the Parliament, though profoundly undemocratic, wished to abide by the rule of law. And to the extent that they were successful in holding Parliament to this aspiration, they lent legitimacy to the legal order as a whole. Indeed, the liberal judges lent more legitimacy than old order plain fact judges like Ackermann who reduced their cognitive dissonance by elevating the formal stakes, or than those judges who experienced no cognitive dissonance at all because they were enthusiastic supporters of apartheid.

It seems then that the liberal judges, who tried to do most from within, also get judged harshly and they get judged harshly precisely because they took the greatest risk. They were vulnerable to being judged by their own standards at the same time as they implied, by their participation, that those standards were the standards of a legal order which required them to participate in administering the legislative machinery of both ordinary and extraordinary violence.

The fact that the liberal judges are vulnerable to this judgment does not, however, lead to the conclusion that their participation was

---

[122] David Dyzenhaus, *Hard Cases in Wicked Legal Systems: South African Law in the Pespective of Legal Philosophy*, n. 80 above, ch. 10, and see my review of Ellman, *In a Time of Trouble: Law and Liberty in South Africa's State of Emergency*: David Dyzenhaus, "Law's Potential" (1992) 7 *Canadian Journal of Law and Society* 237.

unjustified. While Wacks was perhaps right in arguing that liberal judges lent more legitimacy than others to the apartheid legal order, the basis of his argument was, as I have shown, wrong. It was not the case that liberal judges always had to interpret the law in the light of the ideology of the powerful.

Moreover, the argument about legitimacy is more complicated than Wacks suggested. Once one sees that the basis of his argument was wrong, one can also see why it was important for liberal judges to stay in office despite the legitimacy they thereby imparted. Here Arthur Chaskalson's "no lamenting the past" statement is, with some editing, instructive. Liberal judges, "despite all the paradoxes . . . somehow held to the infrastructure and . .. kept alive the principles of freedom and justice which permeate the common law. [T]he notion that freedom and fairness are inherent qualities of law lives on . . . That is an important legacy and one which deserves neither to be diminished nor squandered".[123]

In sum, the judicial debate about whether to stay in office could not be conducted by merely weighing benefits derived from participation against legitimacy lent to the system. In addition, one had to take into account the future—what were the prospects for a democratic transformation in a country where there was little or no respect for law? And, perhaps even more important, one had to take into account the point we saw Etienne Mureinik make, one quoted in part by Chaskalson *et al.*, "If we argue . . . that moral judges should resign, we can no longer pray, when we go into court as defence counsel, or even as the accused, that we find a moral judge on the bench".[124]

4. Preliminary Conclusion

I will return to the main themes of this chapter—judicial independence and accountability to the rule of law—in Chapter 4. But there is one issue which deserves immediate treatment, and it was succintly raised by Carmel Rickard, South Africa's leading legal journalist, who attended the Hearing and published her impressions under the title "The judiciary goes on trial for its apartheid past".[125]

---

[123] Arthur Chaskalson, "Law in a Changing Society" (1989) 5 *South African Journal on Human Rights* 293, 295.

[124] See n. 50 above.

[125] Carmel Rickard, *Sunday Times*, 2 November 1997, p. 16.

Rickard came away with this jaundiced view:

"[W]hile the judiciary and other participants had been assured there would be no "witch hunt" and that the focus of the hearings would be a collaborative search for what had gone wrong in the past, that is not what happened in practice.

After the adversarial questioning of the first two days, judges may feel they made the correct decision to stay away. Legal organisations and individuals appeared intent on scoring points off each other in trying to show how much they had done to oppose injustice. Individual judges were named—and damned or praised".

I have shown here that Rickard is right in saying that the proceedings did turn into a kind of trial. But I have also tried to show how the judges could not feel that their failure to appear is vindicated by that fact. For the atmosphere of confrontation was in part created by the impression that judges considered themselves beyond the reach of truth and reconciliation.

But even had some judges appeared, confrontation of the sort Rickard describes would have happened. And in the debates leading up to the Hearing, the thought was often expressed that the Hearing would only be productive if it would focus on the institutional level and not attempt to "pigeonhole" individuals, judges or others, into simplistic categories of good and bad.

In my view, some of those who decided not to participate at all or were very reluctant to do so rightly saw that an inquiry at the institutional level alone is not possible. Take for example a recurrent issue so far, the merits of different understandings of the rule of law. Such understandings shape the institutions of the law and they are developed and maintained by individuals who have important roles within the institutions. It made an important difference to law who was Chief Justice and whom he appointed to hear appeals on challenges to executive action.

In short, one cannot discuss the rule of law under apartheid without discussing individuals who exemplified different understandings of the ideals of the rule of law. And we will see in the next chapter how the choices of one South African lawyer, Bram Fischer, dramatically illuminate the issue of the rule of law under apartheid.

It is inevitable that such a discussion will become to some extent personalised—fingers will get pointed, accusations will be made. But if the overarching aim of the discussion is an understanding of what went wrong with a view to constructing a better future, then individuals who are committed to that future should be prepared to take the knocks.[126] The reluctance of most judges to participate at all, and the willingness of the others to participate only by sending written submissions, contributed to the process of personalisation by suggesting that judges considered themselves somehow beyond the reach of truth and reconciliation.

Of course, there are factors that make judges special; judges do need to be independent of political influence if they are to do their job and they need to be independent in order for them to be accountable only to the law. But in an exceptional situation, one which starkly raises the issue of what accountability to the law required, an appeal to independence has little weight. It has no more weight than a claim that a plain fact approach was appropriate in conditions where such an approach clearly lacked any legitimacy.

I do not think one should underestimate the risks of full participation. As we will see in the next chapter, those who did subject themselves to the Hearing found themselves even more exposed than the judges who did not attend. But had the judges participated fully in the Hearing, not only would the tone have been different but a discussion would have started in a more auspicious way about the substance of judicial independence.

Indeed, I argued in my submission to the TRC that the special role and situation of judges made it even more incumbent on them than on other lawyers to appear at the TRC.[127] In this regard I pointed to the contrast between the judicial world and the world of those men in the security forces whose appearance before the TRC was to apply for amnesty.

The security world was populated by people on the ground who performed appalling acts often, it seems, with little understanding, even now, of the moral consequences of their action. It was also populated by those who gave them orders, whether their direct superiors, or those in the highest echelons of security, or their political masters. And these people were either complete ideologues, impervious to moral argument, or had complex views about the moral justification for deeply immoral acts. But what united them all

---

[126] See on this issue, Jürgen Habermas, "What does 'Working Off the Past' mean today?", in Habermas, *A Berlin Republic: Writings on Germany*, Peter Uwe Hohendahl trans. (Lincoln: University of Nebraska Press, 1997) 17, pp. 18–21.

[127] Dyzenhaus Submission, pp. 5–7. I drafted the submission in the anticipation that the judges would probably not appear.

was that the only law in their world of shadows and secrecy was the order or command of one's superior and that disobedience to command could be followed by fatal consequences, or, at the least, would mean the end of one's career.

Judges during the apartheid era operated in almost the exact converse of the security world. They sat in open courtrooms, listening to carefully reasoned arguments often from the most distinguished members of the Bar, and their qualification to do that job required university degrees that trained one in argument and practical experience in making such arguments. They had the benefit of exposure to the academic writings in professional journals and in monographs which analysed their role, writings which gave them the opportunity to reflect out of the courtroom about their duty in it. In this regard, the plain fact judges had the benefit of exposure to the judgments of the minority; and this exposure was particularly important since it showed them that one could do on occasion otherwise in office. Further, while judicial advance through the ranks under apartheid might have depended on not incurring the political displeasure of politicians, as judges at any level they were guaranteed the complete security of tenure and a salary thought appropriate to maintaining the independence and impartiality of the judiciary. Finally, they were given an unique opportunity to observe at close quarters both those who led the struggle against apartheid and its footsoldiers. Other white South Africans were subjected to a one-dimensional picture of the opponents of apartheid as the devil's fanatical followers. But judges had the opportunity, often over months, to observe carefully and listen to people whose moral case for opposition is today recognised as unassailable and many of whom are regarded today as moral exemplars of the human spirit under stress.[128]

In short, judges were doubly privileged. They could carry out their duty without fear of serious personal repercussions and their

---

[128] For an exploration of how this exposure could have results, see Nelson Mandela, *Long Walk to Freedom* (Boston: Little, Brown and Company, Abacus, 1996), pp. 199–261, on the Treason Trial, a process which lasted from 1956–1961, and in which 156 activists, including Mandela, were charged with high treason. All accused were acquitted, and Mandela comments, p. 261, that "the consequence of the government's humiliating defeat was that the state decided never to let it happen again. From that day forth they were not going to rely on judges whom they had not themselves appointed. They were not going to observe what they considered the legal niceties that protected terrorists or permitted convicted prisoners certain rights in jail. During the Treason Trial, there were no examples of individuals being isolated, beaten and tortured in order to elicit information. All of those things became commonplace thereafter".

duty was not one which required following orders; it required careful consideration of argument and careful attention to the particulars of cases.

South Africans were therefore entitled to know how and why the majority of judges failed so miserably in keeping to their oath of office. They needed to know how men in so privileged a position, with such an important role, and with so much space to do other than they did, made the wrong moral choice, one which I will argue to be clearly in dereliction of their judicial oath of office.

3

Memory's Struggle

The effacement of memory is more the achievement of an all-too-wakeful consciousness than it is the result of its weakness in the face of the superiority of unconscious processes. In this forgetting of what is scarcely past, one senses the fury of the one who has to talk himself out of what everyone knows, before he can talk them out of it.

Theodor Adorno.[1]

1. Introduction

This chapter focuses on the struggle of certain parts of the South African legal community to come to terms with their role in the apartheid legal order: the advocates, the attorneys, legal academics and the Attorneys-General.[2] Recall that the legal profession in South Africa is divided between the Bar of advocates who during apartheid enjoyed an exclusive right of audience before the Supreme Court and the side-Bar of attorneys whose extra-curial work included instructing the advocates. The Attorneys-General are the civil servants in each province who control prosecutions.

During the apartheid era, the Attorneys-General were regarded with grave suspicion by the legal profession. The view of the Attorneys-General was that they were enthusiastic participants in enforcing apartheid rather than occupants of an independent office committed to the ideal of the rule of law. But opponents of apartheid, including lawyers, had their own concerns about the commitments of the professional bodies which controlled advocates

---

[1] Theodor Adorno, "What Does Coming to Terms with the Past Mean?", Geoffrey Hartman trans., in Geoffrey Hartman (ed.), *Bitburg in Moral and Political Perspective* (Bloomington: Indiana University Press, 1986), p. 114, at pp. 117–18

[2] The order of treatment in this chapter reflects roughly the order in which the lawyers on whom I will focus appeared. On day two of the Hearing, the General Council of the Bar (the advocates) was followed by the Association of Law Societies (the attorneys) and then the Law Faculties. On day three, the Attorneys-General appeared.

and attorneys. Indeed, these concerns led to the formation of groups of lawyers like the National Association of Democratic Lawyers (NADEL) and the Black Lawyers Association (BLA). And concerns about the willingness and ability of the professional associations to mount an effective critique of apartheid law and to use the law to oppose apartheid led to the foundation of the Centre for Applied Legal Studies at the University of the Witwatersrand and the Legal Resources Centre.

Many of the lawyers who made written and oral submissions to the Hearing fell prey to the phenomenon which the philosopher Theodor Adorno described above; the temptation to try to manage public memory in their own self-interest. The quotation is from Adorno's classic 1959 essay, "What Does Coming to Terms with the Past Mean?", in which, writing from the perspective of a German Jew who had returned to teach in Germany after the Second World War, he examined German attempts to come to terms with the Nazi past.

We will see that Adorno's point about such attempts also applies to the presentations of many lawyers at the Hearing. The management of memory—the attempt both to forget what is uncomfortable and to persuade others to forget—is not, Adorno suggests, an unconscious process. It requires deliberate decision from the vantage point of one who does in fact remember. And we will see that even those lawyers at the Hearing who made the most courageous efforts to remember, and who, not coincidentally, had most to be proud of, were not entirely immune from the temptation to manage memory.

2. Independence and the Rule of Law

The General Council of the Bar (GCB) is the national body which seeks to represent the members of the advocates' profession in South Africa. Advocates practice at regional Bars, each of which is located in a city in which there is a provincial or local division of the High Court. Each Bar, while not homogeneous, has something of its own character. The Johannesburg Bar is considered more liberal since among the advocates practising there were the leading human rights advocates. The Pretoria Bar is not only more conservative, but over the years actively supported apartheid policy.

There are of course plenty of exceptions to these loose generalisations. For example, the Johannesburg Bar at one time included within its ranks both Joe Slovo, a leading communist, later head of the African National Congress's military wing, and John Vorster, who as Minister of Justice crafted South Africa's security legislation. Nevertheless, the Bars do have quite distinct characters, which is why some advocates would have preferred Bars to have made individual submissions.

The GCB began its written submission by noting that it came into being in 1946 on the basis of a compromise. Advocates wanted an effective body to represent them, but in order to include all the Bars, the GCB accepted that each Bar could determine issues like racial exclusivity of membership and that no policy could be adopted or public statement made without consensus. The result was that advocates paid a high price for a federal voice. They accepted apartheid within their ranks and that they would not be able to speak in one voice on many of the occasions on which individual Bars wished to protest the erosion of the rule of law, political harassment of lawyers, and the obstacles which apartheid threw in the path of black lawyers. The Pretoria Bar in particular thwarted most attempts by the GCB to speak out against executive action or legislation which under-mined the rule of law and voluntarily confined membership of its Bar to whites until 1980, when it changed its policy only under threat of exclusion from the GCB. The GCB thus adopted, as it said, "a 'lowest common denominator' position on matters of controversy", leaving it to individual Bars to protest and make representations in regard to erosions to the rule of law and state abuse of human rights.[3]

The GCB seems to suggest that this was not a matter of great importance, since protests against government policy were rejected and "most, if not all of the representations made were ignored".[4] But, as we will see, the decision of the individual Bars to speak to the TRC through the federal body resulted in ambiguities and evasions which perpetuate the problems of the past.

Unlike the judges, the written submission made by the GCB made the issue of legitimacy central. They put as their frontispiece the following quote from an address by Sidney Kentridge S.C. to the New Zealand Law Society in 1978:

What are we, as counsel, doing . . . —are we really defending the rule of law or what remains of it or . . . are we helping to give a spurious air of respectability and fairness to a procedure which is fundamentally unfair?

---

[3] GCB Submission, vol. 1, pp. 3–6, at p. 5.   [4] Ibid., p. 5.

Here is the conclusion to their submission:

We have tried to present our history, good and bad. Thus we expose for the public record the racism which existed in certain Bars. We have also recorded the endless protests, objections, and delegations to Ministers seeking to combat yet further inroads in the administration of justice. In the circumstances which prevailed, there is an echo of what Alexis de Toqueville wrote in Democracy in America: "No man can struggle with advantage against the spirit of his age and country, and however powerful a man may be, it is hard for him to make his contemporaries share feelings and ideas which run counter to the general rule of their hopes and desires."

Inevitably the record is imperfect. There is, the TRC has written to us, no judgement to be passed in these proceedings. But in the inquiry of how it was that gross violations of human rights could have occurred in South Africa during the years 1960 to 1994, there is inevitably an assessment of the Bar's role. In that regard, it is not for the Bar to pronounce upon itself. What however it would wish to do, taking pride in those instances in which it, in the ways and on the occasions described above, challenged inroads upon the administration of justice, is also to acknowledge and regret that there were occasions on which yet more could have been done. At times so impregnable did the legislative and executive fortress seem to be that Bar leaders despaired. Just ten years before a commitment to transition to democracy was announced, Kentridge S.C. wrote (in (1980) 128 University of Pennsylvania Law Review *621) quoting William the Silent: "Is there any hope of restoring what has been lost? It would not be realistic to say so. But realism, however sombre, is not to be confused with silence or acquiesence. 'It is not necessary to hope in order to work, and it is not necessary to succeed in order to persevere'".*

The GCB then quoted in full an apology made by the Pretoria Bar Council:

During the period which is covered by the submission of the General Council of the Bar to the Truth and Reconciliation Commission (1960–1990), the government of the day steadily eroded civil liberties, interfered with the rule of law and passed increasingly repressive legislation. While other constituent Bars of the GCB voiced their concern, the Pretoria Bar failed to do so and, on more than one occasion, refused to join its fellow members in condemning executive excesses which brought the administration of justice into disrepute and prevented the courts from protecting civil liberties.

Although the vast majority of the Pretoria Bar's present members do not share the sentiments of the majority during the period under discussion, it cannot be gainsaid that the Pretoria Bar as an institution failed in its duty to fulfil the legal profession's role of custodian of individual rights and the rule of law. Its refusal to join the other Bars in protest also prevented the GCB from speaking on behalf of the entire profession with one voice.

We apologise to our colleagues, to the judiciary, the attorney's profession, the public at large and in particular the victims of unjust laws for these failures.

As is the case with the apology which we tendered in regard to the racial discrimination which our Bar practised until 1980, we should have offered our expressions of regret at a much earlier stage. We apologise for this remissness.

We are grateful for the opportunity which our fellow Bars and the Truth and Reconciliation Commission have given us to set the record straight in public.

Dated at Pretoria this 17th day of October 1997.

GL Grobler S.C.

Chairperson: Pretoria Bar.

The GCB closed with these words:

All advocates whom the GCB and its constituent Bars represent would wish to rededicate themselves to promoting the administration of justice in the future. In Milan Kundera's phrase, the struggle against the abuse of power is the struggle of memory against forgetting.[5]

These issues were also the ones highlighted in the GCB's oral submission, made by Jules Browde S.C. whose career had spanned the period with which the TRC was dealing, and a man of impeccable liberal credentials.

However, both the GCB's written and oral submissions showed just how difficult is memory's struggle. Recall that the GCB had had to deal with some resistance of members, who thought the GCB should not make any submission. In addition, it was well known that the stance the GCB had adopted—the highlighting of the question of legitimacy—was controversial within its ranks. In particular, one topic which the GCB discussed in detail, both in the written and the oral submission, was considered highly sensitive.

[5] Ibid., vol. 2, pp. 209–11.

This topic concerned the striking off of Abram "Bram" Fischer from the roll of advocates, a move initiated by his own Bar, the liberal Johannesburg Bar. Fischer, as the GCB's submission notes, was son of the Judge President of the Orange Free State and the grandson of the Prime Minister of the Orange River Colony, the political entity which came into being between the end of the Boer War and the establishment of the Union of South Africa in 1910. He became one of South Africa's leading advocates, a position he maintained in the 1950s and early 1960s despite the fact that he was a prominent member of the South African Communist Party. In 1964 he was charged with various offences under the Suppression of Communism Act 1950, in reaction to which the Communist Party had dissolved itself and gone underground. Fischer was permitted to leave South Africa on bail to argue a case before the Privy Council in London since the court accepted that a man of his integrity would not estreat (break the conditions of) his bail. Fischer returned to stand trial, which commenced in November 1964. In January 1965 he failed to attend his trial, leaving a letter for his legal representative explaining his reasons. Here are some extracts:

I wish you to inform the court that my absence, though deliberate, is not intended in any way to be disrespectful . . . I have not taken this step lightly. As you will no doubt understand, I have experienced great conflict between my desire to stay with my fellow accused and, on the other hand, to try to continue the political work I believe to be essential. My decision was made only because I believe that it is the duty of every true opponent of this government to remain in this country and to oppose its monstrous policy of apartheid with every means in its power. That is what I shall do for as long as I can . . . Cruel, discriminatory laws multiply each year, bitterness and hatred of the government and its laws are growing daily. No outlet for this hatred is permitted because political rights have been removed. National organisations have been outlawed and leaders not in gaol have been banned from speaking and meeting. People are hounded by Pass Laws and by Group Areas Controls. Torture by solitary confinement, and worse, has been legalised by an elected parliament—surely an event unique in history . . . Unless this whole intolerable system is changed radically and rapidly disaster must follow. Appalling bloodshed and civil war will become inevitable because, as long as there is oppression of a majority such oppression will be fought with increasing hatred . . . These are my reasons for absenting myself from court. If by my fight I can encourage even some people to think about, to understand and to abandon the policies they now so blindly follow, I shall not regret any punishment I may incur. I can no longer serve justice in the way I have attempted to do during the past thirty years. I can only do so in the way I have now chosen. [6]

Just two days later, the Johannesburg Bar Council instructed its attorneys to prepare an application to court for the removal of Fischer's name from the roll of advocates. Shortly afterwards Fischer wrote another letter to his legal representative, expressing his dismay at the haste with which the Johannesburg Bar Council had acted. He was also distressed by the fact that the decision had been taken without any attempt to get his side heard. Indeed, his daughters testified, immediately after the GCB's submission, that this action was one of the most traumatic of his life.[7] And Fischer's life was not exactly trauma-free. In 1963, only a year before his arrest, his wife Molly died in a car accident when he was at the wheel. After estreating bail in his trial on charges under the Suppression of Communism Act, he was captured after almost a year on the run from the police, convicted and sentenced to life imprisonment. Shortly thereafter one of his children died and he was not permitted to attend the funeral and he was released from prison only in the very last stage of a fatal cancer, to which he succumbed in 1975.[8]

In his letter, Fischer strongly defended himself against the charge of conduct "unbefitting that of an advocate" entailed in an application to strike off:

The principle upon which I rely is a simple one, firmly established in South African legal tradition. Since the days of the South African War,[9] *if not since the Jameson Raid,*[10] *it has been recognised that political offences, committed because of a belief in the overriding moral validity of a political principle, do not in themselves justify the disbarring of a person from practising the profession of the law. Presumably this is so because it is assumed that the commission of such offences has no bearing on the professional integrity of the person concerned.*

When an advocate does what I have done, his conduct is not determined by any disrespect for the law nor because he hopes to benefit personally by

---

[6] Ibid., pp. 190–1.

[7] Transcript, p. 243.

[8] See Stephen Clingman, *Bram Fischer: Afrikaner Revolutionary* (Amherst, Mass.: University of Massachussets Press, 1998).

[9] The war between the British and the Boer Republics.

[10] A raid into the Transvaal Republic in December 1895, instigated by Cecil John Rhodes in a botched attempt to get rid of President Paul Kruger.

"any offence" he may commit. On the contrary, it requires an act of will to overcome his deeply rooted respect of legality, and he takes the step only when he feels that, whatever the consequences to himself, his political conscience no longer permits him to do otherwise. He does it not because of a desire to be immoral, but because to do otherwise would, for him, be immoral.

Fischer went on to say that he had returned to South Africa determined to see his trial through. But his experience of facing trial on evidence extracted from detainees held under the 90-day detention law—the "gross injustice (apart from the cruelty) of this barbaric law"—convinced him that no prosecution which depended on evidence "extracted" during such detention could be considered fair. In addition, he thought he might be facing the kind of "indeterminate sentence" which the Minister of Justice had discretion to impose and of which he said "we have already seen how European [i.e. white] public opinion has failed to register any protest against this arbitrary, indefinite incarceration and has complacently accepted this total abolition of the rule of law". He thus found himself compelled, he said, into a stance of:

open defiance, whatever the consequences might be, of a process of law which has become a travesty of all civilised tradition: A political belief is outlawed, then torture is applied to gather evidence and finally the Executive decides whether you serve a life sentence or not.

I cannot believe that any genuine protest made against this system which has been constructed solely to further apartheid can be regarded as immoral or as justifying the disbarment of a member of our profession.[11]

However, the Johannesburg Bar went ahead with its application to have him struck off and at the hearing advocates Kentridge and Chaskalson represented him. The Court held that he should be struck off: he had been guilty of dishonest conduct because he had used his status as senior counsel to get bail and someone who took an attitude of defiance to the law could not serve the law.[12]

The GCB comments:

Those who took the decision to apply for the striking of Fischer's name from the roll of advocates must have been confronted with an invidious problem. They namely recognised that Fischer had been "regarded by the

[11] GCB Submission, vol. 2, pp. 193–7.
[12] *Society of Advocates of SA (Witwatersrand Division)* v. *Fischer* 1966 (1) SA 133 (T).

Courts of the Republic, by the members of the Johannesburg Bar and by other legal practitioners as a most honourable and trustworthy member of the Bar" who had at all times "observed the highest ethical standards of legal practice" and had been "in every respect a worthy and distinguished member of the legal profession".[13] *They believed that notwithstanding the esteem in which Fischer was held by all, the deception to the Court, coming as it did from a senior practitioner, justified the striking off. There is no doubt that even in 1965, the issue was painful and divisive for those involved. Many of the leaders of the Johannesburg Bar felt that their personal relationship with Fischer was such that they would not be willing to appear in the application for his striking off. Thus it was that the then chairman of the GCB who practises in Durban, was approached to move the application. For him, the task was a distressing one, since he too had a great respect and liking for Fischer . . .*

Today, with the benefit of hindsight, there is a different perspective. Fischer was confronted with an acute dilemma. He was torn between his fidelity to law, which he had served faithfully for many years and his profound commitment to opposing the injustices of apartheid. He acted not out of self-interest but from political and moral conviction. Far from securing any personal advantage, he realised that his actions would result in increased punishment.

The GCB then reported that the Johannesburg Bar Council believes now that "a grave injustice" was done to Fischer and it apologised to his family.[14]

The full presentation of the record here is to the credit of the GCB for it shows just how difficult memory's struggle is and how great is the temptation to manage it. Unexplained in the GCB's submission is the phrase "with the benefit of hindsight". That phrase does not mean that one is engaging in a simple act of memory but that one can see things now that one was not able to see earlier. But since Fischer made the situation crystal clear, hindsight is not required for gaining the "different perspective" but for understanding why the Bar chose to evade the issues presented by Fischer. And this perspective was not unique to Fischer; Leslie Blackwell Q.C., a former judge of the Supreme Court, published an article in the *Sunday Times* sympathetic to Fischer's case.[15]

The GCB not only invited the question of how hindsight was

---

[13] The quoted words are from the founding affidavit supporting the striking off.
[14] GCB Submission, vol. 2, pp. 201–4.
[15] See Clingman, *Bram Fischer: Afrikaner Revolutionary*, n. 8 above, at p. 371.

relevant when Fischer, whose moral stature it recognised both in 1965 and at the Hearing, had presented the moral complexity of his situation fully at the time. It also failed to deal with the fact that Fischer's situation was morally complex in part because of legal factors. Although Fischer had estreated bail, he had not clearly estreated the conditions imposed on him when he was initially granted bail. He had come back to stand trial and, as he explained, it was his detention on his return which had led him to view his situation in a different light. More important, the argument he made based on that experience was one about the absence of the rule of law in South Africa. Not only were his concerns related to the fact that the majority of South Africa's population had no political rights and to the fact that legal political opposition had been closed to them, but also to the fact that his trial, as well as the sentence he might face, were in violation of his understanding of the rule of the law. That is, even if it were the case, as he was prepared to grant, that his decision to go underground was in violation of his initial undertaking, the reasons for his decision could not reflect negatively on his integrity as an advocate.

The "invidiousness" of the Johannesburg Bar's situation was one entirely of their own making. Their "indecent haste", as Fischer's daughters termed it,[16] to get Fischer struck off meant that the Bar took the initiative from the government in discrediting Fischer, thus helping to obscure the message he hoped to send his fellow white South Africans. As Fischer himself said in his letter, though the GCB did not quote this particular sentence, his "contention" was that "if in the year 1965 I have to be removed from the roll of practising advocates, the Minister himself and not the Bar Council should do the dirty work".[17] The culpability of the Johannesburg Bar is only increased by the fact that their personal discomfort with this action led them to try to avoid the appearance of doing the dirty work by getting an advocate from another Bar to argue the matter in court.

To this day, the advocate who argued the application in court on behalf of the Bar, Douglas Shaw Q.C., maintains that there is no basis to the allegation that the application was inspired by political motives.[18] And the GCB emphasises in its submission that the fact

[16] Transcript, p. 243.
[17] Clingman, *Bram Fischer: Afrikaner Revolutionary*, n. 8 above, p. 371.
[18] See his memorandum, dated 2 October 1997, in GCB Submission, vol. 3, p. 134.

that "Fischer was facing charges of a political character" formed no part of the basis for the application for striking off.[19]

But the Minutes of the Bar Council meetings on the subject of the application to remove Fischer, reproduced in volume 3 of the GCB's submission, reveal a process of communication with the Minister of Justice on this topic which suggest a negotiation about how best to play down the politics of the application.[20] And while it is true that, technically speaking, the application for striking off referred only to Fischer's decision to break the conditions of his bail, the Bar's narrowing of the issue to one about the personal integrity of an advocate, entirely abstracted from the political context of South Africa, was a deeply political act. It was and is a way of refusing to confront the wider political and rule of law implications of Fischer's decision, implications which were intimately connected to the charges he was facing and the "legal" process of a political trial. One can only conclude that when one of the Bar's number tried to force them to see over the apartheid divide, they reacted by sacrificing him in order to avoid the view.

How the GCB was at risk of losing memory's struggle was even more apparent in its oral submission to the Hearing. For Browde, who presented the oral submission, sought to present the Fischer story as if Fischer's dilemma about how best to serve the rule of law was the same dilemma as that faced by the Johannesburg Bar in deciding whether or not to apply to have Fischer struck off.[21] The GCB was ill served both by this aspect of Browde's presentation and by the responses to the TRC's questions by the outgoing Chairman,

---

[19] GCB Submission, vol. 2, p. 198.

[20] See the Minutes for 2 November 1965, GCB Submission, vol. 3, p. 135: "Festenstein had informed the Minister of the reasons why the affidavit suggested by the Minister had not been filed by the Bar Council. The Minister advised that he understood the position".

The Minutes also reveal much about white society of the time. As Lee Bozalek pointed out to me, on the same page where the Council records its process of getting rid of the embarassment of Fischer's association with them, occurs the minute titled "Pension for Elijah", where the Bar Council discusses how best to pension off some faithful black retainer—black, we can know, because he is not dignified with a surname. No doubt the minutes of any corporate body would have read in exactly the same way on this last topic at this time and until very recently, if not still today. But there is a special irony in that this minute appears in proximity to the minute of the striking off of a man who was seeking public recognition of the humanity of the Elijahs of South Africa. It is worth recording here that Fischer's own path from scion of an Afrikaner nationalist family to communist revolutionary began when as a student he had to shake hands with a black man at a party: see Clingman, *Bram Fischer: Afrikaner Revolutionary*, n. 8 above, pp. 50–1.

[21] Transcript, pp. 208–9.

Malcolm Wallis S.C. who had been appointed to answer them.[22]

Wallis had already made it plain in his comments as a panelist on day one that he had a rather condescending attitude to other participants in the Hearing. For example, he dismissed my argument about judicial dereliction of duty on day one, then repeated the point on day two, as "the rhetoric which academe entitles him to employ".[23] He claimed that the record of the judiciary was quite different, as those on the inside—advocates like himself—knew.[24] But, as I could point out in the panel at the end of day two, my charge of dereliction of duty merely rephrased quotations in my submission from eminent legal practitioners engaged in human rights work, though they were not advocates but attorneys.[25]

Wallis refused consistently to engage with the TRC's questions, especially those put by Hanif Vally, the legal officer. One exchange in particular was indicative of the whole. Vally referred to the following passage from Judge Pius Langa's submission:

I was admitted as an advocate [in] 1977 and became only the fourth African practising at the Natal Bar. None of my three predecessors were silks.[26] My induction was relatively smooth; unlike the reception which the first and second of my predecessors received on admission to the Natal Bar. Both Advocates Tshabalala and Skweyiya had not been allowed to serve pupillage; according to Justice Tshabalala, the reason given was that since he was a black person, it would be embarassing for his Master's white clients to have him sit in during consultations in chambers.[27]

Vally wanted to know from Wallis, a senior member of the Natal Bar,

---

[22] Several people who commented on a draft of this manuscript expressed concern about my treatment of Wallis. The suggestion has been that not only do I give the impression that I am retaliating against Wallis for his hostile remarks about me but that I am inappropriately personalising the important substantive issues. After much thought, I have decided not to change some of my initial treatment. There were other participants whose demeanour at the Hearing was more inappropriate than Wallis's. But the fact that they usually represented either insignificant or even notional constituencies and made submissions that were not taken very seriously meant that they had no impact on the proceedings other than creating irritation. Wallis, in contrast, was the person the advocates of the GCB chose to represent them in the 1990s both as the head of their body and as their main spokesman at the Hearing. (Browde's role was a more or less honorary one, as for the most part he simply read from a submission drafted by others.)

[23] Transcript, pp. 165 and 235.

[24] Ibid., pp. 234–5.

[25] Ibid., p. 439.

[26] Advocates who had attained the rank of Senior Counsel.

[27] Langa Submission, p. 7.

what one could surmise from the fact that African advocates at that Bar at one time could not get the only professional training available to advocates—the period of pupillage in which a beginning advocate learns the profession from a "pupil master", a more senior advocate.

But Wallis refused to answer the question. His response was that at that time pupillage was not compulsory and that, since the time when pupillage had become compulsory, no advocate had been refused pupillage. On being asked the question again, he said he had no knowledge of the truth of the claims and would have to investigate them.[28] He also refused to express any regret for the fact that the Bars had submitted, as they were required by law to do, to the racial exclusions enforced by the Group Areas Act.[29] And he said, in answer to a question about the attitudes of the advocates from whose ranks judges had almost exclusively been recruited under the old order:

If you want to know whether white judges who went onto the Bench had, across the spectrum, the range of views which white people in South Africa entertained, I wouldn't have thought it was necessary to ask me that question. The answer is rather too self-evident.[30]

What he could not bring himself to say is that by and large the advocates of even those Bars with a reputation for liberalism were content to practice law in the comfort many whites gained through accepting the economic rewards of apartheid. They were not prepared to run the risk of losing even part of those rewards by refusing to pander to racist clients. Langa's claims were of course hearsay—he had not personally experienced the treatment he describes. But Wallis was not contesting facts in a criminal trial and it would have been gracious to accept the allegation for the sake of giving an answer to the question.

Further, no-one doubted that Wallis personally abhorred the racist statutes which excluded black advocates from access to the same facilities as their white counterparts. But an explicit acknowledgment that advocates participated in and reaped the benefits of a system designed to advantage whites was not inappropriate, given that he represented a body of professionals who had been generally content to benefit from that system.

[28] Transcript, pp. 220–8.
[29] Ibid., pp. 218–20.
[30] Ibid., pp. 221–2.

Now one senior advocate's refusal to state the obvious, other than to say that the obvious is obvious, may not appear significant. But this problem, one of barely disguised hubris, was not the preserve of one advocate. It was a problem endemic in the GCB's written submission.

There is in that submission much criticism of apartheid, of the Attorneys-General, of magistrates, the security forces, and of Ministers of Justice. There is, as we have seen, criticism of the public exclusion of blacks at the Pretoria Bar and the Johannesburg Bar's treatment of Fischer. There is also criticism of judges since "so few of the judiciary sought to mitigate the effect of [apartheid] laws or expressed their revulsion of them".[31] Finally, there is criticism of attorneys who had a dismal record in taking on cases on behalf of the opponents and victims of apartheid.[32]

But the impression is created that advocates faithfully adhered to the "cab-rank rule", whereby an advocate is ethically obliged to accept any brief as long as there are no special circumstances which justify its refusal.[33] The GCB comments:

The independence of the Bar as an institution and that of its members facilitates fearless advocacy. It ensures that everything that can possibly be said for a client will be said without fear of adverse consequences. The "cab-rank" rule ensures that advocates accept briefs, no matter how unpleasant and the advocate's duty to his or her client ensures that the case will be presented without fear or favour.[34]

The GCB's written submission not only criticised the attorneys on this score but saw fit in a later section to reinforce an impression of a collective sense of superiority. In a section titled "Lessons for the Future", the GCB, quoting from Sidney Kentridge, said that "it is the independent Bar inseparably from the independent Bench which is the protection of the citizen against the state". The GCB continued:

The hallmark of the Bar, it has been stated above, is the duty of the advocate to argue a cause, however unpopular, unconstrained by any concern for the loss of an existing clientele or the sensitivities of partners. This is not to denigrate the attorneys' profession; its members may be expected to continue high standards of professionalism and a wider service

---

[31] GCB Submission, vol. 2, p. 18.
[32] Ibid., pp. 78–9.   [33] Ibid., pp. 77–8.   [34] Ibid., p. 80.

to the administration of justice. The point however is that the structure of the Bar inherently fosters greater independence and in so doing, imposes a concomitant higher obligation.[35]

This attempt to distinguish the advocates from the attorneys by claiming greater independence for the advocates in virtue of the duties of the latter under the cab-rank rule are examples of a less than frank exercise of memory. As I pointed out in the panel at the end of day two, it was the case that for much of the period of the TRC's inquiry—the 1960s and 1970s—it was well known that there were very few human rights lawyers (in those days known as "political" lawyers); there were, that is, very few lawyers prepared to take on the defence of those whom most white South Africans would have viewed as subversive of the regime they supported. Further, not only is the cab-rank rule easily evaded—an advocate merely has to say that he has too much work to take on another matter—but no-one accused of a political offence would want to challenge such a refusal or even to approach an advocate who might be thought to be reluctant to appear in such a matter.[36]

In this regard, let me recount one small but revealing episode from the history of the Bar. The GCB mentions an adverse comment on the Bar in 1976 by Bernard Levin, the influential columnist of the London *Times*. In a column criticising the Yugoslav Bar for failing to support a lawyer who took on political cases and who had consequently himself been victimised, Levin invited a comparison with "the similar divergence between the individual courage and honesty of those South African lawyers who dare to defend the regime's victims and the craven and shabby collective behaviour of the South African Bar".

---

[35] Ibid., pp. 206–7.
[36] Transcript, p. 440 and see the Legal Resources Centre Submission I, pp. 4–5. This situation started to change after the early 1980s as students who had been involved in political opposition to apartheid turned to the law as a site of political struggle and as funds became available for human rights work. It was pointed out to me that at this time human rights work became quite popular, and that a not inconsiderable number of lawyers involved in the work were considered to be involved in milking a lucrative cow, often quite unscrupulously. It was also pointed out to me that before this time there were some advocates who would take on political cases, not because of their personal beliefs but because of their honest adherence to the principle of the cab-rank rule. Finally, it was pointed out that the rule did provide a significant measure of protection against political interference for those who desired to take on political cases. I take all of these points, but wish that the GCB had dealt with them explicitly.

The GCB reports this episode in the section of its submission which details the record of the Bar in speaking out against legislation and executive action which undermined the rule of law. As noted, it was often the case that the GCB could not speak out because of its unanimity rule, which meant that it was left up to individual Bars to make their protest. "On occasion", says the GCB, "the Bar spoke out strongly in relation to public comments on the role of the Bar itself". It cites the Levin episode, and refers to the "response published by Van Heerden S.C.".[37] But the Annexures which comprise the third volume of the GCB's submission tell a different and more interesting story.

It was in fact a judge, none other than Judge Didcott, who brought the Levin reference to the attention of Gerald Friedman, then a senior counsel at the Cape Bar, suggesting that the Bar should respond, failing which he might himself come to the defence of the Bar. This matter was debated by Friedman, Chaskalson, and Hendrik van Heerden, the Supreme Court of Appeal Judge, then Chairman of the GCB. A draft letter was produced which contained an indignant response to Levin. But it was never sent for a reason outlined in a letter from Friedman to Didcott—the Bar feared that their letter would "stir up a hornet's nest":

[N]either Hennie van Heerden nor Arthur Chaskalson are entirely convinced that it would be in the interest of the Bar to become involved in a debate about the matter . . . in The Times . . . They feel that Bernard Levin would have the last word and that he may well be able to point out instances where the S.A. Bar (collectively) has not always been as outspoken as it might have been, largely because of the unanimity rule.

Didcott expressed his disappointment and again offered to respond himself, but Friedman rejected this offer:

Firstly, as to the wisdom of your writing, I feel it would highlight the absence of a statement from the G.C.B., which could only make matters worse than they are. Secondly, as to the propriety, I do not think it would be proper for you, as a member of the judiciary, to intervene in what is, after all, primarily a matter which directly affects the Bar.[38]

Here we have perhaps the most innovative judge of the apartheid era seeking to initiate a response to a critique of the collective behaviour of

---

[37] GCB Submission, vol. 2, pp. 125–6.
[38] GCB Summission, vol. 3, pp. 349–64.

the Bar, but he is turned down by Chaskalson and Friedman, clearly because they are not so sure that the Bar can be defended. In other words, Levin's harsh words are recognised to have some substance to them, and the reluctance to have that substance debated in public— the fact that it is only a few courageous individuals who are taking political cases—deters the response.

The GCB did allude to these issues in its section on the striking off of Fischer. For there it quotes from an article which describes Fischer thus:

the story of Bram Fischer dramatises and illuminates the difficult questions of what the duty of conscientious lawyers is, when the government (and particularly a non-representative government) represses its citizens. Many options present themselves. Does one simply go about one's business, hoping that this unpleasantness will go away? Should one work within the (immoral) system as a lawyer, trying to mitigate the evils of the system and to assist those who are its victims? Or should one distance oneself completely, and attempt actively to undermine and subvert the system? [39]

Human rights lawyers took the second option, and for that they had to be able to see over the apartheid divide. We have seen how a liberal old order judge had to walk a tightrope between his sense that Parliament was illegitimate and that it was his duty to hold Parliament to the rule of law values which are part of what makes a legitimate parliament so. Similarly, an advocate who was to give effective representation in a political matter had to understand that the accused had sound reasons for considering wholly illegitimate the state which tried them. That required not just an act of intellectual projection, but an act of emotional and moral empathy without which one could not start to translate arguments about the illegitimacy of the state into a form which made them effective in a forum which presupposed the legitimacy of the state.

For example, a lawyer had to recognise the illegitimacy of apartheid in order to see the need in the Zondo trial to call as a witness in mitigation a well-known sociologist who could describe to the court what it was like for an intelligent and sensitive youth like Zondo to grow up in a devout Christian and law-abiding family and to try to reconcile his family values with the brutal facts of

---

[39] G. Budlender, "Bram Fischer—The Man and the Lawyer" 1995 *Consultus* 161 at 162, quoted in GCB Submission, vol. 2, pp. 202–3.

apartheid.[40] And two of the most significant legal victories of the 1980s, significant because they are two of the few oases of fidelity to the rule of law in the desert created by the Appellate Division during that era, were won by the Legal Resources Centre, which was staffed by lawyers (advocates and attorneys) who were committed to using the law to end apartheid.[41]

Finally, in those political trials in which the leadership of the liberation organizations were put on trial as much for their beliefs as for their conduct, the leaders insisted on controlling the presentation by their lawyers of the defence. As Joel Joffe, attorney for Mandela and several others in the 1963 trial that ended with life sentences for Mandela and all but one of the accused, explained:

> "From our very earliest discussions with the accused . . . one thing stood out clearly. None of them was prepared to deny associations with the bodies to which they belonged . . . In their eyes, they made clear, this was less a trial in law than a confrontation in politics. They were all conscious of the fact that, in the eyes of their followers and supporters at least, they were public representatives of and spokesman for organisations which were illegal, deprived of any public platform and banished from publicity in the columns of the South African press. They would be speaking in court as the defendants, almost the gladiators of their cause. And they intended to speak as they would expect representatives of such a cause to speak when they appeared in public outside a court - proudly in support of their ideals, defiant in the face of their enemies. This was their intention from the start, and the spirit of their general instruction to us".[42]

And lawyers—attorneys or advocates - who would act in such trials, usually in the face of deeply hostile white opinion, were few and far between. Joffe, for example, tells of how he was about to emigrate from South Africa because he found the political situation intolerable, though he had not been involved in politics or in legal work on behalf of opponents of apartheid. He was approached by the wife of one of the detainees who told him of how she could not find any lawyer prepared to take the case. Joffe, "sickened" by the tale of

---

[40] See the excerpts from the evidence by Fatima Meer reproduced in her book, *The Trial of Andrew Zondo* (Baobab Books: Harare, 1988), pp. 133–41.

[41] *Komani NO* v. *Bantu Affairs Administration Board, Peninsula Area* 1980 (4) SA 448 (A) and *Oos-Randse Administrasie Raad* v. *Rikhoto* 1983 (3) SA 595 (A).

[42] Joel Joffe, *The Rivonia Story* (Belleville, South Africa: Mayibuye Books (UWC), 1995) 36.

the reception she had got, agreed to take the case but warned her that public opinion would be against the accused. He then describes how his world was turned upside down by her response: "Mr Joffe, I think we speak a different language. You're talking of white public opinion. I'm talking of majority public opinion, which is not against but *for* the . . . accused."[43]

It is certainly true, as both the GCB and some of the judges emphasised, that the behaviour of honourable individuals at the Bar meant that the ideal of the rule of law was never abandoned, even during the worst years of apartheid. As Chaskalson *et al.* say:

For all the deep injustices perpetuated by law, there remained a real sense in which the techniques and procedures of law remained independent from the gross manipulation of the executive and in which justice was seen to be done. But no account of these years would be accurate if it were not accepted that justice was done and seen to be done in some cases. In this way, principles and values central to the rule of law and a just legal system were not entirely lost . . . The maintenance of such values during the years of apartheid facilitated the transition to a constitutional democracy and provided an important foundation for the legal system in that democracy.[44]

But the fact that for most of the apartheid era there was only a very small number of such honourable individuals is significant. That the GCB's submission did not deal with this fact means that it permitted the lustre of the few, for the most part a minority at one Bar, to shine on the GCB as a whole. And so it never properly addressed the question of legitimacy of participation we have seen it raised by citing in the frontispiece to its submission Sidney Kentridge's question:

What are we, as counsel, doing . . . —are we really defending the rule of law or what remains of it or . . . are we helping to give a spurious air of respectability and fairness to a procedure which is fundamentally unfair?

The GCB thus seemed to lose the struggle against the tendency to forget what is uncomfortable by making itself complicit in a further unreflective act of legitimation. The only indication of the GCB's awareness of the risk of legitimating the many by focusing on the few is the way in which it placed the quotation from Toqueville in the

---

[43] Ibid., p. 10.
[44] Chaskalson *et al.* Submission, p. 13.

conclusion to its submission. For that placing makes the GCB's point ambiguous between the claim that one should not have expected a few advocates to have had much much influence on their peers and the claim that one should not have expected the body of advocates as a whole to have had much influence on their fellow white South Africans.

We may well wonder about the peers. Is it significant in this regard that the GCB omitted to make any apology for the fact that, by and large, its members either actively supported apartheid or did not in any way oppose it? Its quotation of the Pretoria Bar's apology both in its written and its oral submission might have been an attempt to indicate that some of its members beyond the Pretoria Bar wished to make a more general apology.[45] But it can also be read as an attempt to suggest that the Pretoria Bar, rather than the GCB, bears the burden of culpability. Clearly the problems that plagued the GCB's founding as a federal body may still persist as it attempts to speak with one voice under the new order.

The most significant failing, however, lies in the GCB's unreflective claims about the virtues of an independent Bar of advocates. When such claims are used in an attempt to maintain a sense of superiority in the legal hierarchy over all except judges, one senses more than a tinge of regret for the fact that advocates no longer enjoy a monopoly on the right of appearance before the superior courts and a virtual monopoly on judicial appointment.

And this regret is not confined to the Bar. In their praise for old order South African judges, Judges Smalberger *et al.* had this to say about the Bar.

The bar is a hard school. It is contemptuous of "yes-men" and prizes integrity and independence . . . [J]udges trained in the cauldron of the bar and used to abuse and hostility when defending unpopular causes or clients, are unlikely to allow such pressure to influence them and to buckle under it.[46]

But the great majority of men at the Bar said "yes" to apartheid, proving themselves content to support and reap the benefits of South African society which, to adapt a phrase from an influential feminist thinker, was designed as an affirmative action plan for white men.

---

[45] Transcript, pp. 213–15.
[46] Smalberger *et al.* Submission, pp. 6, 16.

In this they were no different than the great majority of the rest of white South Africans but for two features of their situation. The federal structure which advocates set up in 1946 ensured that they had a body which would effectively maintain their monopoly on highly priced legal services and so ensured an especially privileged place in the sun of the South African economy. And, at the same time, they prided themselves, as Smalberger *et al.*, tell us, on their independence and integrity in maintaining the rule of law. In view of both that special privilege and the failure of most advocates to live up to their own standard, a more introspective discussion of the virtues of the independence of the Bar in the new South Africa would have been appropriate.[47]

At least, however, the advocates came to talk to the TRC, even though their oral presentations and presence may reveal some deeply problematic features in their sense of role. The fact that much is revealed and illuminated when people take the witness stand, something obvious to trial lawyers and judges, is of course yet another reason to regret the absence of judges on day one; and this reason could only be strengthened by the appearance of the other lawyers.

[47] It is of course unobjectionable to argue for the virtues of an independent legal profession, especially when one invites debate about the substance of independence. As a recent study suggests, an independent legal profession was a crucial element in the development of the idea of the rule of law—the idea that government, however powerful, is subject to principles which ensure accountability of government to citizens: see Terence C. Halliday and Lucien Karpik (eds.), *Lawyers and the Rise of Western Political Liberalism* (Oxford: Clarendon Press, 1997), especially the introductory essay by Halliday and Karpik, "Politics Matter: a Comparative Theory of Lawyers in the Making of Political Liberalism", ibid., p. 15. (Halliday and Karpik argue that although lawyers were quite often more motivated to retain control over their profession by their wish to achieve a profitable monopoly on legal services than by more noble desires, nevertheless their independence was crucial to maintaining an independent judiciary, itself crucial to maintaining principled constraints on government.) But the independence of a professional body of advocates, distinguished from attorneys by advocates' monopoly over more highly priced and socially esteemed legal services, is a relic of the hold a now archaic British social hierarchy gained over the legal profession. To assume that that hierarchy is essential to maintaining the rule of law betrays not only a highly parochial view of legal order, but one ill suited to a society attempting to escape from an era of dominance by white elites.

3. Dismalness Compounded

We have seen the GCB suggest that the attorneys had a dismal record when it came to opposing apartheid. And the oral and written submissions of the Association of Law Societies (ALS), the professional body which represents attorneys, to the Hearing served only to compound this judgment. If anything, the ALS made things worse for itself, for it attempted to combine an apology for having failed South Africans during apartheid with the following claims: it in fact did a lot to oppose apartheid, though not enough; doing a lot risked a reaction by government which would have destroyed the independence of the profession; in any case, opposition to the apartheid monolith was futile.[48] In particular, it did not seem to occur to the ALS that it could not excuse itself by claiming that the apartheid legal order seemed an impregnable monolith if its own supineness in the 1950s and 1960s, indeed, at times its own active support for apartheid during that time, had contributed to the appearance of impregnability.

Revealing here is the way in which the ALS invoked the supremacy of parliament defence. It said that it:

admitted that when the Association's efforts came up against the ultimate brick wall of the sovereignty of Parliament which completely blocked further lawful protest, the Association considered that it had little, if any, option other than to accept the position. Every attorney had sworn an oath of allegiance upon his or her admission to practice. Unlawful action in further protest could well have meant breach of the oath. This was all part of the dilemma facing attorneys.[49]

In the context of its discussion of parliamentary supremacy, the ALS dealt with its own counterpart to the story of the Johannesburg Bar and the striking off of Fischer. In 1954, the Transvaal Branch of the Association, the Transvaal Law Society, attempted to get Nelson Mandela struck off the roll of attorneys after he had been convicted under the Suppression of Communism Act because of his part in the Defiance Campaign, a campaign to persuade black South Africans to engage in non-violent defiance of racist laws. Judge Ramsbottom rejected this application on the ground that nothing Mandela had done reflected on his fitness to remain in the profession.[50]

---

[48] ALS Submission, at D 2–4, D 17–18.   [49] Ibid., C–D.
[50] *Incorporated Law Society, Transvaal* v. *Mandela* 1954 (3) SA 102 (TPD).

The ALS says that the lesson attorneys learnt from this judicial rebuff was the following:

its members were not inevitably bound to follow slavishly the laws of parliament and that the breach of a law not involving anything dishonourable did not necessarily mean disloyalty to or violation of the allegiance to which every attorney swears or solemnly affirms on his or her admission to the profession.[51]

The ALS then quoted from an English judgment[52] which discusses how judges should approach the conflict between the "law of the land" and the "moral imperative", and it comments that Mandela, "[i]n disobeying a law that he believed to be unjust . . . in yielding to the moral imperative, may well have demonstrated one of the very rare instances in which the moral imperative is truly just and justifiable".[53]

We see here more than that the ALS cannot bring itself in 1997 to say that the law was in fact unjust, or that the moral imperative here was in fact justifiable. Worse is that its description of the situation, in the context of a discussion of parliamentary supremacy, is clearly akin to the judicial strategy we observed in Chapter 2 of ascribing responsibility elsewhere. The ALS is trying to suggest that it was merely following the law of the land in bringing the application for Mandela's removal. As Hanif Vally pointed out in his questions, what was wrong was not the attorneys' "slavish" following of apartheid law, but the fact that without any legal duty at stake, they initiated their own campaign of harassing opponents of apartheid.[54]

Moreover, in taking this stance, the ALS failed to see the distinction which was pointed out by Vincent Saldanha, one of the representatives of NADEL in the panel at the end of day two. Saldanha, commenting on the ALS's applications to have political dissidents struck off the roll of attorneys on the ground that they had violated

---

[51] ALS Submission, p. 18.

[52] *Francome* v. *Mirror Group of Newspapers Ltd* [1984] All ER 415.

[53] ALS Submission, p. 20.

[54] See Transcript, p. 292. The reply Vally received (ibid., pp. 293–4) from an ALS representative failed entirely to address the point. Note that the Natal Law Society made a separate submission, which was annexed to the ALS Submission. In contrast to the ALS, the Natal Law Society took pains to point out that in applications for striking off one has to avoid denying the "pivotal role of the Society as Applicant and a litigant which actively pursues an order"; ALS Submission, A4.

their oath of allegiance, had this to say about the lawyers involved in the radical opposition to apartheid:

[While we] took an oath of allegiance to the state, we certainly did not take an oath of allegiance to the apartheid state. If anything, we took an oath of allegiance to undermine the apartheid state, and I think a distinction must be drawn. That's why we distinguish ourselves from the establishment lawyers or the lawyers who operated within the Law Societies under the particular milieu and ideological context they did. We worked with these lawyers, we used the law as a terrain of struggle, unashamedly, and to that extent would continue to use the law as a terrain presently in furtherance of the principles and the values of the new Constitution.[55]

Most damning is that to the extent that the record of the ALS revealed any opposition to apartheid, it was a record of minutes of meetings, of polite approaches to cabinet ministers and of articles in the attorneys' law journal, *De Rebus*. Put differently, it was not a record of lawyers who had taken an active part in using legal means to oppose the apartheid legal order. It was not that there were no attorneys who were committed to the struggle against apartheid, but that they were even thinner on the ground than human rights advocates and often found themselves marginalised by their own profession. As Zunaid Husain of NADEL pointed out in the panel at the end of day two:

One wonders whether there was in fact a genuine desire to look introspectively at the operation of the organised profession or whether it was simply a review of the minutes to find exculpatory resolutions and the like . . . The expressions of regret and apology, such as they were and which came through today, from our point of view seemed to be lost amidst the endeavours to find defences and justifications and rationalisations for their positions . . . The only reason that you had organisations such as the Democratic Lawyers Association, Democratic Lawyers Congress, Community Law Centres and the like, throughout the country, was because the organised profession was not a home to people who sought to use the law as a terrain of struggle, who sought to be legal activists and no amount of pointing to minute books is going to change that from our point of view.[56]

---

[55] Transcript, p. 450. I have corrected certain inaccuracies in the Transcript from my notes.

[56] Ibid., pp. 444–6.

4. Academic Amnesia

Universities were required by law to be racially segregated for most of the apartheid era. The universities set aside for groups other than whites were widely and justifiably regarded as "bush colleges", second-rate educational institutions staffed by faculty whose main qualification was their commitment to National Party policy and to policing the student body.[57] And there was segregation within the white universities, though not enforced by law, since they were divided between English and Afrikaans. The Afrikaans universities were openly committed to the ideology of apartheid, some more fervently than others, while the English universities, again some more so than others, attempted to sustain liberal opposition.

Many Law Faculties simply failed to respond to a letter of invitation from the Society of Law Teachers to make a submission to the TRC about the past and future of legal education. The letter requested among other things information about faculty who had actively opposed apartheid.

One of the most conservative of the Afrikaans law faculties, the Faculty of Law at the University of the Orange Free State, responded so evasively that we can infer that the Dean clearly thought that there was nothing worth responding to:

Your letter dated 26 September 1997 refers. The letter was circulated in our Faculty and our opinion is that many academics over the years criticised court decisions and inappropriate or unreasonable legislation. To state that the legal academic profession did not respond appropriately to violations of human rights and corruption of the legal system would be to assume that the profession were aware of such violations. In general we believe legal academics have always been prepared to criticise court decisions etc. We would not like to single out any specific individuals.[58]

The Dean of the Faculty of Law at one of the former bush colleges, the University of Zululand, said "we always had a lively debate in the classes on current issues, the legal system and the role of our courts. I think we succeeded in encouraging our students to think critically . . . We do not have any staff member to nominate in particular".[59]

---

[57] These universities are now known as HDUs "Historically Disadvantaged Universities". The old guard still dominates the administration at most of them.

[58] Extract from letter from Professor D.W. Morkel to Roshni Maharaj, Secretary of the Society of Law Teachers, 8 October 1997. I have corrected several typographical errors.

[59] Letter from Professor M.G. Erasmus, dated 1 October 1997.

The Faculty of Law at the Rand Afrikaans University committed itself collectively to the ideals of the new order. But it also attempted to fudge the fact that it owed its existence to a government sense that Johannesburg needed an ideological counterweight to the most liberal of the English-speaking universities, the University of the Witwatersrand. For the Dean said that the "Faculty came into being in the apartheid era and, by its very existence as a state-subsidised institution, the *perception could have been created* that it reconciled itself with the system and structure of apartheid".[60] He also claimed that individual members of his faculty did speak out against the injustice "inherent in the philosophy of apartheid" and said that "more could have been done in the teaching and research of the law, to expose the structural injustices inherent in the legal system and in the administration of justice brought about by apartheid legislation". But before the end of apartheid was clearly in view, it is a safe bet that he would have been hard put to find a single example of a public statement against apartheid by a member of his Faculty or an example of a course taught at his Faculty which dealt with apartheid law, let alone intimated its injustice.

It was clear that when there was someone who could be named or an example that could be cited of opposition, that person or that example was mentioned.[61] Even those Law Faculties at English universities which made submissions and which could plausibly claim to have been involved in opposition to apartheid, Witwatersrand and Natal, could cite only a few individuals with an active public record of opposition during the bulk of the apartheid era.[62] And, during this same period, there were very few courses taught at these universities

[60] Letter from Professor Derek van der Merwe, dated 23 October 1997, (emphasis added).

[61] The Faculty of Law at the University of Potchefstroom attached the lengthy curriculum vitae of two academic lawyers to prove its credentials as not having been part of apartheid's Afrikaans educational monolith. But only one of these, that of Professor Johann van der Vyver, displayed a record of serious critique of apartheid. Moreover, he had left the University because of the reaction of his colleagues to his critique, a fact which got scant mention in the University's submission.

[62] Hence the absurdity of the claim of the Dean of Law at UNISA (University of South Africa), Professor Joan Church, in a letter dated 9 October 1997, that she was prevented from naming names only by her fear that she might leave some names off the list of the "many" in her Faculty (one with no reputation at all for opposition to apartheid) who spoke out against apartheid. Indeed, the only publication from this Faculty of which I am aware which dealt with apartheid and injustice was a poorly argued apology for South African judges: Adrienne van Blerk, *Judge and be Judged* (Cape Town: Juta & Co., 1988). Publication of this work was subsidised by the trust fund of the ALS.

which made the injustice of apartheid a central theme. For the most part, these Law Faculties tried their best to function as if the legal order of South Africa was no different in nature from that of the United Kingdom.

One has to be careful here not to look at the period from 1948 to the mid-1980s through the rose-tinted glasses of the late 1980s, a care missing from the Annexure to the University of the Witwatersrand's Law Faculty's written submission to the TRC. For there it is claimed that:

the academy played an enormously important part in contributing to the efforts to maintain the ideal of judicial independence. From the pages of the law journals issued repeated appeals to recognise the degree to which the common law can and should be used to protect the individual from the exaggerated, arbitrary or discriminatory exercise of state power. The sustained industry of outrage and criticism which forms the basis for much of this analysis rendered it increasingly difficult for those teaching and learning law to indulge in the unfortunately prevalent tendency to regard human rights and a concern for liberty as a frivolous pastime, or one that bore little relation to the serious business of law. Pioneers of this admonitory role, like Anthony Mathews, and particularly John Dugard, whose work is the essential starting point of any examination like this one, succeeded in taking the debate into the mainstream of legal academia, to the credit of the academic profession and the long term health of the integrity of the judiciary. Judges were increasingly pressed to respond to the challenges and criticisms put, and, although these responses did not always delight, they certainly represented an essential process of engagement with human rights jurisprudence on the part of the bench.[63]

Much more accurate is the observation made by the Dean of the Witwatersrand Faculty of Law, Carole Lewis, in her oral submission:

It is true that more and more academics entered the battle against apartheid in the late 80s and in the early 90s, but the decades of ignoring the edifice of injustice within which we have all worked had a marked effect . . . Even in the sphere of private law, in the sphere of law affecting things like contract and property there were gross injustices. It would be true to say that the whole of the law of property was permeated and poisoned by racial legislation. It is true also that in enforcing influx control and in enforcing the provisions of the Group Areas Act the courts

[63] Annexure to Lewis Submission, pp. 11–12, footnotes omitted.

had a marked effect on those areas of law as well. It was possible to write about this to expose the injustices, to expose the effect in every area of the legal system of racial legislation and some people did so. Others claimed and continue to claim now that they were involved in different areas of the law, that gross violations of human rights if they existed were not their concern, and that claim of course is untenable.[64]

Further, it is clear that during this time, say, 1960 until the mid-1980s, these institutions were far from encouraging the efforts of critics of apartheid. It was much more the case that the critics were able to do what they did because their institutions were precluded by their principles from preventing critics from speaking out or from teaching courses critical of apartheid. In other words, the liberalism of the institution consisted in its allegiance to principles which made it possible for a few individuals to pursue their liberal ideals without grave personal cost.

Indeed, Edwin Cameron, who in the late 1970s and 1980s taught at the University of the Witwatersrand, has criticised the two dominant figures at the Faculty during the apartheid era, H.R. Hahlo and Ellison Kahn, for cultivating an ideological atmosphere which encouraged deference to authority.[65] In the Annexure to the Law Faculty of the University of the Witwatersrand's submission, the following comment is offered in response to Cameron's criticism: "The fact that such an overwhelming proportion of the writings highly critical of the judiciary, including those by Cameron, stemmed from the Wits Law School might fairly elicit the observation that more is expected of those who have given more".[66]

But again, this is to confuse the heyday of critique with the period before the mid-1980s. Take, for example H.R. Hahlo and Ellison Kahn's 1968 publication *The South African Legal System and its Background.*[67] At the beginning of this immmensely learned book, the authors deal with debates about legal positivism and natural law and the relationship between law and justice. They even advert to Gustav Radbruch's famous critique of German lawyers for having permitted an allegiance to legal positivism to help pave the way for

---

[64] Transcript, pp. 269–70.
[65] Cameron, "Lawyers, Language and Politics—In Memory of JC De Wet and WA Joubert" (1993) 110 *South African Law Journal* 51.
[66] Annexure to Lewis Submission, p. 11, note 69.
[67] (Cape Town: Juta & Co., 1968, 2nd impress. 1973.)

Hitler's accession to power.[68] But apartheid does not figure as a topic in the book, nor is security legislation discussed. In so far as cases which deal with racial segregation are discussed, there is not the slightest hint of criticism.[69] The overall impression the authors seek to give is that the South African legal order is only unusual in its combination of Roman-Dutch sources with English common law.

There is, however, a valid point to be gleaned from the picture which the University of the Witwatersrand Annexure paints. The ideal of judicial independence is one which academics no less than practising lawyers should help to sustain. If one values the rule of law, and understands the role of judges in upholding that rule, then the importance of an independent legal academy is clear. But that independence is instrumental to the rule of law. And as I will argue in Chapter 4, unexercised independence is worse than worthless; it legitimates oppression which seeks to operate under the guise of the rule of law. Hence, legal academics who fail to take up a role of critics of the law and of the legal institutions of their society fail in their duty, as by far the majority of such academics failed in South Africa, a failure still largely unacknowledged today.

5. Truth-Tellers, Bunglers or "Sweepers"?

In a letter to the *Mail and Guardian* in 1996, Professor George Ellis of the University of Cape Town raised the issue of Natal Attorney-General Tim McNally's failure to prosecute three "hit-squad" cases which had been brought to his attention, that is, assassinations in which it appeared that serving or former members of the South African security forces were implicated.[70]

Ellis pointed out that McNally's refusal followed hard on the heels of the failure of his prosecution in the trial of General Magnus Malan, former Chief of the South African Defence Force and Minister of Defence, and 19 others, who had been charged with murder and conspiracy to murder in connection with the 1987 massacre of 13 people in a township near Durban. Ellis then suggested three possible explanations of why McNally's prosecution had failed: he simply did not prosecute the case "with sufficient

---

[68] Ibid., pp. 6–24.
[69] See for example, ibid., pp. 59–60.
[70] George Ellis, "McNally Must Tell the Truth", letter dated 26 November 1996.

vigour", though he wanted it to succeed; he only instigated the case
because a Parliamentary Committee had put pressure on him because
of his record of previous inaction in such cases and so did not care
whether it succeeded; he did not want the case to succeed, as
suggested by statements on South African Broadcasting Radio by
Dirk Coetzee, one of apartheid's most notorious assassins, that
McNally is now the "sweeper", the person "who comes behind and
hides evidence of covert activity after it has taken place". Indeed, we
will see that a wholly innocent explanation is just as likely—that
Mcnally wanted the prosecution to succeed and did his best to
ensure convictions, but simply failed. But the relevance of these
events which took place after the cut-off date for the TRC's inquiry
is that McNally is one of the many civil servants who served
apartheid but kept his job in the new order. The question that is
posed by his conduct after that date is whether it is of a piece with his
conduct and that of other Attorneys-General during apartheid. For
not only McNally but almost all the other serving Attorneys-General
are survivals from the old order. They, as well as one Attorney-
General who had retired, testified at the Hearing. Each claimed that
during his office as an Attorney-General under the old order, he had
been fiercely independent, not subject to the political influence of the
National Party government and resilient to political pressure
whatever its source.

For example, the retired Attorney-General, Klaus von Lieres und
Wilkau S.C., Attorney-General of the Transvaal from 1983 to 1995,
said that he had not intended to make an appearance; he had been
driven to it by press reports of what other submissions had said of
the Attorneys-General. He said:

> *Mr. Chairman, I am here today because I believe it needs to be said that
> we owe a debt of gratitude to many of the fine prosecutors, past and
> present, who discharged their prosecutorial tasks with integrity, courage
> and professionalism. I believe that they have been severely maligned by
> unfounded generalised propaganda . . . We took our decisions to prosecute
> or not to prosecute on facts and not on the basis of ideological convictions.
> Had the latter been the case, our reputations as competent prosecutors
> would have been severely dented.*[71]

Contrast this with the GCB's identification in their submission of

---

[71] Von Lieres Submission, p. 8.

"two areas of particular concern" about the role of the Attorneys-General:

The first is the very substantial vigour with which the Attorneys-General and their departments prosecuted cases with political overtones. The proper function of a prosecutor is to present to the court with reasonable impartiality the evidence on behalf of the State in support of a conviction. In terms of ethical rules which bound prosecutors they were obliged to make available to the defence material in their possession which indicated that the accused might be innocent. They were also obliged to hand over statements by witnesses where those conflicted in material respects with their testimony. The general experience of members of the Bar was that prosecutors were reluctant to do this.

In addition in political cases the State always opposed endeavours by the defence to have access to statements, including statements by the accused themselves. Every major political prosecution involved complex charge sheets in which full reliance was placed on statutory presumptions against the accused. These equally inevitably brought forth demands for particularity which had not been furnished by the State. In general there was an overwhelming sense that the prosecutors in these types of cases identified with the police and the security apparatus in pursuing convictions at all costs. (As with everything there were exceptions to this but we believe the above general view is a fair reflection of the experience of advocates defending clients in cases with political overtones.)

The second problem area relates to the power initially given to Attorneys-General in 1959 and expanded from time to time thereafter to withhold bail and subsequently to cause witnesses to be detained. These powers were exercised time and again without any apparent restraint. In any case with political overtones it was routine to refuse bail and inevitably witnesses were detained. This was criticised by the Bar and on occasions roundly condemned from the Bench. It is the view of the GCB that the ostensible independence of the Attorneys-General during the critical apartheid years was more apparent than real. The conduct of political cases was such as to convey that the prosecutors concerned were intent at all costs on procuring convictions which seems to have been viewed as part of a responsibility to uphold the State at all costs. We are unaware of any objections by the Attorneys-General to the methods adopted to procure evidence, the detention of witnesses and accused persons without the right of access to lawyers, doctors or family, the breadth of definition of statutory offences, the presumptions in favour of the prosecution or the excessive reliance by the police in all cases (not only political ones) on confessions.

The matters we have mentioned, in our view, at the very least facilitated the abuse of power by police officers and those responsible for detentions and the enforcement of security legislation. A refusal by Attorneys-General and their staff to pursue prosecutions on the distorted basis which security legislation established would have been a considerable help in preventing human rights abuses in South Africa. Even resistance to the introduction of such measures or simply not using them, as in the case of the bail provisions, would have improved the situation to some degree.[72]

It was easy to know whom to believe. Von Lieres, overcome by indignation at the thought that anyone could think he had been other than a fiercely independent upholder of laws of which no-one need be ashamed, departed from his written text and delivered a strident lecture to the TRC on the need to understand the revolutionary situation during the last years of apartheid.[73]

In giving this lecture, Von Lieres used the military jargon in vogue in South Africa in the 1980s of how to defend a country faced with a revolutionary "total onslaught". I had informed Hanif Vally just prior to the start of the session that Von Lieres had been my commanding officer during much of my compulsory military service; he commanded and continues to command the 7th Infantry Division, which was a very active part of the South African Defence Force's citizen force combat capability.[74]

Vally and the Commissioners asked Von Lieres how he could reconcile his two roles. Von Lieres saw no problem here, which was precisely the problem. "Rommel", he said, "was a Field Marshal but that didn't make him a Nazi, did it?"[75] There was significant doubt in the room that Von Lieres was capable of making the distinction between the no-holds-barred total military response supposed to be warranted by a total onslaught and the response of an Attorney-General.

Von Lieres's fellow Attorneys-General tried to indicate both in their written and their oral submissions that they were cut from different cloth. In this regard, they apologised for their role in

---

[72] GCB Submission, vol. 1, pp. 71–3.

[73] See the Transcript, pp. 457–9.

[74] White conscript soldiers who had completed their initial military training were still liable for "camps" each year.

[75] Transcript, p. 465.

prosecuting violations of laws which they now recognised as illegitimate. But their attempts to portray themselves as a different kind of human being failed, because like Von Lieres, they wished to a man to claim that they had been wholly independent and upstanding officers of the law. At most, they would make the following sort of concession, taken from the submission by D.J. Rossouw S.C., former Attorney-General of Cape Town:

As a product of . . . [the apartheid] environment, on occasion I may have believed accusers too readily or may have been insensitive to hearing or investigating claims of injustice. I confess to my imperfections and I ask forgiveness of those persons who suffered as a result.[76]

Not one of them of them could, however, recall an instance of having been swayed by political influence, or a prosecution that was over-zealous, or even usage of the mechanisms which the state made available to them to put extraordinary pressure on the accused and state witnesses. And they, like Judges Smalberger *et al.*, relied on what we can term "the 95% defence"—the claim that most of their work had nothing to do with prosecution of violations of apartheid laws.

In the case of the Attorneys-General, the defence is a convenient gloss over the fact that for black accused, by far the majority of those they prosecuted, the law and its enforcers looked like a monolith designed to process them as quickly as possible from arrest to jail. For the South African police had an enviable record in solving ordinary crime under apartheid: instead of using conventional detection, they tortured confessions out of black suspects. The Johannesburg Murder and Robbery Squad, for example, was more feared than the security police because of the notoriety of its "Waarkamer" or truth chamber. (Such practices persist to this day as hundreds of people still die while in police detention and the problem of lack of ordinary police skills is stark.) The confessions were then relied upon to procure convictions of undefended accused by magistrates whose record for impartiality is generally considered rotten.[77]

Rossouw in his oral submission repeated the apology he had made earlier in private to Michael Hendrickse, who had served under him

---

[76] Rossouw Submission, p. 2.
[77] For a discussion see "Why McNally Lost the Malan Trial", *Mail and Guardian*, 18 October 1996.

as a prosecutor, for his insensitivity to Hendrickse when the latter, a coloured man, had indicated that he wanted to be excused from prosecuting violations of the Group Areas Act.[78] But Hendrickse's submission later that day revealed more than past insensitivity on Roussow's part. The prosecutions had, he testified, been initiated after a period in which there had been an unofficial moratorium on such prosecutions. And that occurred because the National Party had been publicly embarrassed about the moratorium by the more right-wing Conservative Party who accused them of not enforcing the law of apartheid. In other words, Rossouw had initiated the prosecutions in response to a government "diktat" that a few people had to be sacrificed in order to preserve its electoral support.

Hendrickse also told how he was required by his senior prosecutor to proceed with a public violence prosecution when he knew there was no basis in law for proceeding; such prosecutions were the main tool of the state in trying to suppress the resistance in the streets of South Africa by the township youth in the 1980s and early 1990s. He went ahead, but when the main witness blatantly perjured himself (Hendrickse suspected at the request of the police), Hendrickse fulfilled his duty and made the witness's contradictory statements available to the defence.

He later refused to prosecute another public violence docket on the basis that the criminal justice system was being "abused by the government of the day to brand people as criminals to enforce their policies and to hold out that persons in the struggle for democracy in South Africa were 'common criminals' who had no respect for the law'":

I was then summoned to the office of the Attorney General, Mr. Rossouw. I explained to him why I could not prosecute these persons. He informed me that he could not allow prosecutors to pick and choose cases. I was told that I was there to do a job, and if I did not, I will be removed from my prosecution duties and transferred to the Clerk of the Court's office to work with the receipt of payment of fines. He added that at that stage, no post existed in the clerk's office. The message was clear—prosecute or be retrenched, the latter allowing him to discharge me without having to defend his instruction that I resign.

This was not a matter of picking and choosing cases—I had a definite and conscientious objection. It may be argued that I owe a duty to

---

[78] Transcript, pp. 520–1.

perform any task given to me. But when this task directly involves me consciously upholding a criminal and unjust policy, then I am entitled not to do so. There were many prosecutors who had no objection to prosecuting such cases.[79]

Hendrickse said of the Attorneys-General and the magistrates:

the very people who abused the rule of law now hold themselves out as the defenders of justice and human rights. If the consequences of their policies were not so tragic, traumatic and dehumanizing, their new-found sense of morality would be laughable.[80]

Further, Jacques Hechter, a former Captain of the Security police and an applicant for amnesty for his part in the murder of two opponents of apartheid, Franklin and Florence Ribeiro, testified that, prior to his appearance in a public investigation into their deaths, he had been fed the questions he would be asked and the answers he should give by a state attorney and a prosecutor.[81] Hechter testified that his impression from his interview with these two officials is that they were completely *au fait* with the real facts of the murder.[82]

Finally, Lee Bozalek, who had represented accused persons charged with political offences in Cape Town, told of how he had given up advising clients who had been assaulted by the police to lay criminal charges because the Attorney-General never followed the charges with a prosecution and would give no reasons for his failure. He also told of how political trials were often set by prosecuting authorities to take place in centres distant from where they would normally take place, in his view, in order to ensure that state witnesses did not testify in front of a public which might provide witnesses to challenge their testimony. Further, he told of a series of arson trials where it became apparent to him that the prosecutor added a juvenile accused to the list of accused in order to make use of

---

[79] Hendrickse Submission, p. 4.

[80] Ibid., p. 5.

[81] For a portrait of Hechter, see Jacques Pauw, *Into the Heart of Darkness: Confessions of Apartheid's Assassins* (Johannesburg: Jonathan Ball Publishers, 1997), passim. Hechter applied for amnesty for 26 incidents, though he is suspected of many more killings; see ibid., p. 198.

[82] Transcript, p. 562. I was struck during the TRC's examination of Hechter by a phenomenon which observers of the TRC often find disquieting. Hechter, a self-confessed murderer, who is likely to get amnesty, has an almost friendly relationship with the Commissioners, while others, for example, advocates who had a decent record during apartheid, were treated with suspicion and hostility.

a provision in the Criminal Procedure Act which permitted the trial to be held in camera, again shielding the evidence of state witnesses. The juvenile accused was then acquitted at the end of the state's evidence in each case, as no evidence was led implicating him or her.[83]

Most revealing though was the public display of moral rectitude by Tim McNally, S.C. The second submission of day two was delivered by Mary Reyner of Amnesty International. Amnesty's submission did not address the period 1960 to 1994, but events in Kwazulu Natal after 1994, in the light of which it made recommendations for the reform of the prosecution service in South Africa. Amnesty's submission focused on the role McNally had played during this time, particularly in the failed prosecution of General Magnus Malan.[84]

The facts surrounding the prosecution are immensely complicated, in part because both the investigation and the prosecution involved an "Independent Task Unit" and an "Investigation Task Board". These had been appointed because of the incompetence of the local police and because of their lack of will to bring to book high ranking officials of the old order.

Amnesty's submission detailed the case that McNally, who led the prosecution in the Malan trial, had failed to mount an effective prosecution. Amnesty could point in particular to rifts that opened between McNally and the Independent Task Unit over McNally's refusal to call certain key witnesses and the fact that the judge, in giving judgment at the end of the trial, had commented very explicitly on his inability to reach conclusions on important issues because of this failure.

After Reyner concluded her submission McNally asked for the opportunity to cross-examine her. He was given this opportunity by the presiding Commissioner, Yasmin Sooka. McNally's case in his own defence was that the witnesses he had not called would have weakened the state's case and that the judge had not meant to criticise him by remarking on the failure to call certain key witnesses,

---

[83] Bozalek Submission, pp. 4–6. Two other submissions by black lawyers who had served in the old order as magistrates and prosecutors also severely undermined the credibility of the Attorneys-General: submissions by advocates J.B. Skosana and A.P. Laka.

[84] Von Lieres, who resigned from office as Attorney-General of the Transvaal on the gounds of ill health, then found himself well enough to go into private practice as an advocate. He represented Malan.

something he said had been confirmed to him privately by the judge.[85]

If one were to confine evaluation of McNally, who is an effective advocate, to the exchange between him and Reyner, one would not be able to conclude beyond a reasonable doubt, even on a balance of probabilities, that he was in any way to blame for his handling of the Malan matter. But the general context set out in the Amnesty submission, made extremely problematic his refusal to contemplate the possibility that he had ever made even the smallest mistake in the past.

If anything, the exchange lends weight to those who argued for the institution of a Truth and Reconciliation Commission rather than the pursuit of the truth about atrocities through the criminal justice system, on the ground that the truth about apartheid's history is more likely to be revealed outside of a strictly forensic context.[86] Curiously, very much the same point was made by McNally in his submission on his role. Unlike the others, he addressed explicitly the relationship between truth and justice. "'What is truth?'", he said, "is a question which has reverberated down the centuries" and he said that the rules of evidence often result in the "baby of truth" being "thrown out with the bathwater of falsity".[87]

He presented himself as having always been opposed to apartheid, using his discretion whenever possible to avoid prosecutions of violations of institutionalised racism. Like the other Attorneys-General, he claimed that it was only the inability to get good evidence that influenced his decision not to prosecute allegations of assault and torture by the security forces. Again like the others, he said one cannot judge the past from the present perspective, which includes the facts revealed only through the work of the TRC. "South Africans", he said, "have shaken the dust of apartheid from their sandals and moved on. The legal profession is known for its conservative approach but its intellectual athleticism has allowed it to embrace the new legal order based on a human rights culture".[88]

He also quoted the extract from King's judgment where King says that "intellectual honesty" compelled him to decide a case under the

---

[85] Transcript, p. 492. I also rely here on my own notes as the recording at this stage was faulty and the exchange does not appear in the Transcript.

[86] See Kader Asmal, Louise Asmal, Ronald Suresh Roberts, *Reconciliation Through Truth: A Reckoning of Apartheid's Criminal Governance* (Cape Town: David Philip, 1997).

[87] McNally Submission, p. 3.   [88] Ibid., p. 9.

Group Areas Act in terms of the law rather than justice.[89] McNally, that is, wanted to claim not only that he is a highly moral man, but that if we were, like him, intellectually honest, we would recognise that he was only doing his duty.

Had McNally then acted, as Coetzee alleged, as a kind of "sweeper" for the security forces, using his discretion to avoid implicating them in their crimes, or was he telling the truth that he had been deeply revolted by such crimes and had done everything possible to prosecute them?[90]

Recall that McNally and several of the others who appeared are still serving as Attorneys-General of South Africa. The fact that suspicions dog McNally even as he proclaims his "athletic" embrace of the new order illustrates the difficulties that order faces as it relies on the skills of those who faithfully served the old.

The Commissioners were clearly troubled by this fact, especially since these Attorneys-General had been opposed to the institution of a National Directorate of Public Prosecutions, a central body establishing policy for South Africa to which all Attorneys-General will be accountable, although this is required by South Africa's Constitution.[91] This constitutional requirement is a reaction to a 1992 statute which formally declared the independence of the Attorneys-General by giving those in office tenure of their jobs for the rest of their working lives.[92] The statute was enacted by the National Party government during the negotiations about the handover of power.

---

[89] Ibid., pp. 2–3. See Chapter 2, text to n. 90.

[90] For discussion of Coetzee's relationship with McNally, see Paauw, *Into the Heart of Darkness: Confessions of Apartheid's Assassins*, n. 81 above, pp. 85, 92 and 168. McNally argued at the Hearing that he had dealt with the problem of conflict of interest by getting his deputy to cross-examine Coetzee. Coetzee, along with another assassin, began to blow the whistle on death squad operations in the late 1980s. McNally, then Attorney-General of the Orange Free State, led a commission of inquiry into their allegations. He found, without interviewing Coetzee, that there was no evidence to suggest that they were telling the truth. He then accepted an assignment to lead evidence at a judicial commission of inquiry, presided over by Judge Louis Harms, who made the same finding, observing that Coetzee had psycopathic tendencies despite no psychological evidence being led. It was argued strongly at the time that McNally should have recused himself from this assignment. Harms was then promoted to the Appellate Division, where he still serves, and McNally to the post of Attorney-General of Natal. See Paauw above. McNally's alleged failure to prosecute or follow up various allegations of high-level official complicity in "third force" activities is detailed in the Amnesty International Submission.

[91] See s. 179.

[92] Attorney-General Act, 92 of 1992.

Clearly, National Party politicians hoped that such independence from central government of the particular men who would continue to hold office would stand in the way of political pressure in the new order to prosecute the crimes committed under the old.

Their opposition to the National Directorate of Public Prosecutions, the Attorneys-General all said at the TRC, should not be regarded with suspicion; they simply wanted to preserve their independence from political control and that desire could not be criticised if one also wanted to decry lack of independence under the old order.[93] But there has to be grave concern about the understanding of the Attorneys-General of their independent role. They are men who suddenly discovered the importance of independence as the order which had nurtured their careers crumbled and as an attempt was made to find a balance between accountability and independence for their office in the new order.

6. Fischer's Challenge

In my view, Bram Fischer's story is central to any account of the choices South African lawyers faced during apartheid. The history of apartheid law can be roughly divided into 10-year periods: in the 1950s the apartheid divide was legislated; in the 1960s, the security apparatus to repress opposition to apartheid was legislated and eventually consolidated; in the 1970s, cracks in the ideology behind the divide and in the law which maintained it started to appear but were patched over by ruthless use of the force licensed by the security legislation; in the 1980s, the divide fractured, was maintained for a while by force, but was eventually destroyed, a feat in which lawyers played a significant role.

In looking back over this period, lawyers like both to dwell on the period of the 1980s, when some of their number were most active in opposing apartheid, and to claim that opposition to apartheid through the law was usually futile, as demonstrated by the fruitless representations to the government which the professional associations on occasion made. Their stance here—one which asserts both power and powerlessness—is reminiscent of the judges' tales of (dis)empowerment.

---

[93] Transcript, pp. 533–4.

In the case of the professional associations, the tension is most exposed for the attorneys. During the 1960s they were almost totally silent about the erosion of the rule of law. For the advocates, the tension comes about because at this same time, the most liberal of the Bars took part in the repression of one of its own, Bram Fischer. Moreover, it took that part in the face of an explicit and powerful challenge which Fischer threw down to South African lawyers.

Fischer did not simply ask these lawyers to confront their role in sustaining the injustice of the law. He tried to get them to see that there was more wrong with the law than that it was being used in the cause of unjust policies. He argued that any lawyer who wished to maintain respect for the rule of law had to question whether the ideal of the rule of law was not in fact better served by violating the letter of apartheid law.

Fischer clearly regarded this question as an open one, to be decided by each individual. As we know, he decided that the only way he could participate in building a society founded on respect for the rule of law was to go underground in order to join the illegal armed struggle. But we also know that he hoped that his example, the example of an Afrikaner aristocrat who had established himself as one of the leaders of the legal profession, would make other lawyers rethink their role *within* the legal order. And that was because he regarded himself as in a genuine dilemma. However repugnant he found the apartheid legal order, it remained a legal order—an order in which there were still the vestiges of the rule of law—and his respect for the law still exerted a pull on him which he found difficult to resist.

As Stephen Clingman shows in his excellent biography of Fischer, Fischer's decision to return from England to stand trial in the face of considerable pressure from his comrades in exile abroad, his courtesy to his legal representative and to the judicial officers presiding at his trial, and his great concern about the uncomfortable situation he had created for his legal representative, were all occasioned by his continuing respect for the law, even as he planned to go underground. And as we have seen, it was the complete lack of understanding of most of his colleagues at the Johannesburg Bar of his position, evidenced by their haste to join in the government's attack on him as a political dissident, which so distressed him.[94] The dilemma which Fischer

[94] Clingman, *Bram Fischer: Afrikaner Revolutionary*, n. 8 above, pp. 344–56, 368–72, 389–91, 400–16.

faced underpins all the other dilemmas thus far discussed and I will refer to it as the rule of law dilemma.

The best description of that dilemma I know, one which seems designed for Fischer, is to be found in an essay by the distinguished philosopher Christine Korsgaard.[95] Korsgaard says the following of a morally upstanding citizen who contemplates joining a revolution against the established order:

> "When the very institution whose purpose is to realize human rights is used to trample them, when justice is turned against itself, the virtue of justice will be turned against itself too. Concern for human rights leads the virtuous person to accept the authority of the law, but in such circumstances adherence to the law will lead her to support institutions that systematically violate human rights. The person with the virtue of justice, the lover of human rights, unable to turn to the actual laws for their enforcement, has nowhere else to turn. She may come to feel that there is nothing for it but to take human rights under her own protection, and so to take the law into her own hands".[96]

Korsgaard suggests that such a decision is ethically different from most decisions we make. It is not the "imperfection" of justice—justice which fails to measure up to our sense of right and wrong—which is the basis for our decision. Rather the basis is the "perversion" of justice, the sense that it is injustice disguised as justice. Given the consequences that likely attend overthrowing an established order, the revolutionary cannot, she thinks, claim that he is justified in resorting to revolution. "That consolation is denied him. It is as if a kind of gap opens up in the moral world in which the moral agent must stand alone".[97] Korsgaard thus maintains that justification in such matters is always retrospective—everything depends on whether the revolutionary is successful in establishing a stable government.[98]

In Fischer's speech from the dock in March 1966 prior to the presiding judge finding him guilty and sentencing him to life imprisonment, he said much the same in explaining why he had refused to enter a plea to the charges:

[95] Christine M. Korsgaard, "Taking the Law into Our Own Hands: Kant on the Right to Revolution" in Andrews Reath, Barbara Herman, Christine M. Korsgaard (eds.), *Reclaiming the History of Ethics: Essays for John Rawls* (Cambridge: Cambridge University Press, 1997), p. 297.

[96] Ibid., pp. 318–19, footnote omitted.

[97] Ibid., p. 315.

[98] Ibid.

"The law, my Lord, under which I have been prosecuted, was enacted by a wholly unrepresentative body, a body in which three-quarters of the people of this country have no voice whatever. This and other laws were enacted not to prevent the spread of Communism, but, my Lord, for the purpose of silencing the opposition of the large majority of our citizens to a government intent upon depriving them, solely on account of their colour, of the most elementary human rights: of the right to freedom and happiness, the right to live together with their families wherever they may choose, to earn their livelihoods to the best of their abilities, and to rear and educate their children in a civilized fashion; to take part in the administration of their country and to obtain a fair share of the wealth they produce; in short, my Lord, to live as human beings.

My conscience, my Lord, does not permit me to afford these laws such recognition as even a plea of guilty would involve. Hence, though I shall be convicted by this Court, I cannot plead guilty. I believe that the future may well say that I acted correctly".[99]

Where Korsgaard goes wrong, however, is in suggesting that the decision has to be made in a moral gap or void. Fischer had no doubt that whatever the future would in fact say, he was at the time justified in taking his step. The difference between his own understanding of his situation and Korsgaard's is that he does not adopt the perspective which we saw, in Chapter 1, Robert Cover term the "perspective of the disobedient", "the perspective of the established order".[100] For although Fischer appealed, like Cover's disobedient, to a "juster justice"[101] beyond the law to justify his disobedience, his perspective on the law was not entirely external. As we have seen, his appeal was also meant to awaken South African lawyers to the possibility for them of the pursuit of the ideal of juster justice within the law. In contrast, Korsgaard's analysis seems to suggest that for the disobedient revolutionary only the external "disobedient" perspective is available. But that would mean that there was no real dilemma.[102]

---

[99] Quoted in Clingman, *Bram Fischer: Afrikaner Revolutionary*, n. 8 above, p. 410.

[100] Robert Cover, *Justice Accused: Antislavery and the Judicial Process* (New Haven, Conn.: Yale University Press, 1975), p. 1. See Chapter 1, text to n. 65.

[101] Ibid.

[102] Korsgaard regards apartheid South Africa as an example of what she has in mind: "Apartheid South Africa horrified us more, perhaps, than more egregious despotisms, because of its outward forms of legality, its caricature of a modern Western democracy"; "Taking the Law into Our Own Hands: Kant on the Right to Revolution", n. 95 above, p. 317. But if the forms were merely outward, if law was but a cloak for naked power, there would be no dilemma. Other elements of Korsgaard's essay also suggest the perspective of the disobedient, one which is ultimately a positivist perspective on law.

Clingman also seems to rely on the external disobedient perspective in his exploration of the nature of Fischer's choice in 1965. He rejects the view that Fischer's life was a tragedy in the classical sense in which a great individual contributes to his fall "through some crucial error or flaw", preferring the idea that Fischer had to pay the price of an uncompromising stand on the side of right against the "unregenerate force of apartheid".[103] Here Clingman suggests that for Fischer the situation was one of a clash between opposites—evil might and total right.

Fischer's choice had of course tragic consequences for him personally. He died in 1975 when those involved in the struggle against apartheid had few grounds for hope. And that choice committed him to an armed struggle which had tragic consequences for others, consequences, as Korsgaard suggests, which attend any decision to engage in revolution. Even if one considers the turn to armed struggle by the African National Congress (ANC) in the early 1960s as a completely justified reaction to government repression, one has to admit that the ANC's decision gave the government the excuse to engage in a no-holds-barred war which escalated into the tale of human cruelty with which the TRC has had to deal. And one can give the ANC the moral high ground in this war and still hold the ANC responsible, as the TRC must do, for its own gross human rights abuses. Indeed, the idea for the TRC was born in an ANC initiative in the early 1990s to appoint commissions to inquire into its record of brutality to its own soldiers in ANC training camps.[104] In other words, the decision to engage in armed struggle was one whose human consequences could be predicted without having been able to predict the ultimate result. And it is unimaginable that someone as far-sighted and ethically rigorous as Fischer took his decision without accepting responsibility for these consequences.

However, at least from the institutional perspective of the rule of law, the idea of a clash between two opposites, and of a decision in a moral void, does not get exactly right the tragic nature of Fischer's choice in 1965.

We can think of a morally tragic situation as being one in which no choice can be made without ignoring the legitimate pull of important moral considerations. We have nevertheless to choose in

---

[103] Clingman, *Bram Fischer: Afrikaner Revolutionary*, n. 8 above, pp. 449–51.

[104] See Daan Bronkhorst, *Truth and Reconciliation: Obstacles and Opportunities for Human Rights* (Amsterdam: Amnesty International Dutch Section, 1995), pp. 82–3.

such situations. And we have to try to make the best choice without the comfort, however the choice turns out, that the ignored considerations will cease to be legitimate. Even when one seems vindicated in retrospect, all one can say is that one did the best one could and that one is deeply sorry about one's complicity in the moral wrongs that resulted from one's choice.

Recall that at the same time as Fischer made his choice to go underground, he hoped by it to encourage others to take a different decision. And it is worth noting that Nelson Mandela seems to have been occupied by the same issue in the 1960s. He says that at the time of the trial which resulted in his own sentence to life imprisonment, he urged Fischer, leader of the defence team, who was already considering going underground, not to take this route. Mandela stressed that Fischer "served the struggle best in the courtroom, where people could see this Afrikaner son of a judge president fighting for the rights of the powerless".[105]

In other words, Fischer and Mandela did not adopt a simple strategy of fighting an illegal war against an unjust state in order to establish a just one.[106] They thought that it was important that at the same time war be fought by legal means in order to keep alive the idea upon which we saw Vincent Saldanha rely.[107] There is a distinction between the apartheid government and the state, since there is a distinction between any government and the state.

And in order for that distinction—one between the government which brings about the enactment of the law and the law of the state to which the government itself is subject—to have any basis, right can never be entirely on the side of one who decides to overthrow an order which still contains vestiges of the rule of law. Indeed, besides the costs to human beings that follow a decision to overthrow an established order, the revolutionary has to take into account the costs which armed struggle imposes on respect for the rule of law.

But the revolutionary can seek to justify his actions here and now

---

[105] Nelson Mandela, *Long Walk to Freedom* (Boston: Little, Brown and Company, 1995), p. 472.

[106] The complexity of Fischer's strategy is illustrated by his secret conduct during the Rivonia trial, the trial which issued in sentences of life imprisonment for Mandela and others. For he used his office as defence lawyer to convey exhibits from the trial (maps of likely targets for sabotage as well as plans for blowing them up) as well as ideas from the accused to the new high command of the military wing of the African National Congress. See Clingman, *Bram Fischer: Afrikaner Hero*, n. 8 above, pp. 310–11.

[107] See text to n. 55.

in making his decision, as long as he recognises the pull of competing considerations and thus the moral worth of the other decision.

That other decision, the decision to use the law to oppose the law, had almost as momentous a result as the decision to turn to armed struggle. In this regard, Clingman takes care to note that lawyers who worked with Fischer and who represented him, most notably Arthur Chaskalson, continued and even extended his work in the courts. Clingman points in particular to Chaskalson's co-founding of the Legal Resources Centre in 1978 and his recent appointment to the Presidency of South Africa's Constitutional Court. And he records that Ilse Fischer, Bram Fischer's daughter, was employed at the Centre as librarian, and "had the pleasure of seeing, on a daily basis, her father's law library, housed at the Centre at a time when so little of Bram's life had any public legitimacy". Clingman continues: "Yet that aspect changed as well: in June 1995 Nelson Mandela gave the first Bram Fischer Memorial Lecture in Johannesburg, and one year later the Bram Fischer Memorial Library was formally opened at the Legal Resources Centre, again by President Mandela".[108]

In sum, while Fischer was a South African of altogether exceptional moral stature,[109] the way he lived his life set an example for all other white South Africans, particularly lawyers. His choice, while tragic, was one which could be justified even at the time he made it, whatever the result. For the manner of its making opened up moral space for those who did not want to follow him; and so, while they cannot be judged negatively for having decided to opt for the politics of legal opposition, they can and should be judged by how they behaved within that space.

---

[108] Clingman, *Bram Fischer: Afrikaner Hero*, n. 8 above, p. 455.

[109] Mandela says of Fischer, "As an Afrikaner whose conscience forced him to reject his own heritage and be ostracized by his own people, he showed a level of courage and sacrifice that was in a class by itself. I fought only against injustice, not my own people"; *Long Walk to Freedom*, n. 105 above, p. 389. And Clingman records this moment during Fischer's trial in the cross-examination of Piet Beyleveld, an Afrikaner who had been a leading figure in the resistance to apartheid, but who turned state's evidence against Fischer and others: "Hanson [Fischer's advocate] . . . continued, 'I don't like to put this in my client's presence, but he is a man who carries something of an aura of a saint-like quality, does he not?' To which Beyleveld's simple reply was, 'I agree' ": Clingman, *Bram Fischer: Afrikaner Hero*, n. 8 above, p. 351.

4

The Politics of the
Rule of Law

"These exclusions [from practising at the Pretoria Bar, from office space and the common room at the Johannesburg Bar, and from the Orange Free State from sunset to sunrise] reinforced a multitude of other exclusions which denied my humanity. They inflicted deep wounds inside me, often revived in the telling, with a special kind of pain without bitterness.

There was a special sting about this form of exclusion. The study and practice of law had appealed to my idealism, because the justification for law was its pursuit of justice and its capacity to resist injustice. But it was through the instrumentality of law itself and the institutions of justice that palpable injustice was inflicted on me and other persons of colour. But this paradox was not without compensation: it enabled me to focus more intensely and consciously on what the philosophical and ethically legitimate ends of justice were, the degree to which they were manifestly inconsistent with the laws which regulated life in the land of my birth, the reason why they should be reversed and never, never be repeated".

Chief Justice Ismail Mahomed[1]

1. Introduction

We have seen how many of the submissions to the Legal Hearing followed a depressingly similar pattern by enlisting most or all of the following defences: "no use in lamenting the past"; "we only know now (through the work of the TRC) what was going on"; "we had no choice because of parliamentary sovereignty"; "95% of our work had nothing to do with apartheid"; and "independence"—"if you want us

---

[1] "Address by the Honourable Mr Justice Ismail Mahomed at a Dinner given by the Johannesburg Bar on 25 June 1997 to celebrate his Appointment as Chief Justice of the Supreme Court of Appeal", (1997) 114 *South African Law Journal* 604, at 605, his emphasis.

to be independent in the new order you must recognise the value of independence in the old order". And we have also seen the tendency to engage in some special pleading, which obstructed useful discussion of how institutions of the new order might best be structured.

My account of the Legal Hearing shows that these defences did no work for those who enlisted them. The "no use in lamenting the past" defence was not only in tension with any submission to the Hearing but usually depended on a problematic and partial account of that past. And the "we only know now (through the work of the TRC) what was going on" defence was either duplicitous or evidence of a diligent refusal during apartheid to confront the facts. And the "no choice because of parliamentary supremacy" defence was often intellectually dishonest since it assumed both that there was no room for interpretative manoeuvre and the democratic legitimacy of the South African Legislature under apartheid.

The "95% of our work had nothing to do with apartheid" defence was deeply misleading. It adopted a convenient definition of what complicity in enforcing apartheid amounted to. For example, it would be interesting to know just how much time judges spent on reviewing—in effect rubber stamping—magistrates' decisions which declared black men to be "idle and undesirable". In addition, that defence was used, as in the Smalberger *et al.* submission, as a basis for the claim that the good that came out of participation outweighed the bad. But used in this way, the defence depended on a false description of the likely consequences of judicial resignation or refusal to take up appointments. It also depended on a mistaken characterisation of the issues at stake since a discussion of the pros and cons of participation hinged on what kind of judge or lawyer the participant would be.

Of the defences, the independence defence was the most important. It underpinned the "no use in lamenting the past" defence since that defence implied that the ideal of independence in the new order would suffer rather than benefit from scrutiny at the TRC. But that in turn implied two highly suspect claims: that the record under the old order was one of independence and that the ideal of independence, whether in the old or the new order, is uncontentious. It was entwined with the "95% of our work had nothing to do with apartheid" defence since judges and other lawyers sensed that complicity with implementing apartheid raised uncomfortable questions about any claim to independence. And to the extent that judges and other lawyers could not deny that they had in fact implemented apartheid, indeed had been crucial agents in that process, they could fall back, though not without tension, on the claim that sometimes true independence requires implementing some laws which one personally detests. Here they combined the "we had no choice because of parliamentary sovereignty" defence with the independence defence.

We have also seen that the judges made the strongest institutional claim to independence, and no judge appeared at the Hearing. I have already touched on judicial independence in Chapter 2, and here I will go deeper into that topic because of the light it sheds on the central theme of this book—the politics of the rule of law.

2. Why Independence?

By not appearing, the judges aroused public anger which resulted in calls from the media and from within the TRC for subpoenas to be issued to some retired judges. For example, the *Mail and Guardian*, South Africa's leading liberal newspaper, in its editorial of the 31 October/6 November edition called for judges to volunteer to appear at the TRC in the light of the debates at the Legal Hearing.[2] In another editorial in its edition of 12/18 December, the *Mail and Guardian* responded to Judge Curlewis's call to bring back the death penalty, a call from a judge who, as we saw in Chapter 1, was known as a hanging judge and who had treated the TRC invitation to participate in the Hearing with scorn. The *Mail and Guardian* urged that the TRC issue subpoenas to judges because of the fact that the judiciary "harbours such as Curlewis".[3]

While the possibility of subpoenas dimmed and then disappeared as the TRC started to wind down its work, it is worth considering for a moment what would most likely have happened. Subpoenaed judges who were mindful to disobey would have used the law to resist being forced to account and their case would inevitably have ended up in the Constitutional Court, since the principal line of resistance would have been that the independence of the courts is constitutionally guaranteed.[4]

---

[2] *Mail and Guardian*, 31 October/6 November, p. 26.
[3] *Mail and Guardian*, 12/18 December, p. 20.
[4] See below for s. 165 of the Constitution.

The Justices of the Constitutional Court would then have found themselves in the invidious position of being judges in their own cause and they would not have been able to avoid dealing fully and frankly with the issue of the substance of independence. They would, in other words, have forced themselves to deal with what they sought to evade by declining the TRC's invitation.

An even more daunting prospect for the judges must be that their apparent sense of non-accountability began a public discussion, after the very first submission, which raised the question whether judges should be made accountable through a public body like the Judicial Services Commission, the body which at present conducts public interviews of lawyers nominated to serve as judges and compiles a shortlist from which the President selects judges. Indeed, Kader Asmal, one of the most influential ministers in the Mandela government, and a former human rights lawyer, has been prompted by the Curlewis episode to call for judges to be made accountable in this way.[5]

One should not think that such issues are confined to South Africa. And I want briefly to digress from the South African discussion in order to consider the Supreme Court of Canada's treatment of of judicial accountability in a situation which does much to illuminate the topic of independence.

In *MacKeigan* v. *Hickman* (1989),[6] the Canadian Supreme Court had to decide whether judges of the Court of Appeal of the province of Nova Scotia could be summoned by a Royal Commission of Inquiry appointed by the Nova Scotian Legislature into the "Marshall Affair". Some of the judicial reactions to the affair chime with judicial response patterns we saw in Chapter 2, while others are suggestive of how the issue of judicial independence could have been resolved, had judges resisted a TRC summons to testify.

In 1971 Donald Marshall, Jr., a 17-year-old native Canadian, was convicted of murder during a robbery in which he was involved and sentenced to serve a lengthy term of imprisonment. He consistently maintained his innocence and was vindicated 11 years later when the Nova Scotian Court of Appeal, in the light of new evidence, ordered his release.

When the Court of Appeal decided on Marshall's release, five

---

[5] Kader Asmal, "Judges are not exempt from review", *Electronic Mail and Guardian*, 22 January 1998.
[6] [1989] 2 SCR 796.

judges heard the matter, including Ian M. MacKeigan, the Chief Justice, and Leonard L. Pace who had, at the time of Marshall's conviction, been Attorney-General of Nova Scotia, and thus responsible for Marshall's prosecution. At the end of its judgment, the Court suggested that in Marshall's case, "[a]ny miscarriage of justice is, however, more apparent than real". The Court said that Marshall had perjured himself at trial, an act for which he could still be charged, and that by "lying he helped secure his own conviction". He had thus obstructed development of the "only defence available to him"—that the death which had occurred was at the hands of one of the victims of the robbery. The Court concluded that there could be "no doubt but that Donald Marshall's untruthfulness through this whole affair contributed in large measure to his conviction".[7] After Marshall's acquittal, he was paid $250,000 compensation by the Province of Nova Scotia, and he then executed a complete release of all claims against the government.

The concluding comments of the Court of Appeal were widely perceived to be but a continuation of the systemic racism in the justice system which had led to Marshall's original conviction. Particular concern attached to the fact that the Court's remarks resulted in a reduced amount of compensation to Marshall, to the fact that the panel which gave the decision was tarnished by the appearance of bias because of the inclusion of the former Attorney-General on the panel, and to the fact that the Court's remarks made it unclear on what evidence it had relied, even implying that it had relied on affidavits which had not been properly introduced into Court.

The failure of the Nova Scotian justice system in Marshall's case, especially because of the racism against native Canadians still endemic in Canada, created a public outcry which prompted the establishment of a Royal Commission of Inquiry. Three judges from outside of Nova Scotia, including T. Alexander Hickman, Chief Justice of the Trial Division, Supreme Court of Newfoundland, were appointed as Commissioners.

The Nova Scotian judges declined to appear before the Commission of Inquiry and it issued orders to attend. The judges refused on the basis of judicial immunity against being questioned about their deliberations; this refusal was upheld by the Nova

---

[7] Quoted in *MacKeigan* v. *Hickman*, n. 6 above, at 817–18.

Scotian courts, and their decisions were then appealed to the Supreme Court of Canada.

Judge Beverley McLachlin gave judgment for the majority of the Supreme Court.[8] For her the issue was whether a standard general power to issue orders to "persons" to attend included the power to compel judges.[9] She held that the principle of judicial independence was an "insurmountable obstacle" in the way of such compulsion.

However, there is a tension in her reasoning on this issue. On the one hand, she suggested that independence is an instrumental value. The independence of the judiciary, she said, is important only because it underpins the judicial virtue of impartiality, the virtue which secures accountability to the law: "What is required . . . is avoidance of incidents and relationships which could affect the independence of the judiciary in relation to two critical judicial functions—judicial impartiality in adjudication and the judiciary's role as arbiter and protector of the Constitution".[10] On the other hand, she said that to "entertain the demand that a judge testify before a civil body, an emanation of the legislature or executive, on how or why he or she made his or her decision would be to strike at the most sacrosanct core of judicial independence".[11] Nothing, she found, in the Act showed that the Legislature empowered the Commission to compel the justices "to testify as to the grounds for their decision, including the record relied on".[12] And in answer to the question whether the Commission could compel a judge to testify as to why a particular judge sat on a particular case, she held that "to allow the executive a role in selecting what judges hear what cases would constitute an unacceptable interference with the independence

---

[8] Two judges concurred in McLachlin's judgment. Bertha Wilson and Peter Cory dissented in part. Antonio Lamer agreed with the principles set out by Cory in his judgment, but said that, on these principles, he reached the same conclusion as McLachlin. Gerard La Forest concurred with McLachlin except for the fact that he disagreed with her on a point not dealt with in the text: unlike her, he considered it beyond the province's constitutional authority to enact a statute which explicitly gave a commission of inquiry the authority to compel judges to testify.

[9] Public Inquiries Act, RSNS 1967, c. 250, ss. 3 and 4. Section 3 provided that "The commissioner or commissioners shall have the power of summoning before him or them any persons as witnesses". Section 4 read: "The commissioner or commissioners shall have the same power to enforce the attendance of persons as witnesses and to compel them to give evidence and produce documents and things as is vested in the Supreme Court or a judge thereof in civil cases".

[10] *MacKeigan* v. *Hickman*, n. 6 above, 828.

[11] Ibid., 831.

[12] Ibid.

of the judiciary. Inquiries after the fact must be similarly barred. . . . [T]he principle of judicial independence which underlies judicial impartiality and the proper functioning of the courts would be threatened by the possibility of public inquiries as to the reason for the assignment of particular judges to particular cases".[13]

The two partial dissents by Judge Peter Cory and Judge Bertha Wilson highlight the tension in McLachlin's reasoning. If independence is instrumental to important ends, then, as long as one has a sound case that those ends are not being served, independence cannot be "sacrosanct"; it cannot stand in the way of an inquiry aimed at promoting accountability to those ends. As Wilson, speaking of the composition of the Nova Scotian panel, put it, "[w]hen there is a real risk that judicial immunity may be perceived by the public as being advanced for the protection of the judiciary rather than for the protection of the justice system, the public interest in my view requires that the question be asked and answered".[14]

In his partial dissent, Cory was anxious to emphasise the nature of the duty to testify. Here he quoted from Wigmore, one of the classic authorities on the common law of evidence:

> "The pettiness and personality of the individual trial disappears when we reflect that our duty to bear testimony runs not to the parties in that present cause, but to the community at large and forever.
>
> It follows . . . that *all privileges of exemption from this duty are exceptional*, and are therefore to be discountenanced. There must be good reason, plainly shown, for their existence".[15]

Cory, of course, recognised that judges have a good claim to such an exemption, indeed, he said, an "absolute" claim in respect of the "adjudicative privilege"—the privilege against "testifying as to their mental processes in arriving at a judgment or as to how they reached a decision in any case that came before them". Here their decisions, and their reasons for their decisions, subject them to scrutiny "on appeal by the legal community and by the public at large".[16]

---

[13] Ibid., 833.   [14] Ibid., 808–9.

[15] Original emphasis, quoted at 840. A similar passage from Wigmore was quoted in an important dissent by Judge Rumpff to one of the Appellate Division's worst decisions; see *Schermbrucker* v. *Klindt* 1965 (4) SA 606 (A) at 615. For discussion see David Dyzenhaus, *Hard Cases in Wicked Legal Systems: South African Law in the Perspective of Legal Philosophy* (Oxford: Clarendon Press, 1991) pp. 112–20.

[16] *MacKeigan* v. *Hickman*, n. 6 above, 68–9.

He also reasoned that it was important that no outside agency be able to select judges to hear particular cases and that judges not be compelled to reveal their conversations with their fellow judges or with their clerks. But it was crucial, he said, to distinguish between the principle of adjudicative independence and the principle of administrative independence. Judicial control over the administration of decisions is important only as an adjunct to adjudicative independence and may be qualified and limited in its scope: "there are exceptional cases such as this one where the qualified privilege of immunity from testifying must give way; this will occur when it is necessary to reaffirm public confidence in the administration of justice".[17] And the Marshall Affair gave rise, in his view, to such an exception:

> "In this case it is appropriate to review some of the administrative decisions. The wrongful conviction of Marshall of the crime of murder in itself called for a public inquiry. Later the composition of the panel which heard his appeal could have been the subject of public criticism. The lack of any certainty as to what material comprised the record on the appeal was disquieting. Like the wrongful conviction, these last two matters are of grave concern. They can probably be readily and completely answered, but answered they should be".[18]

Despite the Supreme Court's ruling, the matter did not end here. In its report, the Royal Commission roundly condemned the Nova Scotian Appeal Court for the attitude it had expressed to Marshall, for the inclusion of former Attorney-General Pace on the panel, and, most important, for attempting to defend the "criminal justice system at Marshall's expense, notwithstanding overwhelming evidence to the contrary".[19] The Attorney-General of Nova Scotia then requested, as was his right, that an Inquiry Committee be appointed under the (Federal) Judges Act.[20] He hoped that such a committee (the internal disciplinary tribunal which considers complaints against federally appointed judges) would be able to examine the judges.

The Inquiry Committee is appointed by the judges who sit on the

---

[17] Ibid., 842–3, at 843.   [18] Ibid., 844.

[19] Quoted in "Report to the Canadian Judicial Council of the Inquiry Committee established pursuant to subsection 63(1) of the *Judges Act* at the request of the Attorney General of Nova Scotia", reproduced in (1991–92) 40 *University of New Brunswick Law Journal* 212, 213–14.

[20] RSC 1985, c. J-1.

Canadian Judicial Council. This particular one was composed of three judges and two lawyers. By the time the Committee was appointed, MacKeigan, the Nova Scotian Chief Justice who had selected the panel and then presided over the decision, had reached the mandatory retirement age and left the Bench and Pace had left the Bench due to ill health. The majority of the Inquiry Committee held that it had no jurisdiction over the two most significant members of the panel. They also expressed their agreement with the majority of the Supreme Court of Canada that the Royal Commission of Inquiry had no authority to summon judges before it and they themselves did not attempt to compel the judges to testify.

The majority suggested that the "real question" raised by the Inquiry was "whether inappropriate language, even grossly inappropriate language, constitutes judicial misconduct in the circumstances of this case". In this regard, they found that the panel had given the impression that "it was ignoring the grossly incorrect conduct of other persons and concentrating on the victim of the tragedy", that it was "not responsive to the injustice of an innocent person spending more than ten years in jail" and that it had committed a legal error in seeming to attribute to Marshall "exclusive responsibility for the wrongful conviction". But they did not find that the remaining three judges had rendered themselves incapable "of executing their office impartially and independently with continued public confidence" and so they did not recommend their removal from office.[21]

In evaluating the report of the majority of the Inquiry Committee, one has to bear in mind that they treated the Marshall Affair as a case of individualised injustice, and remained completely silent about the factor which prompted public outrage and a collapse of confidence in the judiciary; they ignored, that is, the allegation that Marshall's treatment was the product of systemic racism that extended into the Nova Scotian Court of Appeal. Indeed, one searches in vain in both the majority and the minority reasons for the barest mention of the fact that Marshall is a native Canadian.[22] Moreover, the majority of the Inquiry Committee half apologised for having made any criticism of the panel:

---

[21] "Report to the Canadian Judicial Council of the Inquiry Committee established pursuant to subsection 63(1) of the *Judges Act* at the request of the Attorney General of Nova Scotia", n. 19 above, 219–22.

[22] See M.E. Turpel, "The Judged and the Judging: Locating Innocence in a Fallen Legal World", (1991–92) 40 *University of New Brunswick Law Journal* 281.

"We do not make out criticisms lightly. We are deeply conscious that criticism can itself undermine public confidence in the judiciary, but on balance conclude in this case that confidence would be more severely impaired by our failure to criticize inappropriate conduct than it would by our failure to acknowledge it".[23]

Still, this was better than the minority report issued by one of the committee members, Judge Allan McEachern, who maintained his stance even more firmly than the majority on one side of a divide internal to Canada, the divide between native Canadians and all others. For he exonerated the Nova Scotian panel on every point except for "one unfortunate error of language" in describing the miscarriage of justice to Marshall as "more apparent than real". "It was", he said, "a bad mistake in choice of words, but that is all it was".[24]

As one commentator pointed out, the majority's claim that innappropriate language was not grounds for removal from office was "pure subterfuge":

"To frame the issue in this manner ignores the fact that inappropriate language reveals a great deal about the biases of those who speak the words. It is ludicrous to suggest that inappropriate language from the Bench does not bring the justice system into disrepute and cannot constitute judicial misconduct. For example, what if a judge were to say, "I find this nigger not guilty"? Would that kind of language be tolerated by the public? Absolutely not. There would be immediate call for his or her removal. Why? Because it is offensive and any justice system allowing that language to go uncensored would fall into disrepute in short order".[25]

In my view, the poverty of the reasons offered by both the majority and the minority of the Inquiry Committee vindicates Cory's argument that the Marshall Affair presented a clear case for an exception to the principle of judicial immunity. The Inquiry Committee was able to avoid the real issue—the complicity of judges in the systemic racism of the criminal justice system. It was able to do that because it could interpret its mandate very narrowly, both by

---

[23] "Report to the Canadian Judicial Council of the Inquiry Committee established pursuant to subsection 63(1) of the *Judges Act* at the request of the Attorney General of Nova Scotia", n. 19 above, 221–2.

[24] Ibid., 233.

[25] Michael G. Crawford, "Canadian Judicial Council v Nova Scotia Court of Appeal: A Judicial Review More Apparent than Real", (1991–92) 40 *University of New Brunswick Law Journal* 262, at 264.

using the majority of the Supreme Court's reasoning in *MacKeigan* v. *Hickman* as a pretext for focusing exclusively on the issue of the remarks which the panel had made in its judgment and by choosing to understand that issue as a case of individualised injustice.

In contrast, the Royal Commission was designed in order to confront the systemic issue and so it did.[26] Moreover, there was an important difference between the Royal Commission of Inquiry and the Inquiry Committee. Although as a matter of fact the commissioners on the Royal Committee were all judges, their mandate was a democratic one; they were appointed by a democratic legislature to inquire into the way in which judges had participated in a failure by the Canadian state to live up to democratic ideals.

As Cory and Wilson suggest, judicial independence should not be made into a fetish by talk of the sacred. One has to ask what independence is for and the answer to that question will have much to do with the distinction we saw drawn in Chapter 3 between the apartheid state—the state in practice—and the state to which radical lawyers were prepared to swear allegiance—the state as an ideal.[27]

A democratic society needs independent judges for the same reasons it needs independent lawyers. Their independence provides the potential to bring the government—the state in practice—into line when it oppresses the people whose interests it is meant to serve. In fulfilling that potential, judges and lawyers play a crucial role in ensuring the democratic accountability of state institutitions.

It follows that when judges make themselves complicit in state oppression they cannot cite their independence as an "insurmountable obstacle" to their being made accountable. It also follows that a judicial inquiry into judicial misconduct, which is in essence the mandate of an Inquiry Committee appointed under the Judges Act, lacks the requisite impartiality. Such an inquiry is appropriate for individual cases of misconduct, for dealing with the bad apples, but not for dealing with a systemic problem which amounts to a failure of the institutions of a democratic state to live up to its ideals.

The Royal Commission was not, of course, prevented from coming to conclusions about the Nova Scotian judges and perhaps its conclusions might have been no different had the judges in fact

---

[26] See Kent Roach, "Canadian Public Inquiries and Accountability", in Philip C. Stenning (ed.), *Accountability for Criminal Justice: Selected Essays* (Toronto: University of Toronto Press, 1995), pp. 268, 280–5.

[27] See Chapter 3, text to n. 55.

volunteered to appear or had their claim to immunity not been upheld. But the Royal Commission's conclusions lacked the force which they would have had had the panel of judges been publicly engaged in a discussion under oath of what went wrong in the Marshall Affair. Thus, the majority of the Supreme Court, by upholding the judges' claim to immunity, left the last word to the Inquiry Committee which was able to dodge, and in fact did dodge, the real issue.

Cory's reasoning on judicial independence is clearly applicable to the South African situation. Not only is there a deep structural similarity between the South African and Canadian legal systems in that both are historically common law legal systems which have only recently had to come to terms with a written constitutional, but that structural similarity has meant that Canadian constitutional jurisprudence is taken very seriously in South Africa.[28] The only difference is that the judicial complicity in injustice which might have seemed exceptional in the Canadian context was general in South Africa during apartheid.

Recall also that in *Azanian Peoples' Organisation v. President of RSA*,[29] South Africa's Constitutional Court ruled against a challenge that the amnesty provisions in the TRC's statute were unconstitutional on the basis of the exceptional nature of the situation with which those provisions were designed to deal. The Court reasoned that not only had a policy of amnesty been mandated by South Africa's Interim Constitution, but the harm to a few who might have got more in the way of retributive justice through the criminal justice system, or more in the way of monetary compensation through the civil justice system, was outweighed by the benefits of the truth and reconciliation process to victims in general and also to all South Africans.[30]

It would, I suggest, have been difficult for the Constitutional Court to resist the logic of the reasoning that starts with the premise of the exceptional nature of the apartheid legal order and the transition to democracy in deciding whether judges enjoyed immunity from testifying before the TRC. Indeed, in *Azanian Peoples' Organisation v. President of RSA*, the principle of judicial independence, as enshrined in South Africa's Interim Constitution, was the

---

[28] Canada's Charter of Rights and Freedoms came into force in 1982.
[29] 1996 (8) BCLR 1015 (CC). See Chapter 1, p. 10.
[30] See Chapter 1, p. 13.

main hook on which the constitutional challenge to the TRC's amnesty provisions was hung. For it was argued that the amnesty provisions were inconsistent with section 22: "[e]very person shall have the right to have justiciable disputes settled by a court of law or, where appropriate, another independent or impartial forum" and with Constitutional Principle VI: "[t]here shall be a separation of powers between the legislature, executive and the judiciary, with appropriate checks and balances to ensure accountability, responsiveness and openness".[31]

A constitutional challenge to the summons to judges would have been put on the basis of section 165 of the Final Constitution:

> "(1) The judicial authority of the Republic is vested in the courts.
>
> (2) The courts are independent and subject only to the Constitution and the law, which they must apply impartially and without fear, favour or prejudice.
>
> (3) No person or organ of state may interfere with the functioning of the courts.
>
> (4) Organs of state, through legislative and other measures, must assist and protect the courts to ensure the independence, impartiality, dignity, accessibility and effectiveness of the courts.
>
> (5) An order or decision issued by a court binds all persons to whom and organs of state to which it applies".

But the Constitutional Court would have to take into account that that section instantiates a constitutional principle already given protection in the Interim Constitution, the same document which the Court had found permitted the design of the amnesty provisions of the TRC. Indeed, Schedule 6 to the Final Constitution, which deals with "Transitional Arrangements", provides in section 22 that the provisions dealing with Amnesty of the Interim Constitution, are "deemed to be part of the new Constitution for the purposes of the Promotion of National Unity and Reconciliation Act [the statute which set up the TRC]".

The main difference between, on the one hand, the situation in *Azanian Peoples Organisation v. President of RSA* and, on the other, our hypothetical case and *MacKeigan v. Hickman* is that in *Azanian Peoples Organisation* the attack was on explicit statutory provisions,

---

[31] These Constitutional Principles were contained in Schedule 4 to the Interim Constitution, and the Constitutional Court was given the task of checking to see whether the Final Constitution lived up to these principles.

whereas in *MacKeigan* and the hypothetical case the question is whether a commission's general authority to summon people includes by implication the specific authority to summon judges. In view of the generally exceptional nature of the apartheid legal order, and the Constitutional Court's endorsement of the constitutional legitimacy of the legislative scheme adopted to deal with the past, it would have been extremely difficult for the Court to assert an absolute immunity of judges from testifying.

It would have been open to the Court to distinguish, as we saw Cory did, between the principles of adjudicative independence and administrative independence and to hold that judges have an absolute immunity from testifying in respect of the former. But in the South African situation, this distinction would have been hard to maintain and I think this shows the difficulty in maintaining it at all. Indeed, it may be that the majority of the Supreme Court in *MacKeigan* v. *Hickman* thought that one had to preserve immunity in respect of administrative independence because of the slippery slope that leads from not preserving it there to having no ground to assert an absolute immunity in respect of adjudicative independence.

For example, no-one would be interested in the composition of Rabie's emergency team were it not for the substance of the decisions given by the Appellate Division in cases where Rabie would not countenance a dissent from a more liberal-minded judge. Questions about the actual thought process of a particular judge on the way to reaching his conclusion would not be helpful. But one could not inquire into the composition of the emergency team without also asking questions about the legal philosophy which Rabie perceived appropriate to deciding such cases and about why he thought it legitimate to pass over judges who adhered to different understandings of the rule of law.

We have seen attempts to portray the apartheid legal order as unexceptional, most notably in the use of the "95% of our work had nothing to do with apartheid" defence. But the exceptional nature of apartheid was not the human rights violations which it perpetrated. Other regimes in Africa and elsewhere have matched or even outdone the white governments of South Africa in this regard. As I will now argue, what made apartheid exceptional was that it was implemented and sustained through law. Moreover, the injustice in which judges and other lawyers were complicit was not only implemented through law, but was often of a kind which subverted the rule of law, thus calling into question any claim to independence made by significant legal actors.

3. Judicial Dereliction of Duty

It is, I think, the idea of dereliction of duty that both explains what is so intriguing about the role of judges under apartheid and reveals an assumption on which the Legal Hearing proceeded. The Hearing was of course concerned with the question of the complicity of judges and others in maintaining the illegitimate system of apartheid. But it was not concerned with that question in the same way as in the Amnesty Hearings, where the details of order-following were at issue. The question of complicity was, rather, used to frame another: given the illegitimacy of apartheid, why did you not use the room made available to you by the law to resist apartheid? And for that question to be appropriately posed, law had to be taken as more than the will of the National Party government, expressed through the Parliament it controlled.

Further, the common thread in all of the submissions, as well as in the Commissioners' questions, was the idea of independence of role. It was assumed by all concerned that independence aspired to something more noble than service to apartheid; independence had to be in the cause of values that were available despite apartheid. Note that the first of the topics for discussion on the TRC's list on the invitation sent out to those from whom it hoped to get submissions was "the relationship between law and justice".[32]

The issues at stake here were succintly described in the written submission of new order judge (and old order human rights lawyer) Edwin Cameron:

The fact that, indisputably, there was leeway to oppose apartheid through the legal system, even through judicial office, was what underlay the most vehement criticism of the Judges under apartheid. Judges were constrained to apply "the law". But that "law" frequently offered them opportunities to curtail apartheid. And, where they could not, they were at liberty, as some did, to criticise the profanation of legal values that apartheid laws represented.

---

[32] See Chapter 1, n. 53.

*The history of apartheid under law . . . reflects a paradox: for law to be effective in enforcing an evil or unjust system, its claim to be at least partially just, or to possess at least a partial internal logic of justice **must** be true. It is precisely the element of legal containment of apartheid, and challenges to its extremities, that kept legal values alive in South Africa.*[33]

In my submission to the Hearing, I attempted to explain what such a partial internal logic amounted to.[34] In nearly all the cases which are regarded as landmark decisions, the basic question the judges had to answer concerned whether they should impose constraints of legality on executive decisions, including decisions about how to implement apartheid policy, decisions about the suppression of political opposition and the detention of opponents, and decisions about the content of regulations made under statutory powers. Examples of the legal principles at issue included the following: the principle that policy should be implemented in a reasonable or non-discriminatory fashion; the principle that someone whose rights are affected by an official decision has a right to be heard before that decision is made; the principle that, when a statute says that an official must have reason to believe that x is the case before he acts, the court should require that reasons be produced sufficient to justify that belief; the principle that no executive decision can encroach on a fundamental right, for example, the right to have access to a court and to legal advice, unless the empowering statute specifically authorises that encroachment; the principle that regulations made under vast discretionary powers, for example, the power to make regulations declaring and dealing with a state of emergency, must be capable of being defended in a court of law by a demonstration that there are genuine circumstances of the kind which justify invoking the power and that the powers actually invoked are demonstrably related to the purpose of the empowering statute.

It is very important to understand why such principles are *fundamental* principles of *legality*. Take the principle that no executive decision can encroach on the fundamental right to have access to a court and to legal advice, unless the empowering statute specifically authorises that encroachment. That principle became particularly important in the period after 1960 in South Africa because the

---

[33] Cameron Submission, pp. 2–3, his emphasis.
[34] Dyzenhaus Submission, pp. 9–11. I go well beyond my submission in what follows.

government sought to insulate detention from the scrutiny of the courts by barring in its legislation access by the courts or any other person to detainees. That meant it became almost impossible to challenge the legality of a particular detention which in turn meant that the violence of the administration could be exercised without any legal warrant. In such circumstances, the courts cannot be said to be administering "the law" because there is no law to which one can hold public officials to account.

Moreover, the law which the courts are failing to enforce does not primarily consist of rules which owe their existence to positive enactment by a legislature or explicit recognition by a court. Rather, this law consists of the principles which make sense of the idea of government under the rule of law, the idea that such government is subject to the constraints of principles such as fairness, reasonableness, and equality of treatment. One will expect such principles to be manifested in statutes and in judgments, but for the reason that it is only in making these principles manifest that legislatures and courts can give some content to the idea of the rule of law, of the accountability of public officials to the law.[35]

In a legal order where the legislature is supreme, judicial scrutiny of official conduct for its legality is of course to some extent conditional on the legislature not saying explicitly that it wishes its administration to act illegally. The qualification is necessary because judges, in meeting their duty to administer the justice of the law, should take pains to find their legislature not guilty of wanting to subvert the rule of law. That duty explains why judges should require very explicit expressions by the legislature of an intention to evade the constraints of legality and why they are prepared to read the most explicit manifestation of such an intention—an ouster or privative clause which seeks to oust judicial review for legality—out of the statute in which it is contained.

In other words, even when there is no written constitution which limits what the legislature can do, the idea of legality or the rule of law in itself limits parliamentary sovereignty. And it is significant that the first major legislative assault by the National government was on such an idea of legality. For in the early 1950s, the government

---

[35] See especially Etienne Mureinik, "Fundamental Rights and Delegated Legislation", (1985) 1 *South African Journal on Human Rights* 111 and both on this point and more generally, "Pursuing Principle: The Appellate Division and Review under the State of Emergency", (1989) 5 *South African Journal on Human Rights* 60.

confronted the Appellate Division with the question whether the sovereignty of the South African Parliament could be reconciled with the provisions of the South Africa Act 1909, which required certain statutes to be enacted by a two-thirds majority at a unicameral sitting of both houses. Here the issue was the attempt by the National government to remove coloured persons (people of mixed race) from the common voters' roll by enacting a statute by a simple majority at separate sittings, when the South Africa Act required the special procedure for such a removal.

At first the Appellate Division resisted. In 1952 in *Harris and others* v. *Minister of the Interior and another*,[36] it held that Parliament had simply failed to express its will in accordance with the formal process prescribed in the South Africa Act. The Court also invalidated the second attempt by the government to bypass the South Africa Act, the passing of a statute which turned Parliament into a "High Court" with review jurisdiction over the Appellate Division's declarations of statutory invalidity.[37] But in 1957 the Court caved in to the third attempt when the majority of the Appellate Division, Judge Oliver Schreiner dissenting, upheld the validity of the Senate Act 1955, which inflated the number of senators in the upper house in order to give the government the requisite two-thirds majority.[38]

Schreiner based his dissent on the proposition that compliance with rules of manner and form does not confer validity when the point of the compliance is to violate substantive constitutional protections. The fact that each step in a fraudulent scheme is in itself legal, he pointed out, does not make the scheme legal. "The same principle should apply where the obstacle is a constitutional protection against legislation and the attempted means of avoiding it legislative".[39]

One can trace a direct line from the reasoning in the first of the decisions on the removal of coloured people from the common voters roll, through the capitulation in the third decision, to the Appellate Division's executive-minded decisions of the 1960s and onward. That line illustrates the inadequacy of an understanding of legality as constraints of pure manner and form, especially when the judicial

---

[36] 1952 (2) SA 428 (A).
[37] The High Court of Parliament Act 1952 was invalidated by the Appellate Division in *Minister of the Interior* v. *Harris* 1952 (4) SA 769 (A).
[38] *Collins* v. *The Minister of the Interior* 1957 (1) SA 552 (A).
[39] See his judgment, ibid., 574.

obligation is conceived of as requiring of judges to submit to any statutory measure that respects such constraints. Put differently, the Appellate Division failed in the first decision to discuss the substantive rule of law reasons for upholding legal limits on sovereign power, and thus laid itself open to more ingenious attempts to evade such limits.[40]

The majority of the Court was also no doubt cowed by the evidence of the government's determination to get its way. After its first decision, the Prime Minister Dr D.F. Malan said:

> "Neither Parliament nor the people of South Africa will be prepared to acquiesce in a position where the legal sovereignty of the lawfully and democratically elected representatives of the people is denied, and where appointed judicial authority assumes the testing right, namely, the right to pass judgment on the exercise of its legislative powers by the elected representatives of the people . . . It is imperative that the legislative sovereignty of Parliament should be placed beyond any doubt, in order to ensure order and certainty".[41]

Moreover, besides the renewed statutory assaults, the government also packed the Appellate Division in 1955, enlarging the court from six to eleven judges, and providing that all eleven had to sit in cases to determine the validity of a statute.[42] The court-packing measure had been presaged by the appointment of L.C. Steyn to the bench in 1951. Steyn was appointed from the civil service, a highly unusual step in South Africa at that time, and he had announced his legal philosophy in a book on statutory interpretation which, as we will see below, made plain his hostility to common law presumptions of statutory interpretation.[43] Steyn was then appointed to the Appellate Division after only three and half years on the bench and was made Chief Justice in 1959, over the heads of two more senior judges, one of whom was Schreiner.[44]

In 1960, Steyn decided a case in a manner which firmly set the stage for the plain fact approach. *R* v. *Pitje*[45] arose because a magistrate had imposed racial segregation in his court room by setting aside

---

[40] See Lorraine E. Weinrib, "Sustaining Constitutional Values: The Schreiner Legacy", *South African Journal on Human Rights* (forthcoming), for a discussion of the constitutional implications of Schreiner's dissent.

[41] 1952 House of Assembly Debates, col. 3124.

[42] Appellate Division Quorum Act 1955.

[43] L.C. Steyn, *Die Uitleg van Wette* (Cape Town: Juta & Co, 1946).

[44] Schreiner retired in 1960.

[45] 1960 (4) SA 709 (A).

a table for "non-European" practitioners. Oliver Tambo, at that time an attorney in Johannesburg, later leader of the African National Congress, had withdrawn from a case after the magistrate had ordered him to address the court from the table set aside by the magistrate for blacks. Pitje, a law clerk at Tambo and Nelson Mandela's firm of attorneys, appeared in the same case at a later date. He insisted on addressing the court from the table set aside for whites—the "European" one—in order to give his reasons for refusing to use the "non-European" table. The magistrate convicted him of contempt for refusing to comply with his order and eventually the decision went to the Appellate Division on appeal.

Steyn, delivering the unanimous judgment of the Court, cited this statement from an affidavit of Pitje.

> "I had good reason to believe that the special treatment meted out to me was because I am an African. If the magistrate had told me that that was the reason, it was my intention to tell the magistrate that neither I nor my client would feel that he had been defended in his best possible interests if he was to be defended by me and for that reason I was going to withdraw".[46]

On the basis of this statement, Steyn found that Pitje had gone to court that day in the expectation of being ordered to address the court from the non-European table and with the intention of refusing to comply with the order. He also found that Pitje had the intention of then withdrawing from the case after making a statement implying that the accused would have a fairer trial if he were not defended by a black lawyer. So Steyn held that Pitje was motivated by an intention to insult the magistrate, even though he had not had the opportunity to do so. Pitje was thus guilty of contempt and Steyn upheld his conviction.

However, if the order had been invalid or incompetent, Pitje would have been entitled to disregard it. So Steyn, on the way to his finding, had to deal with the competency or validity of the magistrate's order that the tables be segregated. Steyn pointed out that the magistrate was in control of his own courtroom and of the proceedings therein. The only ground, he said, on which the order could be attacked was unreasonablenesss, "arising from alleged inequality in the treatment of practitioners equally entitled to practice in the magistrate's court". He upheld the validity of the order for the reason that the

[46] Ibid., 711.

practitioner would not be hampered by this court-imposed racial segregation in the performance of his professional duties.[47] He thus ignored—or perhaps, we might say, invited—the inference which would inevitably be drawn from his decision: that the highest court of the land did not perceive a black lawyer as equal before the law.

Steyn sought to justify his conclusion by saying that, although no action had been taken under the Reservation of Separate Amenities Act 1953 (the statute which permitted public authorities to reserve the use of public amenities for one race):

> "the fact that such action could have been taken is not entirely irrelevant. It shows that the distinction drawn by the provision of separate tables in this magistrate's court is of a nature sanctioned by the Legislature, and makes it more difficult to attack the validity of the magistrate's order on the ground of unreasonableness".[48]

A commentator observed at the time that Steyn's approach in *Pitje* suggests that an official act which would otherwise amount to unlawful discrimination can be validated because "of a kind of empathy" between the Legislature and the official.[49] This comment seems to me to hit the mark, for in Steyn's book on statutory interpretation, he recommended a version of "analogical interpretation" as the method for resolving doubts about legislative intention. Here is his description of the method: "When a law applies to certain cases, and the legislator's intention, undoubtedly present in those cases, is also present in another case, then the requirements of the law must be extended to that other case".[50]

He cited as an example of the correct use of such analogical interpretation Judge De Villiers's lone dissent in a 1920 Appellate Division case *Dadoo, Ltd* v. *Krugerdorp Municipal Council*.[51] There the issue was whether an Indian could evade a statutory prohibition, in an 1885 law of the Transvaal Legislature, on people of his race owning property in the Transvaal. The majority of the court held that Dadoo's device for evading the prohibition, forming a private company to own the land, was legitimate. The case is well known in South African law for this dictum of Chief Justice Innes:

> "It is a wholesome rule of our law which requires a strict construction to

---

[47] Ibid., 710.   [48] Ibid., 710.
[49] R.J.P. Jordan, "Separate Tables", (1961) 78 *South African Law Journal* 152.
[50] *Die Uitleg Van Wette*, n. 43 above, p. 39, my translation.
[51] 1920 AD 530.

be placed upon statutory provisions which interfere with elementary rights. And it should be applied not only in interpreting a doubtful phrase, but in ascertaining the intent of the law as a whole".[52]

De Villiers, dissenting, held that the Legislature had not aimed merely at prohibiting ownership of land by Indians in these areas, but intended to prevent Indians from doing "what they pleased" with the land.[53]

In his book, Steyn strongly criticised the majority decision. For him it was a "striking example" of a case where the non-extension of the terms of a statute to analogous cases creates "anomalies and inequality of treatment which offend one's sense of justice and [which are] damaging to one's legal consciousness". The right method, he thought, was exemplified in De Villier's decision:

> "First the *ratio* [rationale] or *mens legis* [intention of the law] is determined in order to apply it subsequently by virtue of the legislator's will from an identity of rationale to the unexpressed case of Asiatic companies. This result is surely more acceptable to our sense of justice (*regsgevoel*)".[54]

So Steyn was not simply recommending reasoning by analogy, he was recommending reasoning by analogy from intentions discovered in the public record in the way considered appropriate by the plain fact approach. The same reasoning, I suggest, lies behind his remark in *R* v. *Pitje* about the relevance of the Reservation of Separate Amenities Act. He held that the magistrate's order was valid because it accorded with the spirit of a certain policy, which had been given legal expression in the Reservation of Separate Amenities Act.

Under such leadership, it was little surprise that in the 1960s and 1970s, the majority of South African judges began to chip away at the foundation of their duty to uphold the rule of law. In decision after decision, they found more or less implicit indications that the legislature wished its administration to act unconstrained by fundamental legal principles.[55] Academics who commented on this process warned the judges in very clear terms that such chipping would

---

[52] Ibid., 552.   [53] Ibid., 566.

[54] Steyn, *Die Uitleg van Wette*, n. 43 above, p. 45. I rely in this paragraph and for the whole indented quotation on Edwin Cameron's translation, "Legal Chauvinism, Executive-Mindedness and Justice—L.C. Steyn's Impact on South African Law", (1982) 99 *South African Law Journal* 38, at 64.

[55] They also often distorted the rules of criminal law and evidence in evaluating the defence on criminal charges of opponents to apartheid: see Michael Lobban, *White Man's Justice: South African Political Trials in the Black Consciousness Era* (Oxford: Clarendon Press, 1996).

eventually result in a complete dereliction of their duty. But the majority of judges ignored these warnings and by the late 1980s, with Rabie at the helm, the judiciary had reached the point where it betrayed the very "principles to which it owe[d] its existence".[56]

Old order liberal judges, as we have seen, adopted a very different approach. They believed that their oath to administer justice bound them to moral as well as legal values. For these judges, the values were the most fundamental norms of the legal order. But such values are fundamental not because they are at a deeper level than the law made by a supreme legislature but because they are constitutive of what the law of such a legislature is. Judge Didcott explained this point in perhaps his most innovative judgment:

> "[the] justification is the judicial assumption, deeply rooted in our legal heritage, that Parliament contemplated no greater infringement of personal freedom than is clearly and unmistakably apparent from the language in which it has expressed itself. Effect is then given to what is taken to be Parliament's intention to limit the area of constraint to the minimum. This, one emphasises, is done as a normal part of the process of interpretation, and not because the Courts have or claim the authority to supervise statute law".[57]

He also, it must be noted, said:

> "It follows, however, that effect must likewise be given to stringent enactments which are positively shown by Parliament's choice of plain words to have been meant, however offensive to conventional legal standards they might be. That too is axiomatic".[58]

But one has then to ask what happens when the words do indeed become plain, when, as Judge Olivier said, the "record shows that the legislator deliberately meant to subvert human freedom and dignity, or the traditional values of Roman Dutch law".[59] In other words, is

---

[56] Mureinik, "Pursuing Principle: The Appellate Division and Review under the State of Emergency", n. 35 above, at 62–3, commenting on *Omar* v. *Minister of Law and Order* 1987 (3) SA 589 (A) and *Staatspresident* v. *Release Mandela Campaign* 1988 (4) SA 903 (A).

[57] *Nxasana* v. *Minister of Justice* 1976 (3) SA 745 (D), 747–8. The case concerned the issue of whether a court could get access to evidence of a detainee's condition when there was reason to believe that he had been assaulted. Didcott found a way to get such evidence in the face not only of the forbidding wording of the statute but of an Appellate Division decision. I discuss the judgment in detail in *Hard Cases in Wicked Legal Systems: South African Law in the Perspective of Legal Philosophy*, n. 15 above, pp. 132–42.

[58] *Nxasana* v. *Minister of Justice*, n. 57 above, 747–8.

[59] See Pierre J.J. Olivier, "The Judiciary: Executive-Mindedness and Independence", (unpublished essay), pp. 18–19, and Chapter 2, text to note 105.

the difference between Didcott and a plain fact judge merely a different estimation of the scope for creative interpretation by judges?

To see why this is not the case, consider the following possibility. Had the majority of judges applied the law in a way that made best sense of their judicial oath, the government would have had to choose one of two options. It could have openly announced that it could not both abide by the rule of law and maintain apartheid as it wanted, thus explicitly choosing a lawless course, or it could have subjected its administration to the constraint of the fundamental legal principles sketched earlier.

The first option would have significantly decreased support for the government both in the international community and at home. And had the government taken this option, judges faithful to their duty could have denounced such statutes for illegality—not for lack of compliance with some extra-legal ideal of justice, but for failing to be law. In other words, judges could then condemn the law not simply because they disagreed with it, but because the law profaned principles fundamental to maintaining legal order. In contrast, the second option, government submission to the rule of law, would have opened up precious space for opposition to apartheid from within.

In either case, the judges would have confronted the government with a dilemma, the dilemma of the rule of law. In Chapter 3, we saw that dilemma manifest itself for Bram Fischer as he contemplated taking his fight against apartheid underground. In his case, the dilemma was a genuinely moral one. His commitment to the rule of law required him to recognise that the values which he decided to pursue by revolutionary means were put at risk by a revolutionary course, and, more important, could still be fought for by legal means. In other words, the moral quality of his dilemma stems from the fact that a commitment to the rule of law informs both of its options.

In the case of the South African government, however, the rule of law dilemma was not moral but strategic. It was a dilemma between accepting the costs as well as the benefits of operation under the rule of law or doing without the legitimacy which attaches to government under the rule of law.

In confronting the government with the rule of law dilemma, judges would have affirmed their commitment to a process that "does not defer to the violence of administration";[60] rather, the process seeks to impose the constraints of legality on a state which licences that imposition by its claim to be a *Rechtsstaat*, to be a state which governs in accordance with the rule of law. Such a commitment exhibits fidelity to the law because it shows that the rationale for having courts is not, or not mainly, that of Judges Smalberger *et al.*—the necessity for preserving us from the war of one against all.[61] Rather, the rationale is the potential of courts to articulate and maintain a "constitutional vision",[62] one informed by an understanding that the duty judges undertook in their oath to administer the law was one to "administer justice to all persons alike without fear, favour or prejudice".

The South African judiciary let the government escape from the rule of law dilemma and for that the judges are accountable, and not only for dereliction of duty. They are also accountable for having facilitated the shadows and secrecy of the world in which the security forces operated and for permitting the unrestrained implementation of apartheid policy. They thus bear some responsibility for the bitter legacy of hurt which has been the main focus of the TRC.[63]

To place the government in the rule of law dilemma would have been a deeply political act and judges do not like to be seen to be engaging in politics. But, as I argued in my submission,[64] when the politics in which judges engage amount to upholding the rule of law, requiring of a government that it live up to ideals which it itself, however cynically, professes, then judges are simply doing the duty undertaken in their oath of office. They are demonstrating their accountability to the law to which governments, who wish to claim the legitimacy of government through the medium of the rule of law, are also accountable.

Judges who assume that a legislature must be taken to intend to respect the rule of law do so in order to make sense of their role as

---

[60] Robert Cover, "Nomos and Narrative", in Martha Minow, Michael Ryan and Austin Sarat (eds.), *Narrative, Violence and the Law: The Essays of Robert Cover* (Ann Arbor, Michigan: Michigan University Press, 1995), pp. 95, 162.

[61] Chapter 2, text to n. 52.

[62] Cover, "Nomos and Narrative", n. 60 above, pp. 162–3.

[63] The judges were warned of this as a likely consequence to their approach to principles of legality in the first major critique of the judiciary published in South Africa: A.S. Mathews and R.C. Albino, "The Permanence of the Temporary—An Examination of the 90- and 180-Day Detention Laws", (1966) 83 *South African Law Journal* 16.

[64] Dyzenhaus Submission, p. 17.

one faithful to the duty to administer the law. And that tells us that the judges' duty is to moral ideals which play a role in constituting what they should take to be the positive law, even in the absence of a written constitution which gives them such authority. If judges fail to do that, the South African example shows that they fail in their duty as judges. Perhaps the best evidence of this is that in some of the exceptional cases which old order judges often wish to view as exemplifying the record, even plain fact judges could baulk at the implications of their approach and join in a judgment which upheld the rule of law.[65]

There was of course only limited room available to judges for interpretative manoeuvre, room which the South African government often attempted to close off in its legislative reactions to judicial decisions which constrained its policies. And it may seem that my claims about what judges could do are unrealistic not only in terms of an estimation of the scope for interpretative manoeuvre but also in terms of what one could expect of them as white South Africans who had, after all, chosen a conservative course within an already conservative profession.

For example, one might think that it was asking too much to expect a judge in the early 1970s—a period when repression was so successful that it seemed opposition to apartheid was futile—to refuse to accept any confession extracted under detention. The likely result of a judge declaring all such confessions as in themselves untrustworthy would have been a successful appeal against his decision to the Appellate Division and such a judge might then have found himself consigned to the mediocre work of his division. So it might seem that it was just too difficult for a judge to free himself far enough from the establishment mindset to take such a step.

But one must take into account that consignment to mediocrity is

---

[65] For example, in *Komani NO v. Bantu Affairs Administration Board, Peninsula Area* 1980 (4) SA 448 (A) and *Oos-Randse Administrasie Raad v. Rikhoto* 1983 (3) SA 595 (A). These decisions pertained to the administrative regime of apartheid in the strict sense—keeping the races apart. In other decisions in the 1980s, the Appellate Division did decide in a way that frustrated the government: for example, *Nkondo v. Minister of Law and Order* 1986 (2) SA 756 (A) and *Minister of Law and Order v. Hurley* 1986 (3) SA 568 (A). But in these, as I point out in *Hard Cases in Wicked Legal Systems: South African Law in the Perspective of Legal Philosophy*, n. 15 above, the Court found in the statute some explicit indication that the constraints of the rule of law were envisaged by the Legislature. (And see the discussion in Chapter 2, at pp. 83–5). The judges I call liberal judges would impose such constraints not only when there was a deafening silence from the Legislature, but even in the face of clear indications to the contrary.

hardly a severe penalty. Further, the record in so far as it is good, is a record of judges departing from the establishment mindset. It is against this background that we can judge the judges. Had the record been relentlessly bad, we would be engaged in a decidedly different exercise. The irony is that when we judge the judges, those who did most seem to get judged harshly, even as harshly as their colleagues.

Had a judge, say a Didcott or a Friedman, in the early 1970s said that evidence extracted from security detention was in itself inadmissible, and had the Appellate Division overruled him, that would have required the Appellate Division to condone the practice of solitary confinement even more explicitly than it had done in *Rossouw* v. *Sachs* [66] and in *S* v. *Van Niekerk*.[67] Had the unlikely happened and the Appellate Division upheld the judgment, the government would then have been faced with the choice of legislating the admissibility of such evidence or doing without it. Had the government taken the first option, it would have had to be explicit about the fact that the rule of law was no more than a facade in South Africa. Had it taken the second, solitary confinement and torture would not have ceased in South Africa—the security forces would still have wanted to get information and to intimidate. But one important reason for continued solitary confinement and torture—securing convictions on the basis of evidence extracted by torture—would have been removed.[68]

One must be careful here not to err on the side of over- or underestimation. Liberal judges could not have stopped apartheid and one can safely say that any significant act of judicial resistance would have been overridden by the government. But we should note that any particular act of resistance by the internal opposition to apartheid or by the liberation organisations was likely to be, and in fact usually was, overridden. Further, many white South Africans did not find it entirely easy to think of themselves as on the beneficiary side of the apartheid divide. Even when they were not enthusiastic supporters of apartheid, they

---

[66] 1964 (2) SA 551 (A).

[67] (1972) 3 SA 711 (A). See Chapter 2 for general discussion.

[68] The Detainees' Parents Support Committees, which were established in the early 1980s in order to support detainees and their families, and which eventually took on a general monitoring role of detention, were convinced that the following pattern existed. After an initial period of interrogation of a detainee, there would be a cessation followed by periods when interrogation was restarted often in an ever more intense way. The explanation seemed clearly to be that the prosecutors in the office of the Attorneys-General were indicating that they did not yet have enough to make out a case in court. This pattern was of course denied by the Attorneys-General at the Hearing: see the Transcript at p. 471 (supplemented by my notes as the recording is defective here).

needed, like Judges Smalberger *et al.*, to think that they were living in—and helping to maintain—a basically civilised society. Each time a person from within the ranks of the white establishment broke those ranks to point out how uncivilised their society was, the others were threatened with being forced to rethink their position.

Bram Fischer's example is the most striking here. And it is worth noting that despite Judge Ackermann's care, even now, in trying to limit the implications of his resignation from the Bench, his resignation was perceived at the time as a severe comment on the injustice of apartheid precisely because he could not be dismissed as a pawn in the total onslaught. There is no doubt that a mass resignation of the few liberal judges, judges who condemned apartheid not only as a repugnant ideology but because of its subversion of the rule of law, would have rocked the government and white South Africans.

However, I believe that the liberal judges were right to remain in office. Their situation was at the time one of tragic moral choice. In Chapter 3 I described the nature of such a situation as one in which no choice can be made without ignoring the legitimate pull of important moral considerations. We have nevertheless to choose in such situations. And we have to try to make the best choice without the comfort, however the choice turns out, that the ignored considerations will cease to seem powerful. In other words, there is in the tragic situation no univocal right answer. Any decision brings with it regret because even when a decision seems on balance the better choice, the reasons for not doing it remain.

It may seem, then, that for liberal judges the crucial moment for any individual judge was the decision whether or not to accept office. But I doubt whether even the most liberal of the judges thought much or at all about this issue in the 1960s and 1970s, when taking office was regarded as the pinnacle of a successful career at the Bar. It is telling that Judge Ackermann's submission is completely silent on one issue: whether he faced any moral problems when he decided to become a judge in 1980.[69]

However, it does not matter so much what an advocate thought on

[69] One judge who went from an exclusively commercial practice at the Bar to a distinguished human rights record on the Bench told me in the mid-1980s that it was only when he was confronted with the fact of having to administer apartheid law that he started to rethink his role. It would, of course, have been very interesting to know from Judge Friedman, for example, how much of the discussion of the difficulties attending the decision to take office dates to the call by Raymond Wacks on judges to resign rather than to the time of his actual appointmeent. (See Chapter 2, text to n. 62.)

taking office as what he did as a judge when in office. Whether as an advocate the judge would have condemned apartheid and thus found it difficult to accept an office which involved administering the laws was not as salient as whether, once in office as a judge, he saw that there was no rigid dichotomy between law on the one hand and morality on the other. Only if he saw that the law itself provided an arena for moral choice—that his choice to become a judge opened up a range of moral choices while ruling out others—could he walk the tightrope I have described earlier.

Using Robert Cover's terminology, we can say that the choice to become a judge was "jurispathic" since it killed off other options, including radically different ways of understanding what it was to pursue an ideal legal order.[70] Think in this last respect of Bram Fischer, who decided that the only way to create a society which respected law was to take the path of illegal action. The choice to become a judge was one which expressed commitment to the morality of judicial office,[71] but that then raised the question of the contours of the moral space in that office.

It is important to see that once in office a liberal judge confronted the rule of law dilemma in a particularly painful way. Even the most liberal judge who took office under apartheid could not avoid implementing its law. He had to accept that even laws whose content he found abhorrent and whose provenance he regarded as illegitimate had a legitimate claim on his duty to administer the law. He therefore not only made himself complicit in an injustice he recognised as such, but gave to that injustice the aura of legitimacy.

What made a liberal judge different from other judges was not, however, the fact of his complicity in apartheid but his conception of fidelity to the law. By refusing to elevate the formal stakes (the parliamentary sovereignty defence), he kept alive the idea that the law provides opportunities to judges to make the law meet its aspiration to treat all its subjects equally. However, as I argued in Chapter 2, in keeping that idea alive, he also helped to legitimate the apartheid government by giving some genuine substance to the claim that the rule of law did exist in South Africa.

For the liberal judges, then, it was very much a case of "damned if you do, damned if you don't". But without them, there would have been little, perhaps no, point to the efforts of those few lawyers in the

---

[70] Cover, "Nomos and Narrative", n. 60 above, pp. 155–63.
[71] Cover calls this the "hermeneutic of jurisdiction", ibid.

academy in the 1960s and 1970s who sought to provide their students with a critical perspective on the apartheid legal order, or to the efforts of those few lawyers in practice, attorneys and advocates, who were prepared to use the law against the law in the fight against apartheid. The distinction between the apartheid state and the ideal state which we have seen even radical lawyers were and are prepared to draw,[72] depended on the efforts of all of these lawyers, but most importantly on the liberal judges, simply because without an occasional victory in the courts no such distinction could have been drawn. And without a basis for that distinction during apartheid, there would have been precious little reason for the African National Congress to take law seriously both during the negotiations about the new order and in the transition to democracy. One cannot therefore argue that John Dugard, the foremost academic critic of the apartheid legal order, or Arthur Chaskalson, the foremost advocate in the fight against apartheid law, were justified in the choices they made and withhold that justification from the liberal judges.[73]

Nevertheless, there is a salient difference between critics and political or human rights lawyers, on the one hand, and liberal judges, on the other. It is not that one legitimates while the other does not, for it is clear that the participation of all serves to legitimate. Rather, the difference is that liberal judges often could not help but allow the injustice of the law to speak through them. Further, this feature of their role was not confined to occasions when they had no choice but to interpret the law as the government wanted it interpreted. Even when a liberal judge had some room for interpretative manoeuvre it was usually the case that he could only mitigate to some extent the injustice of the law.[74]

---

[72] See Vincent Saldanha, Chapter 3, text to n. 55.

[73] For good discussion of the issues around legitimacy of participation, see Stephen Ellman, *In a Time of Trouble: Law and Liberty in South Africa's State of Emergency* (Oxford: Clarendon Press, 1992) and Richard L. Abel, *Politics By Other Means: Law in the Struggle Against Apartheid, 1980–1994* (New York: Routledge, 1995).

[74] This claim needs some qualification. Consider the following story Nelson Mandela tells in his account of his legal practice in Johannesburg in the 1950s. He was asked to represent a coloured man who had been mistakenly classified as black by a white bureaucrat on the man's return from army service during the Second World War. Mandela says: "This was the type of case, not at all untypical in South Africa, that offered a moral jigsaw puzzle. I did not support or recognize the principles in the Population Registration Act, but my client needed representation, and he had been classified as something he was not. There were many practical advantages to being classified Coloured rather than African, such as the fact that Coloured men were not required to carry passes": Mandela, *Long Walk to Freedom* (Boston: Little Brown and Company, 1995), p. 151. (Mandela recounts

That liberal judges had on occasion to come to the same conclusion as plain fact judges shows that the dichotomy I draw between plain fact and liberal judges is often too crude to capture all of the complexity of the South African judiciary. It is also true that judges minded to walk the liberal judges' tightrope had varying degrees of proficiency and boldness.

And of those who did not step on to the tightrope at all, there were no doubt many judges who personally abhorred apartheid, who accepted judicial office because of their love for the law, and who thought that in the small number of cases that required them to administer apartheid law that they had no option but to apply the law in accordance with a plain fact approach. Recall here that Judge Ackermann said that he could not remember a case which he would have decided differently, given the supreme legal norm of the time.[75]

Such judges must have adopted the view that their duty lay in the plain fact approach because that approach is most likely to determine what in fact law is in accordance with the actual intentions of the majority of the legislators who voted for the statute. But the legitimacy of that approach depends on a democratic theory which says that the people speak through their elected parliamentary representatives, and thus the statutes enacted by the legislature must be applied by judges so as best to approximate what those representatives actually intended. In other words, the legitimacy of an approach which requires judges to ignore in their interpretation of the law their substantive convictions about what the law should be requires a substantive commitment at a deeper level to the intrinsic legitimacy of that law. However, the Parliament whose statutes they interpreted was illegitimate by the criteria of any democratic theory and so the substantive justification for their approach was absent.

Nevertheless, because the plain fact approach operates in deliberate detachment from the substantive values which justify it, it had come to assume a life of its own in democratic legal orders in which the legislature was considered supreme. And those South African judges who adopted the approach because it seemed right for judges

---

that the magistrate who heard the matter was uninterested in his evidence and arguments. He decided in Mandela's client's favour on the basis that the slope of the man's shoulders was typically coloured. Mandela comments: "And so it came about that the course of this man's life was decided purely on a magistrate's opinion about the structure of his shoulders": ibid., p. 152.) There is still, I suggest, a salient moral difference between a lawyer assuming the validity of the law in general in an attempt to get a judicial officer to mitigate the injustice of a particular law and a judicial officer declaring that an unjust law is valid.

[75] See Chapter 2, text to n. 107.

to ignore their substantive convictions about the law may seem less culpable than the others, if only because such judges did not think that it was their moral duty to support apartheid. But once it was pointed out to them in different ways—by academics, in the judgments of their judicial colleagues, by the lawyers who appeared before them, and by the opponents of apartheid whose fate turned on their decisions—that the substantive justification for their approach was missing, they should have reconsidered. Moreover, there was much more wrong with this group's adoption of the plain fact approach than the absence of a substantive justification for it.

In the context of a democratic legal order, a plain fact approach can find support in a respectable view about the place of judges in democracy and, in addition, the approach will not generally be tested in the same way as it was under apartheid.[76] The powerful in a democratic legal order will, as a matter of character and account-ability, not be quick to test the limits of legality in their statutes. As a result, while there might be much to criticise in the actual decisions reached by plain fact judges in a democratic legal order, these decisions will not as often put the judges at risk of dereliction of duty. But adjudication in the apartheid context shows what is wrong with the plain fact approach as an approach to legal interpretation. Under abnormal conditions—under conditions which are the opposite of those in which the approach is designed to work—it is destructive of legality. For that reason, old order judges who adopted the approach because it seemed the right approach to interpretation and not because of their support for apartheid should have dropped it once its consequences had been vigorously pointed out to them.

It is interesting to note here that judges in other less troubled places than South Africa have in times of trouble adopted the plain fact approach in interpreting security legislation, often as relentlessly as Rabie's emergency team. Thus it has been pointed out that the Rabie Court's deference to executive emergency authority resembled the positions taken in prominent decisions of other courts, in countries such as the USA and Britain.[77] And Malcolm Wallis S.C.

---

[76] Though see Murray Hunt, *Using Human Rights Law in English Courts* (Oxford: Hart Publishing, 1997).

[77] See Stephen Ellmann, *In a Time of Trouble: Law and Liberty in South Africa's State of Emergency*, n. 73 above, pp. 166–71. I deal in detail with the judicial record in the United Kingdom in Chapter 8 of *Hard Cases in Wicked Legal Systems: South African Law in the Perspective of Legal Philosophy*, n. 15 above. As I point out in Chapter 4, ibid., South African courts found a ready made approach to security legislation in the majority of the House of Lord's decision in the war-time case of *Liversidge* v. *Anderson* [1942] AC 206.

suggested that the Legal Hearing should not be occupied by discussion of the merits of the plain fact approach; after all, he said, the House of Lords had just used such an approach to exclude any bearing the European Convention on Human Rights might have on the legality of detentions in Northern Ireland.[78]

But surely what goes wrong in these other places is that judges are misled by the fact that the legislation they are interpreting emanates from a democratically elected government into thinking that the intention of the legislature must be taken to coincide with plain facts about the government's position? What was especially perverse about the use of the plain fact approach in South Africa was that even this questionable inference could not be made.

The plain fact judges who did not support apartheid also have to take responsibility for the fact that they helped to provide an important smokescreen for an illegitimate government which, though generally defiant of the moral condemnation of its policies, craved legitimacy. This point is best made by considering a second group of judges who adopted a plain fact approach because it so clearly served apartheid and its security apparatus.

This group equated the reference in their oath of office to the "customs of the Republic of South Africa" with the customs of the unreformed National Party, to the extent that, as we have seen, one of their legal pioneers, L.C. Steyn, as the first National government appointed Chief Justice, was prepared to inject racial prejudice into South Africa's courtrooms because of his sense of justice, his "*regsgevoel*".[79]

It is only this group's ideological commitments that can explain the fact that benches were systematically put together in order to secure at least majorities, preferably unanimities, for the result that served government policy best. For such machinations were no different than the actions of the various National Party Ministers of Justice who sought to pack the courts with judges they thought could be relied on to produce the right results. Nevertheless, when the judges who were enthusiatic about apartheid felt compelled to defend their record in the face of academic criticism, they argued that they

---

[78] Transcript, p. 165.

[79] There were, of course, much earlier examples, notably Lord De Villiers's judgment in *Moller* v. *Keimos School Committee* 1911 AD 635 and Judge Beyers's dissent in *Minister of Post and Telegraphs* v. *Rasool* 1934 AD 167. For analysis, see *Hard Cases in Wicked Legal Systems: South African Law in the Perspective of Legal Philosophy*, n. 15 above, pp. 53–63.

were simply doing what they were required to do as judges—interpreting the law without regard to their substantive convictions.[80]

When they took this step, they mimicked their political masters, who saw that one cannot coherently claim both a commitment to the rule of law and that the judicial duty is to follow the orders of the government. In other words, since the politicians wanted the legitimacy that goes with the claim that one is governing in accordance with the rule of law, they too adopted the plain fact approach: the judge's duty is to put aside his substantive convictions about justice when interpreting the law.

In sum, a more complex account of the South African judiciary requires a more complex set of evaluations. Plain fact judges who adopted their approach because it served unrestrained government policy best should be judged harshly because they put ideological commitment before their official duty. Plain fact judges who abhorred apartheid can also be judged negatively, though not because their complicity was zealous. Rather, they are judged for not questioning an approach which their opposition to apartheid gave them reason to question.

Since the great majority of South African judges were plain fact judges, the story of law during apartheid supports Cover's suggestion that it is easier by far to adopt a plain fact or positivist approach to interpretation:

"Judges are surely right that the issue of power will rarely be in doubt if they pursue the office of jurisdictional helplessness before the violence of officials. The meaning judges thus give to the law, however, is not privileged, not necessarily worth any more than that of the resister they put in jail. In giving the law *that* meaning, they destroy the worlds that might be built upon the law of the communities that defer to the superior violence of the state, and they escalate the commitments of those who remain to resist".[81]

But, as we have seen, this is not the whole story; the issue of power *was* put in doubt by the participation of the liberal judges. And, as I have already argued, liberal judges also have to accept that they were complicit in—and lent legitimacy to—a legal order which was not

---

[80] See for example, L.C. Steyn, "Regsbank en Regsfakulteit", (1967) 30 *Tydskrif vir Heedendaagse Hollandse-Romeinse Reg* 101 and the interview with then Chief Justice Rabie, *Sunday Star*, 3 May 1987, quoted in Dennis Davis, "The Chief Justice and the Total Onslaught", (1987) 3 *South African Journal on Human Rights* 231.

[81] Cover, "Nomos and Narrative", n. 60 above, p. 163, original emphasis.

only morally abhorrent but which for the most part, on their understanding, maintained only the facade of the rule of law. However, at
the same time as they assisted in maintaining that facade, they gave
some substance to it. And that substance did more than open up
space for opposition from within. It also, as we can see in retrospect,
provided a basis for law and judges to play a role in building a decent
political order.

Again we can see that such judges faced a tragic choice while at the
same time we should commend the choice they made. Though they
seem vindicated in retrospect, they still should regret their
complicity in the moral wrongs that resulted from their choice.

As Judge Edwin Cameron in his written submission to the TRC
put it: "*all lawyers and all judges*, whatever their personal beliefs and
the extent of their participation, were complicit in apartheid". But
this, he said, did not conclude the answer to the question about
whether judges and lawyers should have refrained from participating. He, a former human rights lawyer, who is widely recognised
as superbly suited to grace one of South Africa's highest judicial
offices, gives an unequivocal "No" to that question. For, as he says,
it was:

*that ambiguous history that laid the foundation for our present constitu-
tional order. That order places high and ambitious reliance upon law. The
importance of legal challenges to apartheid, and of lawyers' participation
in the system, must therefore not be undervalued.*[82]

We have seen here that the TRC invited judges and others to take
the opportunity to explore the tragic nature of the choice to be a
South African lawyer between 1960 and 1994. We have also seen that
even those who accepted the invitation were unwilling to take advantage of the opportunity. And this is true even of liberal judges, those
who carried the burden of South African expectations since their
understanding of the judicial role promised most.

It might be thought that one does not need judges on the witness
stand to answer such questions. After all, Rabie's speeches out of
court, his uncompromising views on state security and liberty
expressed in the report of the Rabie Commission, as well as his
appalling record as Chief Justice tell us most of what we might learn
from him. That is, we might suppose that the conclusions of a TRC

---

[82] Cameron Submission, p. 3, original emphasis.

with Rabie's participation might have been no different from the conclusions one could draw from one's armchair.

But the appearance of some old order judges at the Hearing would not have been merely symbolic. It would not be a mere symbol for judges to acknowledge that they are subject, like other South African citizens, to the law and in particular to the duty to testify in the process of truth and reconciliation. This would also have been an acknowledgement that they accepted responsibility for implementing the law of apartheid, whether they did so willingly or not. And, in the cases where there was room for interpretative manoeuvre which judges failed to exploit, or where they failed to see over the apartheid divide, they could publicly acknowledge that they failed in their duty to do their best to do justice within the framework of the law.

It was not enough in these regards that some old order judges made written submissions. For in exempting themselves from the process of discussion at the TRC they provoked a discussion from which they then held themselves aloof, thus demonstrating their sense that judges are not accountable like other citizens.

Had even a few judges accepted the TRC's invitation, not only would this have imparted a different tone to the Hearing as a whole, but it would have done more for respect for the law and for the judiciary than any attempts to present their record in its best possible light. Accepting the invitation would have shown that judges acknowledged that they are not above the legal process that seeks to bridge South Africa's awful past to a democratic future. And only such an acknowledgment could have demonstrated a proper awareness that one of the things that made that past so singular was that the injustice of apartheid was implemented through what judges like to consider the vehicle for justice, the law.

In particular, such an appearance would have demonstrated that judges understand that they too are citizens in a democracy, citizens with special responsibilities, of course. But the weight of those responsibilities in the context of a fraught transition to democracy argued for their appearance. By appearing judges would have accepted their commitment to a practice, well described by Paul W. Kahn in an essay on judicial independence during transitions to democracy as the practice of the "morality of citizenship". They would have seen themselves as part of an attempt to articulate in public a sense of responsibility for the past and the future which makes sense of the relationship between state, court, and individual.[83]

Kahn argues that the courtroom is a "political theatre" but that does not make it the "theatre of politics". There is a distinction between law and politics, which is the distinction we have already encountered between the state and government, or the state as an ideal and the state in practice. At the moment that a court accepts jurisdiction over a controversy between government and an individual, government is demoted—it loses its claim to be the exclusive representative of the state. At the same time, the individual is promoted into a public role, to one with an equal claim to represent the state. The court, then, in deciding between these claims articulates a vision of what the state is and publicly draws the line between law and politics.[84]

In order to articulate this vision, the court needs to be independent. But Kahn plausibly suggests that what matters is not the formal structures of independence, which might differ from country to country, but "the informal tradition of norms and expectations that develop around political and legal institutions".[85] In a functioning democracy, courts and political institutions support each other; the "courts provide a kind of legitimacy to the political institutions and the political institutions return the favor to the courts".[86]

Now South Africa under apartheid was not a functioning democracy, though the courts had a kind of formal independence and were engaged in the reciprocal relationship of legitimacy with political institutions which Kahn describes. The enforced divide between racial groups in the service of white supremacy meant that it was impossible to develop an "informal tradition of norms and expectations . . . around political and legal institutions" common to most South Africans. In addition, I have argued that judges for the most part failed in the role which independence protects because they confused government with the state, thus permitting the government to fail to live up to the responsibilities that attend a claim to be a democratic state. Having failed in their duty, judges could not claim the immunity from testifying that normally attaches to the judicial

---

[83] Paul W. Kahn, "Independence and Responsibility in the Judicial Role" in Irwin P. Stotzky (ed.), *Transition to Democracy in Latin America: The Role of the Judiciary* (Boulder, Colorado: Westview Press, 1993), pp. 73, 85. And see Owen Fiss, "The Right Degree of Independence", ibid., p. 55, arguing that the substance of independence is regime-dependent.

[84] Kahn, "Independence and Responsibility in the Judicial Role", n. 83 above, 77.

[85] Ibid., p. 84.   [86] Ibid., p. 85.

role, since, as we have seen, even on the majority's reasoning in *MacKeigan* v. *Hickman*, independence is a value instrumental to judges' properly performing their role.[87]

In a fraught transition a tradition of judicial independence can at best be said to be in the process of being forged. Hence, it was incumbent on judges committed to a democratic future fully to take part in the opportunity offered them to debate both their past and their future.[88]

Moreover judges' participation would not have been confined to these important acknowledgments. While the time allotted to the Hearing was hardly generous, and while the need to look at other legal actors precluded an exclusive focus on the judiciary, a debate on issues of great importance could at least have been initiated.

Take, for example, the issue of judicial appointment. Why was it illegitimate for the National government to "leapfrog" L.C. Steyn into the Chief Justiceship in 1959 but legitimate for the ANC-dominated government to "leapfrog" Ismail Mahomed in 1997? The answer to that question requires an elaboration of the substance of the ideal of the rule of law and of the personal qualities that will display such commitment. It is the difference between Steyn's *"regsgevoel"* and Mahomed's sense of the "ethically legitimate ends of justice". Only an open discussion of that difference could allay the concern that new order South Africa is doomed to repeat the mistakes of the old order.

A similar discussion could have informed the issue of how judges should be assigned to cases. It is uncontroversial that a judge who has extensive experience of tax law or criminal law or family law should be assigned to hear a matter arising in one of those fields. But should a judge with a feminist history be assigned to hear a case on the constitutionality of abortion regulation? Should a homosexual judge who was involved in activism for gay rights be assigned to hear a matter about the constitutionality of assigning public benefits only to mixed sex couples? I cannot make the case here for the legitimacy of both these assignments. But I believe that one can make that case and still argue that it was wholly illegitimate for Rabie to construct his

---

[87] For further discussion of the instrumental and contextual nature of judicial independence, see Peter H. Russell, "Towards a Theory of Judicial Independence", draft paper at 4–6.

[88] A similar point was forcefully argued by Graeme Simpson for the Centre for the Study of Violence and Reconciliation in the last oral submission of the Hearing: Transcript, pp. 637–42.

emergency team, a team which he doubtless thought was best suited by its understanding of the ideals of legal order to decide cases on the legality of executive action.

Finally, judges could have initiated a more general discussion which would have set the stage for sketching the legitimate role of judges in the new South African legal order, one in which the Constitution gives them enormous scope for shaping the moral direction of government. That discussion could then have framed more particular discussions about the role of the magistracy, the role of the legal profession, advocates, attorneys and public law advocacy centres, the kind of independence required by the Attorneys-General, and the type of legal education required in the new South Africa.

Such a general discussion would have to go well beyond suggestions that all is well now that South Africa has abandoned parliamentary supremacy for a legal order in which a written constitution, under judicial guardianship, protects the rights and liberties of all South Africans. As Edwin Cameron observed:

If lawyers and Judges were complicit under apartheid in enforcing injustice and inequity, they have no less responsibility for doing so under the present system. It is true that formal apartheid has been abolished. But we still live in a society characterised by extreme disparities of wealth and power. Our social system is democratic, and its political institutions now, fortunately, representative. But we live in a society still distinguished by extremes of dispossession. As a judge who proudly holds office under the Constitution of the Republic of South Africa, I am nevertheless party to the injustices that still exist in our society; and my role in the enforcement of a system that contains injustices necessarily makes me complicit in them. We run the risk, in looking back at apartheid, of adopting an inappropriately complacent view of our present social order and of the legal system that upholds and enforces it. The transition to democracy has not created nationwide justice in our country. Judges still participate in a system which, in many diverse and complex respects, perpetuates injustice.

That perspective, and the humility and anxiety that ought to derive from it, should not be lost from view. I hope that this sense of present and continuing injustice, and of lawyers' and judges' responsibility for it, will not be lost in your hearings.[89]

---

[89] Cameron Submission, p. 3.

Cameron's profound observations should, however, be qualified in one important respect. Cameron fails to draw a distinction between different kinds of injustice, one illuminated by a recent decision of South Africa's Constitutional Court.

In *Thiagraj Soobramoney* v. *Minister of Health (Kwazulu-Natal)* (1997),[90] the Constitutional Court dealt with an issue which occupied the media for some weeks. Mr Soobramoney, who died shortly after the decision, suffered from several grave diseases and in addition his kidneys had failed so that his life could only be prolonged by means of regular renal dialysis. He could not afford private medical treatment and he did not fall within the guidelines for dialysis at public expense; the scarcity of publicly-funded medical resources had prompted a decision by the hospitals to offer treatment only to patients whose condition was reversible. Soobramoney brought a constitutional challenge against the refusal to admit him for treatment on the basis of section 27(3) of the 1996 Constitution ("[n]o one may be refused emergency medical treatment") and section 11 which stipulates that "[e]veryone has a right to life".

President Chaskalson for the majority of the Court[91] held that the treatment required was not emergency treatment and that the issue was whether Soobramoney was entitled to access to health care services in terms of sections 27(1) and (2) of the Constitution which entitle everyone to access to health care services provided by the state "within its available resources". He found that the criteria devised by the hospital were reasonable in the light of the scarcity of resources available: "The state has to manage its limited resources in order to address [such] claims. There will be times when this requires it to adopt a holistic approach to the larger needs of society rather than to focus on the specific needs of particular individuals within society".[92]

In a concurring judgment, Judge Albie Sachs said:

"If resources were co-extensive with compassion, I have no doubt as to what my decision would have been. Unfortunately, the resources are limited, and I can find no reason to interfere with the allocation undertaken by those better equipped than I to deal with the agonising choices that had to be made".[93]

---

[90] Case CCT 32/97.
[91] Judges Madala and Sachs gave separate concurring judgments.
[92] *Thiagraj Soobramoney* v. *Minister of Health (Kwazulu-Natal)*, n. 90 above, 21.
[93] Ibid., 37.

Recall that Judge Mervyn King, in explanation of his failure to come to the assistance of an appellant who had raised a common law defence of necessity to a charge under the Group Areas Act of unlawfully residing in a "white" area, said the following:

> "An Act of Parliament creates law but not necessarily equity. As a judge in a court of law I am obliged to give effect to the provisions of an Act of Parliament. Speaking for myself and if I were sitting as a court of equity, I would have come to the assistance of the appellant. Unfortunately, and on an intellectually honest approach, I am compelled to conclude that the appeal must fail".[94]

Structurally, the two passages might seem the same. Both Sachs and King suggest that in a world of perfect justice, they would have come to the aid of the individual before the court; and they express their regret at having been party to an injustice required by the law. But there is, I suggest, a difference between the kinds of injustice in issue.

In the cases where I have argued that an old order judge should have used common law presumptions of statutory interpretation to mitigate the effects of a law designed to wreak injustice, the injustice was of a kind which subverted a particular ideal of the rule of law. That ideal holds that individuals subject themselves to the law—accept the authority which the law claims for itself—only on condition that they are treated equally, fairly, reasonably and so on. A law which subverts equality, or which results in gross unfairness, or can only be implemented unreasonably, is suspect from a moral perspective which is also a perspective inherent in the law. In other words, when a statute is suspect in this way, not only its morality but also its legality is in doubt. If a judge is complicit in sustaining this kind of injustice, then he will find himself complicit in undermining the role to which he has sworn fidelity.

By contrast, in Thiagraj Soobramoney's situation the injustice was one created by lack of public resources, and a judgment about how to distribute the resources was one legitimately made by those responsible for allocating medical resources. The Constitutional Court, in upholding the legitimacy of that judgment made themselves complicit in a social injustice but not in such a way that undermined their role. Indeed, in explicitly recognising both the injustice and the limits of their role, they pointed out that, other things being equal,

---

[94] *S* v. *Adams* 1979 (4) SA 793 (T), at 801. See Chapter 2, text to n. 90.

the dilemma of how to distribute scarce public resources was not a dilemma of the rule of law.[95]

King wanted to make just this kind of point, but in the circumstances in which he made it, it constituted an evasion rather than an acceptance of responsibility. For when a judge finds himself in a rule of law dilemma, if he finds that he cannot do other than uphold a law which strikes at legality, he should go further than pointing out the injustice of the law. He should point out that the law is a perversion of justice, or, in Cameron's words, that the injustice of the law is a "profanation" of *legal* values.

Of course, it will be controversial how to draw the line between these two kinds of injustice. For example, it is not clear how to characterise the situation of a judge who is deeply sceptical about the good that sending a convicted criminal to jail can do either that individual or society, but nevertheless continues to sentence people to terms of imprisonment. Here the goals of the criminal justice system are goals of the legal order which are deeply and perhaps inevitably compromised by the institutions which are supposed to implement those goals. In sentencing people to terms of imprisonment, judges may well make themselves complicit in a kind of legal injustice. And, if it is the case that this example is one of legal injustice, then it is the judges' duty to make public their disquiet.

In sum, the difference the new legal order of South Africa will make to South Africa's future does not so much depend on the formal differences between a legal order based on legislative supremacy and one based on a liberal democratic constitution. It depends much more on how those who make the legal order work do their jobs. And when a body is set up to bridge the old and the new in the service of constructing democracy, it is the democratic duty of all citizens, including judges, fully to assist the deliberations of that body.

We saw that Cameron expressed his hope that his sense of "present and continuing injustice, and of lawyers' and judges' responsibility for it" would not be lost in the Legal Hearing. I believe that he had good grounds for hope because, as I will now argue, the Hearing was on balance a success.

---

[95] The qualification here is necessary because it is of course the case that the judgment could not be made on the basis of constitutionally suspect criteria: the hospital authorities could not, for example, solve the scarcity problem by reserving dialysis for members of a particular racial group.

4. Judging the Legal Hearing

"Treason is a crime in a very special category. Where the ideas and political aspirations of those charged are part of the issue in this very strange and complex society of ours as set out at the beginning of this judgment—and given the spectrum of politics of our citizens from Black to white and from far left to far right—with their grievances and aspirations—in most cases legitimate, and the often intemperate and exaggerated language and liberally spiced with political cliches, most of these citizens just striving for a better South Africa—a charge of treason should be very carefully considered and reconsidered before it is brought before the court".

Judge Piet J. van der Walt, in the course of his judgment aquitting the "Alexandra five" of the charge of treason, Johannesburg, 1985.[96]

In the passage just quoted, the judge recognises that the crime of treason is special; it should not be used to characterise the activity of legal subjects when what they are doing is basically organising local communities on the basis of a legitimate aspiration, the aspiration to give people living in those communities some control over their lives. He also recognises that the complexity and strangeness of South African society will lead to that aspiration being expressed in the florid language of the resistance to apartheid—the language of revolution. Finally, and most important, he takes the resisters before him to be part of a larger political community, one united by a desire for a "better South Africa" even if divided on every detail about how to achieve that desire.

It has been convincingly demonstrated that the South African judges who presided over political trials in the 1970s rejected outright the last assumption, which led them in turn to reject the first two.[97] Their own main assumption was that black South Africans were not part of the same political community as white South Africans, and so it was legitimate to close off to blacks legal channels of political opposition to the South African state. From that assumption it followed that any attempt by blacks to organise political resistance to the state inherently threatened an illegal and violent

---

[96] Quoted in Abel, *Politics By Other Means: Law in the Struggle Against Apartheid, 1980–1994*, n. 73 above, p. 369.

[97] Lobban, *White Man's Justice: South African Political Trials in the Black Consciousness Era*, n. 55 above.

overthrow of the state, in short treason. With this assumption in place, the aspiration by blacks to achieve political control over their lives in areas of white political control is by definition illegitimate. Talking about achieving such control, or any conduct that seems directed to this end, is always but a hair's breadth away from incitement to revolutionary overthrow of the state. So Van Der Walt's views represent the beginnings of a sea change in the South African judiciary's understanding of opposition to the apartheid legal order. The idea on which he implicitly relies is that it is a perversion of justice to use the law to punish individuals who are attempting to sustain a value—the value of political community—when that value is one which the law itself is supposed to sustain.

The virtue of the Legal Hearing is that it both brought that idea to the surface and, through its own legal process, showed how law can play a role in building political community. My claim is not that the Hearing was anything close to an ideal inquiry. But it had the merit of participating in establishing an archive, as Professor Pamela Reynolds observed in her inaugural lecture at the University of Cape Town, "Truth and Youth—An Anthropologist Observes the Truth and Reconciliation Commission".[98] The presence of the archive, she says, means that the country's "raw pain" is exposed—"no-one can now deny the cruel nature of much of the past".

Reynold's lecture is a lament for the way in which the pain of the youth of South Africa—pain suffered because of both the ordinary and the extraordinary violence of apartheid—did not, perhaps could not, get fully articulated at the TRC. As she shows, that criticism of the TRC should not obscure that the archive which a TRC Hearing establishes is more than an obstacle in the way of forgetting the past. The archive is an invitation to do better; indeed, in understanding the flaws of any particular hearing, one gets a sense of how to continue the work of elaborating the archive. One can opt to treat the trauma of the past, and the problems in retelling it, as a promise.[99]

Reynold's comments are about the Victim Hearings, but they are pertinent also to the Legal Hearing. The snapshots of that Hearing which have been given here—the absence of the judges, the hubris of the advocates, the dismal record of the attorneys, the amnesia of the academics, and the display of rectitude by the Attorneys-General—

---

[98] I am grateful to Professor Reynolds for her permission to quote from the draft of her lecture.

[99] I owe this phrase to Scott Veitch.

are now part of an archive, and an archive has an independence and potential which escapes the control of any contributor to it. We have already seen this demonstrated in the facts of the record which the advocates presented, facts which are sometimes at odds with their own account of that record, raising questions about their role which they did not fully answer.

Particularly important is the public nature of the event, part and parcel of the TRC's commitment to transparency. The paradoxes of the apartheid legal order have been explored in several comprehensive monographs. But, in the nature of things, their audience is the legal academy, their focus is limited to particular institutions or to a particular period, and they were written at a time when the future was too uncertain for their authors to attempt to link exploration of the past to future illumination.

In contrast, the Hearing was public both in its media coverage and in the sense that it addressed all South Africans. It also raised questions about the role of all important legal actors in a way designed to link the past to the future. The fact that the range of defences enlisted by many of those who appeared, or who declined to appear, got in the way of discussion cannot detract from the fact that at the same time they initiated a discussion. Indeed, the very fact that these defences were raised should prompt and then aid a discussion of what sort of institutional change is required in a process of reconstructive justice, one which seeks to establish democracy in South Africa.

There is little doubt in my mind that without the Hearing such issues would not have been so firmly placed on the public political agenda. In *Divided Memory: The Nazi Past in the Two Germanys*,[100] Jeffrey Herf shows how conservative forces in post-war West Germany deliberately weakened memory of the Holocaust and delayed bringing Nazis to justice (thus eventually letting them escape justice) because of the perception that too much memory and justice might produce a right-wing revolt that would destroy a "still fragile democracy".[101] In contrast, in East Germany, memory of the Holocaust was suppressed in order to portray the past as a simple battle between good and evil in which the good—communism—had triumphed over the bad—capitalism/fascism. Indeed, this suppres-

---

[100] Jeffrey Herf, *Divided Memory: The Nazi Past in the Two Germanys* (Cambridge, Mass.: Harvard University Press, 1997).
[101] Ibid., pp. 6–7.

sion of memory allowed the East German government to make the small Jewish community that survived in East Germany a convenient scapegoat for the sins of cosmopolitan international capitalism.

Herf points out that in order to suppress memory or to attempt to create a weak public memory, those who seek to control memory must themselves remember.[102] Much of Herf's book is devoted to exploring the attempts by individuals and groups within West and East Germany to resist official suppression of memory. In the East, the attempts backfired, resulting in the silencing of those who wanted to remember or even in increased anti-semitism. In the West, the attempts eventually gained ground, largely through the efforts of the Social Democratic Party. Of great significance here is Chancellor Willy Brandt's gesture in the late 1960s, when he knelt at the memorial for Jews killed in the Warsaw Ghetto uprising to symbolise public acknowledgment of and repentance for German war crimes.[103]

Herf argues that the restoration of memory in West Germany was not a threat to a fragile democracy in the process of making a democratic state. Indeed, his conclusion seems to be that the delay in restoration of memory in the West together with the suppression of memory in the East is what renders the attempt to democratise the East after reunification so problematic.[104]

Similarly, in a work which focuses on the role of law in creating collective, public memory, Mark Osiel argues that public memory of past wrongdoing has to be established for a transition to democracy to be successful.[105] However, in his examination of several important attempts to use the law in such a way, the Nuremberg Trials, the Tokyo Trials, the Eichmann prosecution and more recent trials in France and Argentina, he suggests that the main mechanism of the criminal law, the trial, is probably not best suited to this task.[106] The

---

[102] Here he quotes (ibid., p. 10) from Theodor Adorno's classic essay, "What does coming to terms with the past mean?"; for the relevant passage, see the opening quote to Chapter 3.

[103] One can contrast here former President P.W. Botha's refusal to appear before the TRC on the ground that an Afrikaner kneels only before God. A particularly repugnant attempt to justify Botha's stance can be found in Rian Malan, "Crises Show Up the Demise of the Rainbow Nation", *Business Day*, 21 April 1998, and see also the critique by Max du Preez, "'Boers' Tired of Reactionism in their Name", *Business Day*, 24 April 1998.

[104] Herf, *Divided Memory: The Nazi Past in the Two Germanys*, n. 100 above, p. 394.

[105] Mark Osiel, *Mass Atrocity, Collective Memory, and the Law* (New Brunswick, New Jersey: Transaction Publishers, 1997).

[106] See on the same issue, Jennifer J. Llewellyn and Robert Howse, "Institutions for Restorative Justice: The South African Truth and Reconciliation Commission as a model for dealing with conflicts of the past", unpublished paper.

risk he finds is that "legal concepts and doctrines" often lose "their normal connection to the underlying moral and political issues at stake". His solution is to "widen the spatial and temporal frame of courtroom storytelling in ways that allow litigants to flesh out their competing interpretations of recent history, and to argue these before an attentive public. Only in this way can the debate within the courtroom be made to resonate with the public debate beyond the courtroom walls".[107]

I suggested in Chapter 1 that at the Legal Hearing the apartheid legal order was put on trial—law found itself before a tribunal. But the legal order was put on trial in order to assist in the transition from apartheid to democracy, in order to help root and nurture a fragile plant. Moreover, the legal order was put on trial before a democratically constituted body, which sought to engage the most important legal actors in both the old and the new orders in a constructive debate, one which would resonate outside of the Hearing in the way Osiel suggests.

The public archive which the Legal Hearing established is in place and this book aspires to be part of its work—the work of, as the General Council of the Bar put it, the struggle against forgetting. In particular, the Hearing showed that we should not forget that questions about the relationship between law and justice are inherently political but at the same time morally loaded. As Richard Abel has argued, the story of law and apartheid tells us that law is "politics by other means" but those means do make a difference.[108] Government under the rule of law amounts to politics under the constraints of legal order, constraints which impose conditions of publicity, obligations to justify official decisions, and a general obligation on judges to find a role for themselves as the enforcers of legality, not just of positive law. Hence, Abel warns against the false conclusion that law "either makes all the difference or no difference at all".[109]

Law, we have seen, can make a difference, even under the very unpromising conditions of apartheid South Africa, and this goes a long way to show that legal order or legality places constraints on the powerful which at bottom are political and moral constraints—the

---

[107] Osiel, *Mass Atrocity, Collective Memory, and the Law*, n. 105 above, p. 296.
[108] Abel, *Politics by Other Means: Law in the Struggle Against Apartheid, 1980–1994*, n. 73 above.
[109] Ibid., p. 549.

constraints of commitment to a community of free and equal citizens. Of course, there will be many ways of understanding that commitment and legal actors will have to take seriously the idea that they have an obligation of fidelity to law before the commitment has effects on legal practice. But at least one should rule out any legal theory or ideology which attempts to reduce our understanding of law to what a plain fact approach determines to be the content of the commands of the powerful.[110] For law is better understood as the expression of a relationship of reciprocity between ruler and ruled,[111] one in which the rulers commit themselves not only to being accountable to law, but to making law before which all subjects are equal. That in turn suggests that the rule of law is best understood as the institutional expression of democracy.

And here, or so I have argued, we have the explanation of why some judges and some lawyers were able, despite apartheid, to provide the basis for a new democratic legal order.

---

[110] And thus to the extent that various versions of legal positivism either require this understanding of law, or invite it, or even fail to supply a good reason for rejecting it, we have reason to opt for an anti-positivist theory of law. Similar conclusions about legal positivism are suggested by Mark Osiel, *Mass Atrocity, Collective Memory, and the Law*, n. 105 above, pp. 299–300, and by Carlos Santiago Nino, *Radical Evil on Trial* (New Haven, Conn.: Yale University Press, 1996), pp. 149–56.

[111] See Lon L. Fuller, *The Morality of Law* (New Haven, Conn.: Yale University Press, rev. edn. 1969).

LEGAL HEARING SCHEDULE

Note: A short description of a submission follows when that submission is not described in the text of the book.

Day one: Monday, 27 October 1997

Opening Address: Archbishop Desmond Tutu.
Submission: Professor David Dyzenhaus.
Submission: Professor Lennox Hinds.
Submission: Liza Key, film-maker.
Submission: Paula McBride, human rights activist.
Submission: National Association of Democratic Lawyers
Submission: Minister of Justice Dullah Omar. Omar outlined his understanding of the new legal order and stressed the commitment of his Department to accountability, constitutionalism, and transformation.

Panel Discussion

Day two: Tuesday, 28 October 1997

Submission: General Council of the Bar.
Submission: Ruth and Ilse Fischer (Bram Fischer's daughters).
Submission: Priscilla Jana. Ms Jana sketched her experience as an attorney during the apartheid era with an exclusively "political practice". She detailed her harassment by the security police and told of her complete lack of confidence in the Transvaal Law Society's willingness to protect her; rather, she alleged, the Law Society actively harassed her.
Submission: Dean Carole Lewis, Faculty of Law, University of the Witwatersrand.
Submission: Association of Law Societies.
Submission: Black Lawyers Association. The BLA dealt mainly with the problems which black lawyers had encountered, and continued

to encounter in the new order, in seeking to gain entry to the white-dominated profession and in making progress within it. These problems had led to the founding of organisations like the National Association of Democratic Lawyers and the Black Lawyers Association.

Submission: Advocate Lee Bozalek.

Submission: Professor David McQuoid Mason, Law Faculty, University of Natal, and President of the Society of Law Teachers. Professor McQuoid Mason summarised the responses of the various Law Faculties and gave a sketch of his own opposition to apartheid while Dean of the Faculty of Law at his University.

Submission: Legal Resources Centre. The Legal Resources Centre presented an account of harassment by the National government of lawyers at the Centre.

Submission: University of Natal law students. The students presented an account of the apartheid legal order and their understanding of how the new legal order could best be transformed.

Panel Discussion

Day three: Thursday, 29 October 1997

Submission: Former Attorney-General Klaus von Lieres und Wilkau.

Submission: Amnesty International.

Submission: Tim McNally and other Attorneys-General.

Submission: Captain Jacques Hechter, security policeman.

Submissions: Advocates A.P. Laka and J.B. Skosana. Mr Skosana had been a prosecutor between 1984 and 1992 in Kwa-Ndebele, a black "homeland" during apartheid where the administration of justice fell directly under the authority of the South African Ministry of Justice. He gave details of government interference in his office and of police control over the Attorney-General. Mr Naka, who had been a magistrate in the same area, corroborated Skosana's account.

Submission: Former prosecutor, Mr Michael Hendrickse.

Submission: Department of Justice. The Department gave a mundane account of the administration of the machinery of justice during apartheid coupled with an apology for having administered injustice. The most interesting feature of the submission was the revelation of details of the operation of an internal Board of

Review, which made recommendations in regard to the release of detainees. In particular, the Commission was interested in the fact that judges sat on the Board.

Submission: Centre for the Study of Violence and Reconciliation. The Centre argued that the scrutiny of the legal order at the TRC could play a significant role in building respect for law and thus in building democratic institutions.

Submission: Lawyers for Human Rights. Lawyers for Human Rights argued that non-governmental organisations had played an important role in resisting apartheid and should play an important role in sustaining a culture of human rights in the new order.

Panel Discussion

BIBLIOGRAPHY

Materials from the Legal Hearing

Submissions

Ackermann Submission: submission by L.W.H. Ackermann (Judge of the Constitutional Court), "Submission to the Truth and Reconciliation Commission. Re: The Role of the Judiciary".

ALS Submission: submission by the Association of Law Societies of the Republic of South Africa, "Submission to the Truth and Reconciliation Commission".

Amnesty International Submission: "The Criminal Justice System and the Protection of Human Rights in South Africa: The Role of the Prosecution Service. Comments and recommendations on the draft National Prosecuting Bill, 1997, in the contexts and controversies surrounding the role of the Office of the Attorney-General for KwaZulu Natal and other concerns".

Bozalek Submission: submission by L.J. Bozalek (human rights lawyer), "Submission to the Truth and Reconciliation Commission on the Role of the Legal System and its Functionaries in Relation to Human Rights Violations under Apartheid".

Cameron Submission: submission by E. Cameron (Judge of the High Court, Johannesburg), "Submission on the Role of the Judiciary under Apartheid".

Chaskalson *et al.* Submission: submission by A. Chaskalson (President of the Constitutional Court), I. Mahomed (Chief Justice of the Supreme Court of Appeal), P. Langa (Deputy President of Natal), H.J.O Van Heerden (Deputy Chief Justice of the Supreme Court of Appeal), and M.M. Corbett (former Chief Justice of the Supreme Court of Appeal), "The Legal System in South Africa, 1960–1994: Representations to the Truth and Reconciliation Commission".

Corbett Memorandum: memorandum by M. M. Corbett (then Chief Justice of the Supreme Court of Appeal), "Presentation to the Truth and Reconciliation Commission".

Dyzenhaus Submission: submission by D. Dyzenhaus (Professor of Law and Philosophy at the University of Toronto), "Judicial Accountability Under Apartheid".

Friedman Submission: submission by G. Friedman (Judge President of the Cape High Court), "Submission to the Truth and Reconciliation Commission on the Role of the Judiciary".

GCB Submission: submission by the General Council of the Bar of South Africa, "Submissions to the Truth and Reconciliation Commission", 3 volumes.

Govender Submission: submission by K. Govender (human rights lawyer), "Injustice under the Apartheid Judiciary".

Hendrickse Submission: submission by M. A. Hendrickse (former prosecutor), "Submission to the Truth and Reconciliation Commission".

Hinds Submission: submission by L. S. Hinds (Professor, Rutgers University) on behalf of the International Association of Democratic Lawyers, "The Gross Violations of Human Rights of the Apartheid Regime under International Law".

Key Submission: submission by L. Key (film-maker), "Tsafendas: A Madman with a Mission", published in full by the *Mail and Guardian*, 31 October/6 November edition, 1997, 23–5.

Laka Submission: submission by A.P. Laka (former prosecutor), "Administration of Justice in the former Kwa-Ndebele Government".

Langa Submission: submission by P. Langa (Deputy President of the Constitutional Court), "Submission to the Truth and Reconciliation Commission on the Role of the Judiciary".

Legal Resources Centre Submission I: "Submission to the Truth and Reconciliation Commission Hearing on the Legal System".

Legal Resources Centre Submission II: "Submission to the Truth and Reconciliation Commission". (This submission dealt with harassment by the state of the Centre.)

Lewis Submission: submission by C. Lewis (Dean of the Law Faculty, University of the Witwatersrand), "Submission on the Legal System" accompanied by an Annexure "Apartheid and the Legal Profession".

McBride Submission: submission by P. McBride (human rights activist), co-authored with Sharon Ekambaram, "The Judges, the Law, and the Sentence of Death".

McNally Submission: submission by A. T. P. McNally S.C. (Attorney-

General, Natal), "Prosecuting Through the Apartheid Years: A Presentation to the Truth and Reconciliation Commission".

NADEL Submission: submission by National Association of Democratic Lawyers, "The Role of Lawyers and the Legal System in the Gross Human Rights Violations of Apartheid".

Olivier, Pierre J. J. (Judge of the Supreme Court of Appeal), "The Judiciary: Executive-Mindedness and Independence".

Rossouw Submission: submission by D. J. Rossouw (former Attorney-General, Cape Town), "Submission on the Role of the Office of the Attorney-General".

Potchefstroom Submission: submission by the Faculty of Law, University of Potchefstroom.

RAU Submission: submission by the Faculty of Law, Rand Afrikaans University.

Skosana Submission: submission by J. Skosana (former magistrate), "Submission to the TRC Pertaining to the Administration of Justice in the former Kwa-Ndebele during 1986–87".

Smalberger *et al.* Submission: submission by J. W. Smalberger, C. T. Howie, R. M. Marais, and D. G. Scott (Judges of the Supreme Court of Appeal), "Submission on the Role of the Judiciary".

Von Lieres Submission: submission by K. Von Lieres und Wilkau (former Attorney-General, Transvaal), "The Role of the Attorney-General".

White Submission: submission by C. S. White (Judge of the High Court, Bisho), "The Judiciary in the Republic of the Transkei".

Letters

Professor J. Church, Dean of the Faculty of Law at UNISA (University of South Africa), 9 October 1997.

C.F. Eloff, Judge President of the Transvaal Provincial Division, 10 September 1997.

Professor M.G. Erasmus, Dean of the Faculty of Law, University of Zululand, 1 October 1997.

Professor D.W. Morkel, Dean of the Faculty of Law, University of the Orange Free State, 8 October 1997.

Other

Transcript: transcript of the oral proceedings of the Legal Hearing.

Works Cited

Abel, Richard L., *Politics By Other Means: Law in the Struggle Against Apartheid, 1980–1994* (Routledge: New York, 1995).

Adorno, Theodor, "What Does Coming to Terms with the Past Mean?, Geoffrey Hartman trans., in Geoffrey Hartman (ed.), *Bitburg in Moral and Political Perspective* (Bloomington: Indiana University Press, 1986) 114.

Asmal, Kader, "Judges are not exempt from review", *Electronic Mail and Guardian*, 22 January 1998.

——, Asmal, Louise and Roberts, Ronald Suresh *Reconciliation Through Truth: A Reckoning of Apartheid's Criminal Governance*, 2nd edn. (Cape Town: David Philip, 1997).

Bindman, Geoffrey, *South Africa and the Rule of Law* (London: Pinter Publishing (International Commission of Jurists), 1988).

Bronkhorst, Daan, *Truth and Reconciliation: Obstacles and Opportunities for Human Rights* (Amsterdam: Amnesty International Dutch Section, 1995).

Budlender, Geoffrey, "Law and Lawlessness in South Africa", (1988) 4 *South African Journal on Human Rights* 139.

Cameron, Edwin, "Legal Chauvinism, Executive-Mindedness and Justice—L.C. Steyn's Impact on South African Law", (1982) 99 *South African Law Journal* 38

——, "Nude Monarchy: The Case of South Africa's Judges", (1987) 3 *South African Journal on Human Rights* 338.

——, "Lawyers, Language and Politics—In Memory of JC De Wet and WA Joubert", (1993) 110 *South African Law Journal* 51.

Chaskalson, Arthur, "Law in a Changing Society", (1989) 5 *South African Journal on Human Rights* 293.

Clingman, Stephen, *Bram Fischer: Afrikaner Revolutionary* (Amherst, Mass.: University of Massachussets Press, 1998).

Cover, Robert, *Justice Accused: Antislavery and the Judicial Process* (New Haven, Conn.: Yale University Press, 1975).

——, "Violence and the Word", in Martha Minow, Michael Ryan and Austin Sarat (eds.), *Narrative, Violence, and the Law: The Essays of Robert Cover* (Ann Arbor, Michigan: Michigan University Press, 1995).

Crawford, Michael G., "Canadian Judicial Council v Nova Scotia Court of Appeal: A Judicial Review More Apparent than Real", (1991–92) 40 *University of New Brunswick Law Journal* 262.

Davis, Dennis, "The Chief Justice and the Total Onslaught" (1987) 3 *South African Journal on Human Rights* 231.

Dugard, John, *Human Rights and the South African Legal Order* (Princeton, N.J.: Princeton University Press, 1978).

——, "The Judiciary and National Security", (1982) 99 *South African Law Journal* 655.

——, "Should Judges Resign? A Reply to Professor Wacks", (1984) 101 *South African Law Journal* 286.

——, "*Omar*—Support for Wacks's Ideas on the Judicial Process?", (1987) 3 *South African Journal on Human Rights* 295.

Du Preez, Max, "'Boers' Tired of Reactionism in their Name", *Business Day* (website) 24 April 1998.

Dworkin, Ronald, *Taking Rights Seriously* (London: Duckworth, 1978 (new impression)).

——, *Law's Empire* (London: Fontana, 1986).

Dyzenhaus, David, *Hard Cases in Wicked Legal Systems: South African Law in the Perspective of Legal Philosophy* (Oxford: Clarendon Press, 1991).

——, "Law's Potential", (1992) 7 *Canadian Journal of Law and Society* 237.

Ellis, George, "McNally Must Tell the Truth", letter to *Mail and Guardian*, dated 26 November 1996.

Ellman, Stephen, *In a Time of Trouble: Law and Liberty in South Africa's State of Emergency* (Oxford: Clarendon Press, 1992).

Fiss, Owen, "The Right Degree of Independence", in Irwin P. Stotzky (ed.), *Transition to Democracy in Latin America: The Role of the Judiciary* (Boulder, Colorado: Westview Press, 1993) 55.

Foster, Don, with Davis, Dennis and Diane Sandler, *Detention and Torture in South Africa: Psychological, legal, and historical studies* (London: James Currey, 1987).

Friedman, Steven, "Commission's Impartiality Under Fire", *Business Day* (website), 23 February 1998.

Fuller, Lon L., *The Morality of Law* (New Haven, Conn.: Yale University Press, rev. edn. 1969).

Habermas, Jürgen, "What does 'Working Off the Past' mean today?", in Habermas, *A Berlin Republic: Writings on Germany*, Peter Uwe Hohendahl trans. (Lincoln: University of Nebraska Press, 1997) 17.

Hahlo, H.R., and Kahn, Ellison, *The South African Legal System and its Background* (Cape Town: Juta & Co., 1968, 2nd impress. 1973).

Halliday, Terence C., and Karpik, Lucien, "Politics Matter: a Comparative Theory of Lawyers in the Making of Political Liberalism", in Halliday and Karpik (eds.), *Lawyers and the Rise of Western Political Liberalism* (Oxford: Clarendon Press, 1997) 15.

Hayner, Priscilla B., "Fifteen Truth Commissions—1974 to 1994: A Comparative Study", (1994) 16 *Human Rights Quarterly* 597.

Haysom, Nicholas, and Plasket, Clive, "The War Against Law: Judicial Activism and the Appellate Division", (1988) 4 *South African Journal on Human Rights* 303.

Herf, Jeffrey, *Divided Memory: The Nazi Past in the Two Germanys* (Cambridge, Mass.: Harvard University Press, 1997).

Hunt, Murray, *Using Human Rights Law in English Courts* (Oxford: Hart Publishing, 1997).

Joffe, Joel, *The Rivonia Story* (Belleville, South Africa: Mayibuye Books (UWC), 1995).

Jordan, R.J.P., "Separate Tables", (1961) 78 *South African Law Journal* 152.

Kahn, Paul W., "Independence and Responsibility in the Judicial Role" in Irwin P. Stotzky (ed.), *Transition to Democracy in Latin America: The Role of the Judiciary* (Boulder, Colorado: Westview Press, 1993) 73.

Karis, Thomas, and Carter, Gwendolen M. (eds.), *From Protest to Challenge: A Documentary History of African Politics in South Africa* (Stanford: California, Hoover Institution Press, 1987), 3 vols.

Korsgaard, Christine M., "Taking the Law into Our Own Hands: Kant on the Right to Revolution" in Andrews Reath, Barbara Herman, Christine M. Korsgaard (eds.), *Reclaiming the History of Ethics: Essays for John Rawls* (Cambridge: Cambridge University Press, 1997) 297.

Kritz, Neil, "The Dilemmas of Transitional Justice", in Kritz (ed.), *Transitional Justice: How Emerging Democracies Reckon with Former Regimes* (Washington, D.C.: United States Institute of Peace, 1995), 3 vols.

Krog, Antjie, *Country of My Skull* (Johannesburg: Random House South Africa, 1998).

Llewellyn, Jennifer J. and Howse, Robert "Institutions for Restorative Justice: The South African Truth and Reconciliation Commission as a model for dealing with conflicts of the past", unpublished.

Lobban, Michael, *White Man's Justice: South African Political Trials in the Black Consciousness Era* (Clarendon Press: Oxford, 1996).

Mahomed, Ismail, "Address by the Honourable Mr Justice Ismail Mahomed at a dinner given by the Johannesburg Bar on 25 June 1997 to celebrate his appointment as Chief Justice of the Supreme Court of Appeal", (1997) 114 *South African Law Journal* 604.

Malan, Rian, "Crises Show Up the Demise of the Rainbow Nation", *Business Day* website, 21 April 1998.

Mandela, Nelson, *Long Walk to Freedom* (Boston: Little, Brown and Company, 1995).

Mathews, A.S., and Albino, R.C., "The Permanence of the Temporary—An Examination of the 90- and 180-Day Detention Laws", (1966) 83 *South African Law Journal* 16.

Meer, Fatima, *The Trial of Andrew Zondo* (Harare: Baobab Books 1988).

Müller, Ingo, *Hitler's Justice: The Courts of the Third Reich*, Deborah Lucas Schneider trans. (Cambridge, Mass.: Harvard University Press, 1991).

Mureinik, Etienne, "No Shelter for Judges" *Sunday Tribune*, 3 April 1983, reproduced in *Lawyers for Human Rights: Bulletin No. 3*, January 1984 (Johannesburg) 19.

——, "Fundamental Rights and Delegated Legislation", (1985) 1 *South African Journal on Human Rights* 111.

——, "Pursuing Principle: The Appellate Division and Review under the State of Emergency", (1989) 5 *South African Journal on Human Rights* 60.

Nietzsche, Friedrich, "On the uses and disadvantages of history for life", in Nietzsche, *Untimely Meditations*, R.J. Hollingdale trans., intro. by J.P. Stern (Cambridge: Cambridge University Press, 1997) 57.

Nino, Carlos Santiago, *Radical Evil on Trial* (New Haven, Conn.: Yale University Press, 1996).

Nolte, Ernest, "The past that will not pass: A speech that could be written but not delivered", in Ernest Piper (ed.), *Forever in the Shadow of Hitler: Original Documents of the Historikerstreit, The Controversy Concerning the Singularity of the Holocaust*, James Knowlton and Truett Cates trans., (New Jersey: Humanities Press, 1993) 18.

Ogilvie Thompson, N., "Speech on the Centenary Celebrations of the Northern Cape Division", (1972) 89 *South African Law Journal* 30.

Osiel, Mark, *Mass Atrocity, Collective Memory, and the Law* (New Brunswick, New Jersey: Transaction Publishers, 1997).

Pauw, Jacques, *Into the Heart of Darkness: Confessions of Apartheid's Assassins* (Johannesburg: Jonathan Ball Publishers 1997).

"Report to the Canadian Judicial Council of the Inquiry Committee established pursuant to subsection 63(1) of the *Judges Act* at the request of the Attorney General of Novia Scotia", reproduced in (1991–92) 40 *University of New Brunswick Law Journal* 212.

Reynolds, Pamela , "Truth and Youth—An Anthropologist Observes the Truth and Reconciliation Commission", Inaugural Lecture, University of Cape Town, 1997.

Rickard, Carmel, "The judiciary goes on trial for its apartheid past", *Sunday Times*, 2 November 1997, 16.

Roach, Kent, "Canadian Public Inquiries and Accountability", in Philip C. Stenning (ed.), *Accountability for Criminal Justice: Selected Essays* (Toronto: University of Toronto Press, 1995) 268.

Russell, Peter H., "Towards a Theory of Judicial Independence", draft paper.

Soggot, Mungo, "Battle Lines Drawn Over Chief Justice", *Electronic Mail and Guardian*, 20 September 1996.

Steyn, L.C., *Die Uitleg van Wette* (Cape Town: Juta & Co, 1946).

——, "Regsbank en Regsfakulteit", (1967) 30 *Tydskrif vir Hedendaagse Romeinse-Hollandse Reg* 101.

Stolleis, Michael, *The Law Under the Swastika: Studies on Legal History in Nazi Germany*, Thomas Dunlap trans. (Chicago: University of Chicago Press, 1998)

Teitel, Ruti, "Transitional Jurisprudence: The Role of Law in Political Transformation", (1997) 106 *Yale Law Journal* 2009.

Turpel, M.E., "The Judged and the Judging: Locating Innocence in a Fallen Legal World", (1991–92) 40 *University of New Brunswick Law Journal* 281.

Van Blerk, Adrienne, *Judge and be Judged* (Cape Town: Juta & Co., 1988).

Wacks, Raymond, "Judges and Injustice", (1984) 101 *South African Law Journal* 266.

Weinrib, Lorraine E., "Sustaining Constitutional Values: The Schreiner Legacy", *South African Journal on Human Rights* (forthcoming).

INDEX